JEWISH LETCHWORTH

JEWISH LETCHWORTH

A Microcosm of the
Jewish Communal Experience

YANKY FACHLER

VALLENTINE MITCHELL
LONDON • CHICAGO

First published in 2023 by Vallentine Mitchell

Catalyst House,
720 Centennial Court,
Centennial Park, Elstree WD6 3SY, UK

814 N. Franklin Street,
Chicago, Illinois,
60610 USA

www.vmbooks.com

Copyright © 2023 Yanky Fachler

British Library Cataloguing in Publication Data:
An entry can be found on request

ISBN 978 1 80371 032 7 (Paper)
ISBN 978 1 80371 033 4 (Ebook)
ISBN 978 1 80371 034 1 (Kindle)

Library of Congress Cataloging in Publication Data:
An entry can be found on request

All rights reserved. No part of this publication may be reproduced in any form or by any means, electronic, mechanical, photocopying, reading or otherwise, without the prior permission of Vallentine Mitchell & Co. Ltd.

This page is dedicated to the memory of

Sir Naim Eliahou Dangoor z"l

Born in 1914 in Iraq, Sir Naim was the grandson of Iraq's Chief Rabbi Ezra Dangoor and son of the world's largest printer of Arabic books. After availing of the opportunity of studying engineering at the University of London, he vowed that if he should succeed in business, he would donate money to education.

Sir Naim fulfilled his promise, and his philanthropic endeavours continue to extend to many different fields including education, cancer research and caring for refugees and disadvantaged communities across the globe.

He founded a journal, *The Scribe*, to network Iraqi Jews since their scattering over the previous forty years.

The second oldest person to be knighted by the Queen, Sir Naim holds a dear place in the hearts of many for helping his fellow Jews.

DANGOOR EDUCATON (dangooreducation.com),
part of the philanthropy of The Exilarch's Foundation

Table of Contents

INTRODUCTION: 'We're from the same village'		1
1.	Ebenezer, the garden city geyser	8
2.	The Bornstein brotherhood	14
3.	'Vaccies' – compulsory and voluntary evacuation	22
4.	Letchworth at war	41
5.	Two parallel congregations	51
6.	The end of the war	66
7.	The David Sassoon Library	80
8.	Rabbi Solomon (Suliman) and Alice Sassoon	88
9.	Rabbi Asher (Reb Oosher) and Flora Feuchtwanger	110
10.	Families Broch, Winegarten and Schischa	120
11.	Hallmead and Mullway	125
12.	Schooldays in Letchworth	136
13.	Letchworth Talmud Torah and Letchworth Yeshiva	151
14.	Families Kirsch, Pollock, Roth, Ward and Vanger	169
15.	Letchworth tales	184
16.	Letchworth pen portraits	201
17.	'Sollerposh' East – the new centre of gravity	210
18.	The Letchworth branch of Cambridge University	221
19.	'No minyan in Letchworth'	230
20.	An outstanding legacy	234
Dedications		243
List of Illustrations		251
Glossary of Hebrew/Yiddish terms		253

Introduction:
'Anachnu me'oto hakfar' – We're from the same village

'I have information about the community and would be pleased to assist anyone who would wish to write the Jewish history of the town. Hurry up, while I still have my memories!'

MURRAY COHEN

If you draw an arc of about 30-50 miles around the Jewish areas of 1930s London, you will identify some 20 pop-up satellite communities where London Jews sought temporary refuge from the Luftwaffe bombing raids at the start of WW2: Amersham, Beaconsfield, Bedford, Berkhamsted, Chesham, Dorking, Epsom and Guildford. Hemel Hempstead, High Wycombe, Hitchin, Maidenhead, Slough, St Albans, Staines, Welwyn Garden City, Woking and Worthing. And of course, Letchworth Garden City in north Hertfordshire.

Developer Abba Bornstein, the son of a Frankfurt banker, had bought a large plot of land on the outskirts of Letchworth. On this plot, Abba built a workers' estate consisting of two parallel streets, Hallmead and the L-shaped Mullway, which were known together as the Aborn (A Bornstein) Estate.

Did Abba, who was a significant mover and shaker in the modern orthodox Zionist Mizrachi / Bachad movement, have any inkling of what was coming down the line? We do know that when he completed the Aborn Estate in 1939, the anticipated post-Depression boom had not yet materialised, and at first the two streets lay almost empty.

And then the Second World War broke out. When Jews in London started looking for a place that was not subjected to bombing raids, they sought somewhere that provided an easy rail commute from London. Abba was able to persuade family, friends and his Mizrachi contacts to move into his estate in Letchworth. When other religious Jews from different parts of London heard of the emerging orthodox enclave, they also descended on the town. This explains why of all the satellite Jewish communities that were established around London when the war started, it was Letchworth alone that emerged with such a high proportion of religious families.

When Judith Weil (Kritzler) was doing her research for her 2011 *Jewish Tribune* article on the Letchworth Jewish community, Rabbi Jacob Feuchtwanger explained why the memory of the Jewish community had all but disappeared in Letchworth itself: 'The community did not leave any physical footprint. The Letchworth Heritage Museum has very little in the way of records of its one-time Jewish community. Maybe this is because the community did not own any buildings apart from the *mikveh* (ritual bath).'

Yossel Schischa adds that with hindsight, it was just as well that the community never had its own synagogue building, since 'having to dispose of a defunct *shul* would have been no light matter.'

In fact, the question of a permanent footprint did exercise the community early in the Second World War. Several committee meetings of Letchworth Hebrew Congregation were devoted to having a permanent communal hall that would house a synagogue, *Talmud Torah*, and accommodation for a kosher canteen and club rooms.

When First Garden City Ltd turned down the idea, the committee felt that the reasons for the refusal were of an anti-Jewish character. The committee wrote to the Council of Christians and Jews, which asked the newly formed Christian-Jewish Council to take up the matter as a major issue. The committee also asked the president of the United Synagogue, Sir Robert Waley-Cohen, to intervene with Mr Macfadyen, chairman of the First Garden City Ltd. In the end, nothing came of the plan.

Over the years, the suggestion has been floated that it was time that 'someone' wrote a book about the Jewish community in Letchworth. Judith Weil (Kritzler) remarked: 'Researching my article was a fascinating experience, and I felt I just touched the tip of the iceberg.

Each of the people I interviewed suggested I speak to someone else, and each new person had something to add.' Judith felt that a book about the Letchworth community could be placed in the Letchworth Heritage Museum, providing a fitting record of an almost unknown, but very special, chapter in the history of the town.

In response to Judith's 2011 article, Murray Cohen wrote two letters to the editor of the *Jewish Tribune*. In the first, he wrote: 'I have information about the community and would be pleased to assist anyone who would wish to write the Jewish history of the town. Hurry up, while I still have my memories!' The following week, he wrote: 'I hope someone younger than me will write the history of the Jewish Community.'

To quote from my son Ashi's favourite children's book, *The Cat in the Hat* by Dr Seuss, 'Someone, someone, that someone was me.' I decided that I would write this book on Jewish Letchworth. Ten years after Murray wrote to the *Jewish Tribune*, he was interviewed for this book. I am happy to report that his memories are as sharp as ever.

The immediate genesis of *Jewish Letchworth* can be traced back to an email I received in 2016 from Philippa Parker of the Letchworth Local History Research Group. She was enquiring about the famous Sassoon Library amassed by David Sassoon, the father of Rabbi Solomon Sassoon. The library resided in Letchworth between 1940 and 1970.

I was able to supply Philippa with the information she sought. In a PS, I asked her whether there was a historical society in Letchworth that might be interested in hearing a talk about the Letchworth Jewish community during and after the Second World War. Philippa emailed me back as follows: 'As it happens, I am the secretary of the Letchworth Garden City Society - and we would be honoured to have you talk to us on this topic.' We fixed a date for several months later, in February 2017.

On my frequent trips from my home in Ireland to visit family in Israel, I have often been a guest speaker at the English-speaking Jerusalem branch of the Jewish Historical Society of England. When they asked me in 2016 to submit a list of possible topics for my next talk, I added the Letchworth talk as an afterthought. To my surprise, the Jerusalem organisers chose the Letchworth talk, and I addressed a standing-room only audience, including several people with Letchworth connections.

When I travelled to Letchworth to deliver my talk there, something similar happened. As Philippa wrote to me later: 'Your talk to Letchworth Garden City Society attracted our best-ever attendance, and definitely broke the rules on room occupancy.'

The Jerusalem and Letchworth talks proved that Letchworth memories are alive and well, and that the Letchworth Jewish community still has remarkable pulling power. The need for a book on the community was further reinforced when I was guest (Zoom) speaker at the North Herts Holocaust Memorial Day event – for North Herts, read Letchworth – in 2021 and 2022. I discovered that none of the organisers had ever heard of the town's Jewish heritage.

In June 2021, during the Covid pandemic, a bunch of enthusiastic 'Letchworth Girls' led by Carol Eini (Roth) organised a global Letchworth Zoom get-together. The response exceeded all expectations. I delivered an introductory address, and close to 100 participants in several countries shared memories of Letchworth via Zoom. The excitement and enthusiasm of the participants confirmed Judith Weil (Kritzler)'s conviction that a book on the community was long overdue.

Once my generation disappears, there will no longer be eyewitnesses to the miracle that was Letchworth. My sincere thanks to everyone who shared their memories. I could not have written this book without the dogged dedication of Carol Eini (Roth), my Letchworth childhood friend and faithful research assistant. My work was aided by published articles as well as published and unpublished memoirs. Yossel Schischa and Nathan Sassoon provided a valuable treasure trove of documents concerning the two Hebrew congregations that existed side by side in Letchworth during the war.

Jewish Letchworth presents a record of a special chapter in the history not just of Letchworth Garden City but of Anglo-Jewry. For a little over three decades, from 1939 to 1971, Letchworth was a microcosm of the Jewish communal experience. The evolution of the Letchworth Jewish community can be divided into three distinct periods.

The first period begins in 1939/40 when hundreds of Jewish families moved into Abba Bornstein's Aborn Estate. Sammy Hollander's hand-drawn map shows some of the Letchworth Jewish families of this era.

The second period begins after the bulk of the Jewish community returned to London at the end of the war in 1945. For the next thirteen

INTRODUCTION 5

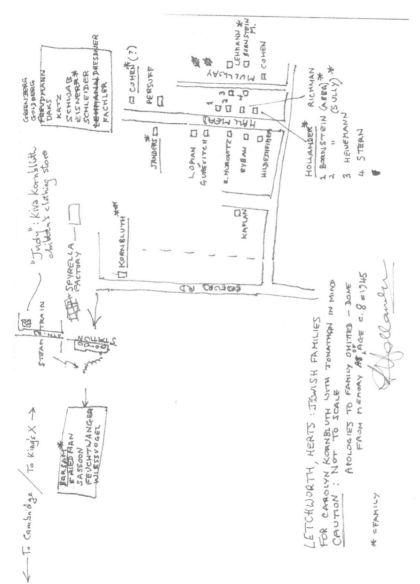

Hand drawn Map of Hallmead by Sammy Hollander

years, an ever-diminishing rump of the community remained in Letchworth until 1958. During this second period, there were three centres of gravity: the Sassoon / Feuchtwanger household in Sollershott East; the 40 Hallmead synagogue, including the small Letchworth yeshiva; and the Shabbat morning kiddush at the home of Shloime (Sali) and Bertha Bornstein at 25 Hallmead.

In the third period, from 1958 to 1972, the centre of gravity shifted from Hallmead to Sollershott East. Shabbat morning services at no. 15 – the Sassoons – were followed by the weekly kiddush at no. 37 – the Fachlers. After the Sassoons and Feuchtwangers left for Israel in 1970, it became a challenge maintaining a Shabbat *minyan*, even with reinforcements from Cambridge students and friends from London. When the last president of the community, my father Eli Fachler, left Letchworth for London in 1971, he appointed Rabbi Yossel Schischa to serve as communal rabbi. The final departure of the Schischas in the Spring of 1972 marked the official end of the community.

The Letchworth glue still retains its powerful adhesive qualities, whether for those of us who were born there, for those of us who were raised there, for those of us who visited there, and even for those who only know of the town by reputation. Something about Letchworth's calming air affected my Israeli-born son, Dr Amit Fachler, a psychotherapist and published author. Although his London-born older brother Ashi spent every weekend in Letchworth for the first four years of his life, Amit had never been to Letchworth. He flew in from Israel especially to attend my 2017 talk. As we strolled through the town earlier in the day, he turned to me and said: 'There's something in the atmosphere here – when I next need time out to write a book, I'd like to do it here.'

This book is largely, but not always, strictly chronological. Some chapters cover themes that span the entire Jewish Letchworth experience. This book is neither an official nor an unofficial history. It is a collection of stories, memories, anecdotes and personal recollections and reflections. Inevitably, these will not always conform to everyone else's recollections, and alternative versions could be incorporated into future editions. I have used a very wide spectrum of public and private sources, so apologies are due to readers who have different memories, whether in terms of spelling of names, dates, quotations or anything else.

INTRODUCTION

My sincere thanks to all those whose generosity made the publication of this book possible. For the sake of transparency, I should point out that to ensure that commercial considerations did not influence the writing or editing decisions, I completed the writing stage before I started looking for funding and sponsorship.

They say that you can take the child out of Letchworth, but you can't take Letchworth out of the child. I have lived in many places – London, Petach Tikva, Raanana, Tel Aviv and Dundalk – but none have shaped me or impacted me as much as Letchworth.

When summing up the Jewish Letchworth experience, two well-known phrases come to mind. One is the proverb, 'It takes a village to raise a child.' Many of the contributors to this book speak of how their lives were shaped by their encounter with Letchworth.

The other phrase is the delightful Hebrew expression: 'Anachnu me'oto hakfar' – literally, we are all from the same village. I think that this phrase encapsulates the sense of identity and the almost mystic attachment that so many people still retain to the village we call Letchworth.

On a personal level, I feel very privileged to have been invited to actively participate for three consecutive years – 2021, 2022 and 2023 – in the North Herts Council's annual Holocaust Memorial Day event organised by Letchworth Council.

I am all too aware that I cannot be fully objective about Letchworth – the town as well as the Jewish community. Here is where my formative experiences played out, and I have never hidden the fact that Letchworth holds a special place in my affections. I hope that readers will indulge me as I shine a very personal light on the world's First Garden City and on the Jewish families for whom Letchworth was home.

Ebenezer, the Garden City Geyser

'At the beginning of the twentieth-century, two great new inventions took form before our eyes: the aeroplane and the Garden City.'

LEWIS MUMFORD,
American philosopher of technology, and expert on cities
and urban architecture

'How could you possibly know that?' Frances Israel (Richman)'s teacher demanded, after he had asked the class to name the oldest road in England. Quick as a flash, Frances had answered 'Icknield Way,' explaining that her wartime Letchworth home was just a few minutes' walk from this ancient pre-Roman trackway that runs from Norfolk to Wiltshire.

Carol (Roth) Eini remembers her headmaster at Hillshott School, Mr Dykes, proudly telling the class that Letchworth is mentioned in the Domesday Book, the great survey completed in 1086 by order of William the Conqueror.

To the west of the town are the remains of Wilbury Hill Camp, a Late Bronze Age hill fort that locals always referred to – probably inaccurately – as the Roman Camp. When my cousin Dovzi Lopian, a frequent visitor to Letchworth in his childhood, was asked about his abiding memories of the town, he singled out the Roman Camp. Almost every child who lived within walking distance of the Roman Camp retains positive memories of this exciting mini-wilderness. Sammy Hollander remembers 'a splendid quarry-like indentation that served as our Sabbath sporting arena.' Vivienne Alper (Gedalla) recalls: 'We all used to play there in the woods and on the small round hills.' Zippy Rosenblatt (Persoff) remembers that her older siblings used to play cricket there.

Here is Zippy's sister Passy describing 'a horrible experience that I will never forget. If our father was free on a Sunday, we'd go to the Roman Camp, where unfortunately I had quite a bad accident. I fell and slit my knee open on a piece of glass and my poor father had to carry me from this camp to somebody's house, the only house that had a telephone near this place, to call an ambulance to schlep me off to hospital.'

Letchworth Garden City owes its genesis to a nineteenth century social reformer, Ebenezer Howard. The London in which he grew up was a dark, fetid place with social inequities, toxic air, filthy water, overcrowding, and rampant infectious disease. After some years in the USA, Howard returned to London and began formulating his revolutionary garden city ideas. His evolving concepts were also shaped by his work as a parliamentary reporter, which brought him into close contact with reports on public health and housing. George Bernard Shaw called Howard: 'Ebenezer, the garden city geyser,' because of his tendency to be a 'spring of benevolent mud.'

In *To-Morrow: A Peaceful Path to Real Reform*, first published in 1898, Howard wrote poetically and prophetically: 'There are not only two alternatives – town life and country life – but a third alternative, in which all the advantages of the most energetic and active town life, with all the beauty and delight of the country, may be secured in perfect combination; and the certainty of being able to live this life will be the magnets which will produce the effect for which we are all striving – the spontaneous movement of the people from our crowded cities to the bosom of our kindly mother earth, at once the source of life, of happiness, of wealth, and of power.'

I think Howard would have been delighted to learn that Lewis Mumford, the American historian, sociologist, philosopher of technology, and expert on cities and urban architecture, would describe Letchworth as follows: 'At the beginning of the twentieth century, two great new inventions took form before our eyes: the aeroplane and the Garden City, both harbingers of a new age. The first gave man wings and the second promised him a better dwelling-place when he came down to earth.'

According to Philippa Parker, The Garden City Association, then the Garden City Pioneer Company, and then First Garden City Ltd. brought Howard's ideas to fruition. Founded in 1903, Letchworth Garden City proposed a new way of living.

The term 'garden city' does not actually mean that every house should have a garden. The term derives from the image of a city being in a belt of open countryside. Howard's idea was that the agricultural belt around the town would provide it with food and that the town would be a market for the produce of the agricultural belt. Many of the older homes in Letchworth have long gardens or green areas in the front or back of the houses where food was grown. My mother Chava Fachler (Becker) may not have read any of Howard's books, but with her twenty-three different varieties of fruits and vegetables, she was a true Howard devotee.

It is no coincidence that the wide, tree-lined boulevard called Broadway has an uncanny resemblance to a particular stretch of the iconic Avenue des Champs-Élysées in Paris. Howard was influenced by Baron George Eugene Haussmann, the city planner behind the renovation of Paris between 1853 and 1870.

Letchworth Garden City is the undisputed flagship that inspired hundreds of innovative settlements all over the world, including Canberra, Australia's purpose-built capital city; the 'new towns' built-in post-war Britain; and hundreds of urban communities and suburbs in countries as diverse as South Africa, France, Finland, Brazil, Canada and, more recently, China and Japan. Closer to home, Welwyn Garden City and Hampstead Garden Suburb were modelled on Letchworth.

The pioneering spirit that we associate with Letchworth mirrors the pioneering spirit of another new city – Tel Aviv – founded in the same decade several thousand miles away on the shores of the Mediterranean Sea. Tel Aviv's planners sought to create a clean and modern garden suburb on the sand dunes north of Jaffa. We know that the British urbanist Patrick Geddes who planned Tel Aviv was directly influenced by the garden city movement.

Howard's sketches are very reminiscent of the iconic layout of Nahalal, the first moshav in Palestine. Nahalal was designed by architect Richard Kauffmann, Chief Architect for the Land Development

Road Sign for Broadway

Company, and a devotee of Howard. Carol Eini (Roth) once attended a course for volunteers at Haifa University. The lecturer, Dr Esther Yankelevitch, mentioned the connection between Nahalal and Howard.

Carol recalls: 'I stood up and shouted, "I grew up in Letchworth Garden City." My classmates thought I was bonkers, but Dr Yankelevich got all excited. "That's fantastic," she said, "please share with all of us what it is like to grow up in a garden city". So for five minutes I gave a potted history about Letchworth.'

The writer George Orwell had a special connection with Letchworth. He lived for several years in the nearby village of Wallington, where he developed many of the ideas espoused in his greatest novels, *Animal Farm* and *Nineteen Eighty-Four*. When I used to decamp to the Letchworth Public Library to study for my A Levels in the early 1960s, I had no idea that just twenty years earlier, Orwell had frequently cycled to that same library to conduct his research.

Orwell famously claimed that Ebenezer Howard's doctrines brought to Letchworth 'every fruit juice-drinker, nudist, sandal-wearer, sex-maniac, Quaker, quack, pacifist and feminist in England.' Letchworth gained a reputation as a mecca for cranks. The Daily Mail ran sightseeing trips to see the idealistic and otherworldly folk of Letchworth. Cockney workers, on their Sundays off, travelled by train from King's Cross to gawp at Letchworth's implausible collection of weavers, potters, yoga fetishists, birth-control fanatics, smock-wearing Esperanto speakers and theosophists. In his poems, *Group Life: Letchworth* and *Huxley Hall,* John Betjeman poked fun at Letchworth's earnest utopianism.

Several celebrities have a Letchworth connection. Actor Laurence Olivier lived in Letchworth between 1918 and 1924 when his father was appointed minister of St Mary's Church. International cricket star Jack Hobbs, holder of the world record for most centuries, played for Letchworth Cricket Club after he retired from first class cricket. Herbert Morrison, the prominent Labour politician who would later hold several cabinet positions, avoided prison as a conscientious objector in the First World War by working as a farm labourer in Letchworth.

Former BBC royal correspondent Jennie Bond, who lived in Spring Road, wrote: 'It was always something to feel faintly smug about; I lived in a 'garden city.' And it wasn't just any old garden city, it was the first of its kind, and made us all feel we had a spurious claim to fame.'

Helen Botschko (Epstein) says that the addition of large numbers of Jewish families in 1939/40 must have been quite a shock for Letchworth residents at a time when multiculturalism was not yet such a distinctive part of the British communal scene. According to Philippa Parker, Letchworth was so accepting of the Second World War Jews because the town had always accommodated people of many faiths and of none. I like to think that Letchworth's pre-war demographic profile as a town full of quirks probably facilitated the garden city's ability to absorb several hundred more quirks – Jewish quirks – after 1939.

Ebenezer Howard lived in Letchworth from 1905 to 1921, and in Welwyn Garden City until his death in 1928. A year before he died, he was knighted. He is buried in a modest grave in Letchworth Cemetery.

For a brief time in the early 1960s, Letchworth was actually owned by a Jewish businesswoman, Amy Rose, through her development company, Hotel York Ltd. One of Letchworth's founding principles was that land should be held in common for the good of all. First Garden City Ltd leased plots to citizens for building houses, and to farmers for growing crops. The rents would provide income for the company, which would then invest the money back into the community.

Changes in British corporate law in the 1950s made First Garden City Ltd vulnerable, since if someone acquired a controlling interest, there was no guarantee that the money would be used for the common good. In December 1960, Amy Rose's Hotel York acquired a controlling interest in First Garden City Ltd. Amy was managing director and her son was on the board. I wonder how many of the few Jews living in Letchworth in the early 1960s were aware of the furious battle which eventually succeeded in thwarting Amy's plans.

Today, Letchworth remains the world's first town that is not fully administered by a town council. The Letchworth Garden City Heritage Foundation is a charity that reinvests all the profits it makes directly back into the community, and has overall control of the town's cultural and environmental issues.

The Bornstein Brotherhood

> *'What could be more fortuitous than the fact that Abba Bornstein, a prominent Hapoel Hamizrachi leader and real estate developer, had just built as yet unoccupied cottages in a working-class area?'*
>
> ZIPPY ROSENBLATT (PERSOFF)

It would be no exaggeration to state that without the Bornsteins, there would be no Letchworth Jewish community to write about. For the first two periods covered by this book – the wartime community and the post-war community – the Letchworth Jewish community and the Bornsteins were interchangeable.

Here is how Zippy Rosenblatt (Persoff) describes the link between Letchworth and the property developer, Abba Bornstein:

'Letchworth Garden City was designed to reduce urban overcrowding by building airy homes with plenty of green – gardens, hedges, trees, green verges and wide streets. What could be more fortuitous than the fact that Abba Bornstein, a prominent Hapoel Hamizrachi leader and real estate developer, had just built as yet unoccupied cottages in a working-class area?

'Abba's estate occupied two parallel streets, Hallmead and Mullway. When the Blitz hit London in late 1939, families realised they needed to evacuate. Word must have spread fast among Abba's fellow Hapoel Hamizrachiites because they flocked to Letchworth. My family—the Persoffs—was one of these lucky families.'

Abba's Aborn (A Bornstein) Estate comprised about 300 small terraced three-up, two-down houses. Abba was the sole landlord, and collected rent from all the houses. According to Norman Oster, 'Abba was very communally minded, but he also was determined to have financial independence. I have this wonderful memory of him riding down Broadway on horseback.'

Abba was the oldest of seven children of Lazar and Golda Bornstein. There is a great photo taken in Letchworth around the end of the Second World War featuring Golda, the matriarch of the family, looking as proud as a peahen; Abba, her son who built Hallmead and Mullway; her son Shloime (Sali) and his wife Bertha; her son Moryce (Moishe); her son Heinrich, who went to live in Israel; her son Idy, who lived in Sweden; and her son-in-law Moishe Sanders, married to Golda's daughter Bertchen (not in the photo.)

Among the Bornsteins who lived in Letchworth either during or after the war were Lazar and Golda; Abba, his wife Hella, and his six daughters; Hella's brother Emile Engel and his wife Nellie and son Joey; Sali and Bertha Bornstein with their son Joshua (Shia), known to everyone as Buby; Bertha's father whom we all called Opa Becker; Bertchen Sanders and her husband Moishe; and Moishe and Ann Bornstein with their daughter Stella.

Zippy Rosenblatt (Persoff) describes the star role that Abba played in her birth: 'I was in utero when my family moved to Letchworth. I was allegedly overdue by about three weeks. It was a Friday. Mum had prepared everything for Shabbat but it was getting urgent to get to the hospital. Mum called our very dear friend Abba Bornstein and said, "Abba, it's time to go to Hitchin." There were two good reasons why she called Abba. One, Dad had not yet come home from his London job. Two, Abba was probably one of the few people who had a car in those days.'

According to Zippy, 'Sali and Bertha's home at 25 Hallmead consisted of two adjacent houses. To access the second house, you had to go through the bathroom of the first house. That always seemed like an adventure to me.' Frances Israel (Richman) remarks: 'A big advantage of living next door to Sali and Bertha was that they had that most precious of commodities – a telephone.'

A newspaper report from the 1960s tells us the story of Tower Clothiers, the Bornsteins' clothing manufacturing business founded in 1933 near London's Tower Bridge. The article, which features Maurice (Moishe) Bornstein, describes that after the London factory was bombed in the Blitz, Moishe's search for a new site brought him to Hertfordshire. 'He spied Weston's old smithy, cleared away 20 tons of metal, and made this Tower Clothiers' new home. He brought the first oil-fired boiler to Weston. The factory was among the first places in the village with electricity and flush toilets. The newly-opened factory brought work and workers to the village, and led to daily bus services from Letchworth, Stevenage and Hitchin.'

Having supplied military uniforms during the Second World War, 80 per cent of Tower Clothiers' output continued to go on government contracts after the war: uniforms for Britain's policemen, firemen, ambulancemen, postmen, chauffeurs and footmen. 'There isn't a uniform we can't make,' Moishe is quoted as saying. The article continues: 'Down in Weston, Hertfordshire's quiet best-kept village, the whir of industry stirs. Behind a screen of greenery, the village's sole factory is starting to turn out uniforms of a different kind – rows of bright green, blue and brown corduroy suits, badge of Carnaby Streetdom, for export to the Continent.'

While the Weston factory was being built, Sali and Moishe lived for a year in the village itself before they moved to their brother Abba's Aborn Estate – Sali to Hallmead, Moishe to Mullway. During the war, many of the factory employees, as well as several widows of Bornstein employees, also lived on the Aborn Estate. Two spinster sisters who worked for the factory, Lily and Esther Davis, lived in Mullway. Another former employee of the Bornsteins was a tailor, Mr Kosminsky, whom everyone called Mr Kaye. His wife later helped my mother Chava Fachler (Becker) when she became cook for the Letchworth Yeshiva.

Esther Herskovics (Munk) remembers: 'My first job, when I had not yet reached the age of sixteen, was in the Bornstein family factory in Weston outside Letchworth. It was a forty eight-hour a week job doing various sewing tasks, but since I was underage, I was only allowed to work eight hours a day, as against ten for the grown-ups. But then I had to hang around until the bus that was our organized transportation arrived to take us back to Letchworth.'

Wallie Tendell got a job as a pattern cutter with Tower Clothiers early in the war. His daughter Pamela Tendell explains: 'In 1946, the family moved into a tied cottage in Hallmead, the hub of the Jewish community in Letchworth. The Bornstein families, the Fachler family, the Tendell family, my uncle, his wife and our cousin, and most importantly the *Shul* were all in this road.'

Stella Bornstein's 3rd Birthday 1948

Golda Bornstein and the Bornstein clan

Bertha and Sali Bornstein in Switzerland

I was a regular visitor to the Mullway home of Moishe and Ann Bornstein when I went to visit my best friend Stella. I visited the Bornstein home every Saturday evening during the winter months. They had television – something my father resisted while we lived in Hallmead. I received an early lesson in human anatomy when the sight that invariably greeted me on Saturday evenings was Moishe lying face down, naked, on his kitchen table, while his Jewish masseur, Mr Barnet from Hitchin, pummelled his back.

My younger brother Chaim was Moishe and Ann's favourite Fachler boy. Moishe always called Chaim 'Herry' – his unique way of pronouncing Harry. Moishe used to tell the story of the time Chaim had a haircut, and kept climbing on a chair to look in the mirror. When Moishe asked Chaim what he was doing, Chaim replied, 'I want to check if my haircut is still there.'

Stella remembers my departure for boarding school. 'Yanky was my constant companion all my life until I was eleven. Suddenly he disappeared from Letchworth after winning a scholarship to Carmel College. My father always referred to Carmel's founder and principal Rabbi Kopul Rosen as "my cousin." In fact, it was Kopul's wife Bella (nee Cohen) from Cardiff who was my father's first cousin.' Stella only revealed to me several decades later how abandoned she felt when I left Letchworth so suddenly.

Sali and Bertha Bornstein's son Buby successfully navigated the role of being the younger brother my father never had, and the older brother I never had. Carol Eini (Roth) is the proud possessor of a Bible that she received from Buby. Inside is a 29 July 1944 dedication from Noach Kaplin on the occasion of Buby's barmitzvah in Letchworth.

One Shabbat when my parents returned earlier than usual from the Bornstein kiddush, they caught my brother Chaim smoking in the back garden. Neither of my parents smoked, so the cigarette could not have come from 79 Hallmead. Buby, himself a heavy smoker, had introduced my asthmatic brother to smoking.

A Buby story that has been passed down through the generations concerns the Seder Night. Buby and his family always finished their Seder much faster than we did. There is a point in the Seder when the children go to the front door and open it to welcome Elijah the Prophet. This particular year, when we opened the door for Elijah, Buby was standing there – and gave us the fright of our lives.

Throughout the 1950s, every Shabbat morning after synagogue services at 40 Hallmead, Sali and Bertha Bornstein hosted a kiddush across the road at 25 Hallmead. While the men argued politics for hours, I had other things on my mind. Bertha was a very special person, and generations of post-war Letchworth children remember both her warmth and her baking prowess. Frances Field (Cohen): 'Bertha made the most fantastic biscuits, and she was such a warm character.' Bertha's onion biscuits were the stuff of legend. No one – not even her daughter-in-law Rachel – ever managed to extract from her the recipe. When Bertha left this world, so did her onion biscuits recipe.

Bertha was the only adult I ever knew who openly and unashamedly read trashy newspapers and comics. Bertha would put aside a week's worth of Daily Mirrors for me. She also bought two weekly comics, TV

Fun and Radio Fun, both of which contained a mixture of two-page prose stories and comic strips. I read them from cover to cover. So my memory of the Bornstein kiddush is of spending hours in my own corner of the room, totally engrossed in my highbrow reading material.

Bornstein cousins who lived in Letchworth during the war included British-born Keva (Akiva) and Ray Kornbluth. Their son Jonathan would tell his family in later life how much he appreciated the opportunity Letchworth gave him to spend so much time with his cousins. One of these cousins was Sammy Hollander, who wrote in his memoir, *The Politics of Political Economy*:

'My first conscious religious experience occurred sometime before age five when I was warned: "Get off that horse, or your father will kill you." It was a milk-delivery van in Letchworth, where my family had been evacuated during the London Blitz. And it was the Sabbath, on which day horse riding – and very much else – is forbidden by Jewish religious law.'

Sammy's London-born mother Lily was an accomplished pianist, but on religious grounds, her father did not allow her to take up a position with the BBC. Sammy remembers his mother taking him and his sister Sally to a local café for cakes that were very doubtful kashrut-wise. His mother explained to the children that it was allowed because 'there was a war on.' She cautioned them to say nothing.

When Sally joined the hachshara kibbutz in Thaxted, her father Yankel discovered that – horror of horrors – Sally was wearing slacks on the kibbutz. He made her return home to Letchworth. My own grandparents, Melanie and Sam Becker, had a more relaxed attitude when their daughter, my mother Chava, wore slacks on her hachshara kibbutz in Buckingham.

All the homes that Abba Bornstein built on the Aborn Estate had a uniform architecture. This could sometimes lead to embarrassing situations, especially since many Letchworth Jewish families did not lock their front doors. Buby Bornstein's son Chaim tells the story of Yankel Hollander coming home from work one evening and absent-mindedly entering the home of Chaim's grandparents, Sali and Bertha. 'When he walked into the living room and sat down, he saw my grandmother Bertha there. Since she was family, he did not think this to be too strange. After a few moments, each of them asked the other if they needed anything. "Why would I need anything?" Yankel asked, "I'm in my own home". My grandmother replied, "Actually you're in mine." '

As a young soldier visiting Letchworth where his girlfriend Chava lived, my father Eli had several encounters with Sali Bornstein. Eli had the unique distinction of being turfed out of the 40 Hallmead *shul* by Sali, not once but twice. First, when Eli turned up for prayers in shorts, and next when he turned up for prayers in open sandals.

Jean Shindler (Pollock) remembers as a child walking to Hallmead and Mullway on a Shabbat and going to the various Bornstein homes. 'My very first taste of gefilte fish was in the home of Moishe and Anne Bornstein.'

The Bornstein tentacles reach the most unlikely places. Carol and Aharon Eini were visiting Hong Kong on their way back from Australia. While at the Night Market, they struck up a conversation with two men wearing kippot, accompanied by an elderly lady. When they asked Carol where she was from, she replied: 'A small town you've probably never heard of north of London, called Letchworth.'

'Oh,' replied the lady, 'My neighbours in Golders Green are Sali and Bertha Bornstein.' 'Then you must know my Auntie Chava - Chava Fachler.' 'Of course,' replied the lady. 'My grandchildren attend the school run by Chava's son-in-law Rabbi Klyne.' When Carol spoke to Chava the following day and gave her regards from Tzipora Mayer, my mother asked: 'Where on earth did you meet her?' 'In Hong Kong's Night Market,' replied Carol. 'Where else?'

Wartime "Vaccies" - Compulsory and Voluntary

"Well, our Maxi looked her over."

MOTHER OF A GIRL EVACUATED TO LETCHWORTH

'Evacuation Begins To-Morrow,' screamed British newspaper headlines on Thursday, 31 August 1939: 'It has been decided to start evacuation of the school-children, and other priority classes, as already arranged under the Government's scheme, tomorrow, Friday September 1st.'

Under an official directive, *Government Order 1939, Section 5(VI), London Schools, Evacuation of*, all schools and colleges had prepared for an eventual evacuation for all children living in London to a safe place in the countryside. The government feared aerial bombardment of cities and towns, like what had happened so recently during the Spanish Civil War.

'No one should conclude that the evacuation decision meant that war was now regarded as inevitable,' the newspapers had reassuringly said the previous day. This misplaced optimism tone was quickly overtaken by events. The evacuation began on 1 September 1939, the day the Germans invaded Poland. On 3 September 1939, Britain declared war on Germany. Within these first three days, under what was codenamed Operation Pied Piper, over one and a half million civilians had been moved out of the cities.

There are no exact figures for how many London evacuees arrived in Letchworth during Operation Pied Piper. A local newspaper revealed that the population of the town increased in two and a half days by over 3,000. Since early 1939, thousands of Women's Voluntary Service personnel had visited millions of homes throughout the country, checking how many people lived there. When the order came to evacuate, a formidable female army was on standby to escort children from their homes to stations, accompany them on trains, pick them up at their destinations, and help billet them. Murray Cohen described the evacuation as a *balagan* – 'organised chaos.'

Arriving in Letchworth was a shock for many inner-city Vaccies, as Letchworth locals dubbed evacuees. Children had never seen cows or pigs, had never been anywhere so green, and had never breathed air free of pollutants. Before Sheila Kritzler (Oster) arrived in Letchworth, she had despaired of the foul air and the smog of London: 'I was very pleasantly surprised to discover in Letchworth Garden City a town that really did have cleaner air.'

While working as a teacher in Letchworth, Keith Stuart wrote his debut novel, *Pied Piper*. He describes how leaflets were posted through letterboxes, simply saying: 'Parents should deliver their children to the station from where they would set off to "somewhere". I struggle to comprehend what that must have felt like, to pack little children off with a case and a gas mask, with no knowledge of where they were going or who they were going to live with.'

Many schoolchildren evacuees to Letchworth were driven around the town in their coaches, distributed to various homes and introduced to their hostesses, who had little choice but to accept them. All the children had been given a postcard to send home with their new address.

My grandparents, Sam and Melanie Becker, and their two daughters Chava (my mother) and Marian, were the lucky possessors of South African/British passports, which allowed them to leave Germany for Britain in 1938 without a visa. The family joined the North London community of maverick Rabbi Dr Solomon Schonfeld, head of the Chief Rabbi's Religious Emergency Council. Rabbi Schonfeld never lived in Letchworth, but he impacted the lives of many Letchworth residents. His son Jonathan told me that the emergency council was a fiction. It was a one-man body created by Rabbi Schonfeld as a vehicle for pressuring the British Home Office to allow Jewish refugees into the country. When Rabbi Schonfeld became Rabbi Hertz's son-in-law, the Chief Rabbi had little choice but to retroactively endorse the emergency council.

A letter in English and German from Chief Rabbi Hertz was circulated to all Jewish refugee children, in Letchworth and elsewhere, who were living with non-Jewish families. Rabbi Hertz's letter said that he was writing 'on behalf of all the good people in England who are working for your welfare. We want you to understand that you have come to a land where you will find love and kindness extended to you from all sides.' Among the specific pieces of advice that the Chief Rabbi offered the youngsters was: 'Try to be considerate to all the people whom you meet in your home. Behave quietly and politely to everyone, including the other people with you. Remember that English people admire quietness and gentleness in behaviour.'

My aunt Marian Becker attended Dr Schonfeld's Jewish Secondary School, where the headmistress was Dr Judith Grunfeld, wife of Dayan Grunfeld of the London Beth Din. When Operation Pied Piper was announced, and the 450 pupils of the Jewish Secondary School had to be evacuated immediately, my grandparents would only allow Marian to join the school if my mother Chava took leave of her studies at Pitman's College to accompany Marian.

The bulk of the school landed up in Shefford, which was close enough to Letchworth to allow contacts between the two towns. The need for secrecy was so strong that teachers and children had no idea where they were going until they got there. Bus drivers were only told their destination after the buses were filled. The school had no say in where the pupils were sent.

In the chapter that Ann Ruth Cohn (Grunfeld) contributed to her mother's book, *Shefford: The Story of a Jewish School Community in Evacuation 1939-1945*, she tells of the time Dr Grunfeld was out cycling, visiting children in the various villages around Shefford. Because there were no signposts, she took a wrong turn and ended up in Letchworth. Someone kindly took her back to Shefford by car, and she collected her bike the following day.

In her book on Shefford, Dr Grunfeld thanked several Letchworth people who helped out at the Jewish Secondary School. The list includes my grandmother Melanie Becker; Flora Feuchtwanger (Sassoon), whose daughter Mozelle Gubbay says that her mother was the school secretary, dealing with visitors to the office and evacuees; and my uncle Jack (Yankel) Lopian, who is listed as a visiting teacher.

When the evacuated schoolchildren arrived in Shefford, one local wife called excitedly to her husband, 'Tom, come quickly, the Children of Israel from the Bible are here.' Another local matron exclaimed in genuine surprise to one of the boys whom she had taken into her house, 'But you have no horns.'

Local Shefford resident Peter Best, whose family took in three boys, recently wrote: 'The Shefford evacuees couldn't speak much English, which made things difficult for the families and the children. All the people of Shefford took as many of the children as they could even though times were tough, with one family taking in six children. Most people had never seen a strict orthodox Jew before.'

Many Shefford families could not understand why these hungry evacuee children refused their tasty *treif* meals. Jack Rosenthal's 1975 TV play, *The Evacuees*, starring Jack's wife Maureen Lipman, captures the confusion, the misunderstandings and the sense of displacement that many child evacuees experienced as they tried to get used to their new surroundings.

Anne Ruth's childhood memories of the confusion surrounding the evacuation probably echo those of many other very young children at the time: 'I felt very frightened. Each of us had a rucksack, a minimum of clothes, and his own gas mask. We were never to be without our gas masks as it was thought by the powers that be that Hitler would attack Great Britain with lethal poison gas. I remember that our children's masks were imaginatively made to resemble Mickey Mouse, Minnie Mouse and other Walt Disney characters.

'As we checked out in long lines and our names called out by a teacher with a loudspeaker, there was frequent panic when newly arrived refugee children who understood only German, Yiddish or French did not answer the roll call; they did not recognise their names pronounced in a very English manner!'

A major challenge facing the organisers of the Shefford evacuation was that there was not enough room in the village to accommodate all the children, several of whom were billeted to neighbouring villages like Clifton, Stotfold and Meppershall. Anne Ruth recalls: 'The nearest primary school was about a ten-minute walk from the little house in the nearby village of Campton in which we were to be settled. We children were sent to this non-Jewish school, and not to Mother's Jewish school in Shefford, because it was considered totally unsafe for us to walk the two miles to Shefford and back each day by ourselves.'

Chava and Marian Becker were billeted in Stotfold with an elderly couple called Carr. As Chava reports: 'In Stotfold we had a kosher canteen, and various school lessons. I was one of the oldest there and helped by giving shorthand lessons. After Marian had settled in, I returned to London. When the siren started up at night, we all had to go down into the shelter until the all-clear sounded. My mother Melanie began to get very nervous, so my father Sam came up with the idea of asking the Carrs if the three of us – my parents and myself – could self-evacuate and join Marian in Stotfold. The Carrs agreed.'

The reunited Becker family was intrigued to hear that there was a thriving Jewish congregation in nearby Letchworth Garden City. One Shabbat, the Beckers walked over from Stotfold to Letchworth, and immediately liked what they saw. They managed to rent a small upstairs flatlet at 6 Hallmead together with Mrs Jones. There were two small bedrooms and a small diner/kitchen where my grandmother Melanie did the cooking on a paraffin stove heater. Chava was delighted to find that her best friend from Frankfurt, Fradel Horovitz, was living in Hallmead, where her father served as the rabbi of a small synagogue.

As Pamela Tendell recalls, for some families the evacuation to Letchworth was unplanned. 'My parents Amy and Wallie married in Hackney in 1936, and I was born in April 1940. That autumn, my parents and I went to stay for a weekend in Letchworth with my mother's brother and his family. What started off as a weekend visit turned into thirty-five years! My parents rented a house in The Quadrant, opposite the Common, and were joined by my grandparents and an aunt. My sister Beryl was born in 1942, brother Donald in 1944 and sister Angela in March 1946 – the same year we moved to Hallmead.'

One of the most prominent evacuee families in Letchworth was the Lopian family. Rabbi Eliyahu Lopian, universall known as Reb Elyah, had been a 9-year-old child prodigy in Poland when he refused to join his parents when they emigrated to the USA because the opportunities to study Torah there were too limited. In 1925, while on a fundraising trip in Berlin for his yeshiva, Reb Elyah was mugged and lost all the money. Penniless, he moved to London where he soon became *Rosh Yeshiva* and *Mashgiach* (spiritual guide) of Etz Chaim Yeshiva.

In 1940, Reb Elyah self-evacuated to Letchworth together with his daughter Liba and her husband Leib Gurwicz; his sons Simcha, Chaim Shmuel, Leizer, Benzion (Benzl) and Yisroel Nachum (Nonni); his daughter Pearl, who was married to Rabbi Barney Klein; and Reb Elyah's youngest son, Yankel Yoel.

Liba and Reb Leib Gurwicz' son Dodi recalls: 'In May 1940, I joined the rest of the Lopian family in Letchworth. Every morning, my grandfather and my father travelled by train to London – Reb Elyah to his yeshiva in Whitechapel, and Reb Leib to his *shul*. On Friday afternoons, Reb Elyah would return to Letchworth to spend *Shabbos* with his children and grandchildren. However, my father remained in London. Right through the Blitz, he spent Friday night sleeping in Whitechapel Underground Station with another Letchworth temporary resident, Rabbi Nosson Ordman.'

As a child, Dodi displayed a keen interest in electronics. 'To a certain degree, I caught it from my father. He was always very interested in technology – he could have been an engineer. In Letchworth during the war, my father used to fix his own radios.' Dodi and his younger brother Avrohom (who would later succeed Reb Leib as Rosh Yeshiva of Gateshead Yeshiva), both attended Letchworth Grammar School together with their uncle Yankel who was the same age as them.

Rabbi Danny Kirsch adds an amusing perspective to the Lopian and Gurwicz families. 'Because the Letchworth Jewish community included so many prominent Rabbis, including Reb Elyah Lopian and his son-in-law Rabbi Leib Gurwicz, any time I mentioned that I'm from Letchworth, people assumed that I must be from one of those illustrious Torah families.'

Efraim Halevy was 6 years old when he arrived in Letchworth with his family. 'I do not remember the exact date we arrived in Letchworth, or the exact procedure that led to us landing there in the area of Hallmead-Mullway. My memory of the very early days is blurred. We travelled to Letchworth by train. A large steam engine pulled the first and third-class carriages. I remember some of the stations on the route, including Welwyn Garden City, Stevenage and Hitchin.

'I remember that after alighting from the train, we found ourselves alone on the platform. As we left the station, there was nobody on the pavement. The neighbourhood we were heading for was seemingly out of town – and out of sight. A lone taxi pulled up and took us to 36 Hallmead, a small semi-detached two-storied house. The street was empty – there were no cars at all in sight.'

Efraim remembers a *haredi minyan* at the top of Hallmead where he sometimes prayed on Shabbat mornings. 'There was an impressive *kiddush* there, despite the privations of rationing. One Shabbat, I spotted a small wineglass with colourless liquid, and I drank it down in one sip. It turned out to be a 96% alcohol. I slept afterwards for eighteen hours, watched over by my worried parents.'

Mordechai Tzvi and Breindel Bindiger, who arrived from Berlin to Stamford Hill shortly before the war, were unusual in that although they were very much part of the Letchworth Jewish community, they were evacuated to Hitchin in 1940. In order to extend the physical distance that would allow them to walk from Hitchin to Letchworth on *Shabbat*, Rabbi Solomon Sassoon organised an *Eruv Techumim* – distance limit – for the Bindigers at the famous Harkness Roses nursery, halfway between the two towns.

Gita Miller (Bindiger) remembers: 'We were billeted with an amazing couple who lived in a large house with several maids. He was a retired sergeant major from the First World War. I had to act as my family's spokesperson, as I spoke the best English. I had to tell our hosts that since we only ate Kosher, we would have to decline their offers of food. I explained that if we could have a little stove with one or two rings in our living room, we would be able to cook for ourselves. Our hosts kindly granted our request.

'Every *Shabbos*, thanks to the *eruv*, we walked to our nearest Jewish neighbours in Letchworth, the Sassoons, who had a *Beis Medrash* in their house. Mrs Sassoon who was very kind to me. With a big smile, she would say, "Gita, stay for lunch!" Often Mrs Sassoon offered that I could stay to read or talk to their guests whilst she had a rest, and then I would join the family for *Shabbos* afternoon tea. Among the people we met at the Sassoons was Rabbi Dessler. I remember that my father, who was Chassidic, was highly impressed by the respect the Sassoons showed to this *Talmid Chochom* – like a king'.

'I went to a good girls-only school in Hitchin where I learnt most of my English. After school, I would cycle to *Cheder* in Letchworth to Rabbi Horowitz's house where classes were held for girls. Our teacher was

Rabbi Wahrhaftig. When I was 15, whilst still at school, I took a private business evening class. My first job was as a secretary in the Amex Publishing Company in Letchworth which published children's books. I worked there for 6 months, and their good references helped me get a job when we moved to Gateshead at the suggestion of Rabbi Dessler.'

Sheila Kritzler (Oster) was a pupil at North London Collegiate when her parents decided that she and her brother Norman would be safer out of London. Their father was very concerned for Sheila's Jewish education, and turned for advice to his friend Rabbi Dr Isidore Epstein. Rabbi Epstein suggested that the children should go to Letchworth where they could stay in a kosher home. The Epsteins had already sought refuge in Letchworth.

12-year-old Sheila spent two happy years living with the Pollocks at 202 Icknield Way. Rabbi Epstein's daughter Helen became Sheila's private Hebrew tutor. Sheila remembers that prayer services were held in the Pollocks' home, especially on the High Holidays. Joe Pollock was closest in age to her, and he looked after her, giving her a birthday date book on her birthday which she still possesses and treasures.

In September 1941, Sheila's younger brother, 10-year-old Norman Oster, arrived in Letchworth from nearby Biggleswade where his prep school had been evacuated. He was first billeted with the family of the rector of the Church of All Saints, an Anglican church in Willian. The rector himself was away on military service, and his two sons did not live up to the name of the church – they were far from being saints.

'For four days,' says Norman, 'They plagued me with the charge of deicide: "You killed Jesus." "Yes," I told them, "All by myself." My objection to their accusation was not on religious grounds. At the age of ten, I simply knew that I had not killed anyone. I insisted that my mother find me alternative accommodation, which she did with another non-Jewish family in Letchworth.'

For the next five months, apart from his sleeping arrangements, and the hours he was at school, Norman's entire day was spent in the company of the members of the Jewish community. 'My mother organised kosher food for me, and I had my lunch every day at the Brochs. On *Shabbat* I was with the Brochs all day. My family knew several families in Letchworth, so I also got to visit Dr Epstein and Dayan Abramsky. My *cheder* teacher after school every day was Dr

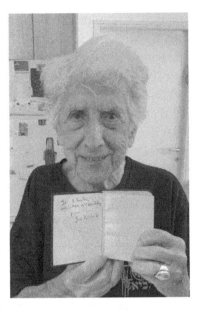

Sheila Kritzler in 2022 holding the birthday date book she received from Joe Pollock in 1941

Pollock House, Icknield Way

Heinemann, and he was excellent. On Sundays, in addition to cheder, there were social activities in the Howard Hall. Habonim was the Zionist youth group – there was no Bnei Akiva in those days.'

Norman's sojourn in Letchworth was cut short in February 1942 when he had a burst appendix and was rushed to London. He never returned to Letchworth. 'I look back on those five months as a very rich experience. I was enveloped by the Jewish community. The standard of Jewish education was incredibly good. My short stay in Letchworth is filled with good and positive memories.'

Sol Cohen (whom everyone called Mustachio – no guessing why) was the headmaster of the orthodox Yesodei Hatorah school in Stamford Hill. He and his wife Sadie arrived in Letchworth with their children, 11 years old son Murray and their daughter Frances, and were joined after the war by their foster daughter Judy Lebrecht, daughter of Sol's late sister.

Murray recalls the circumstances of the family's evacuation: 'I was born in Stepney where my mother had a chemist shop. There was no room in the premises for a corrugated steel Anderson air raid shelter. When the sirens sounded, we ran to my grandmother who lived seventy yards away. Stepney Borough Council workers had dug a big hole in her small garden and put in an Anderson, which my mother furnished with rugs, chairs and a table. We spent many a night in the shelter, with my grandmother forever preparing food and drink.

'One night our home was destroyed in a bombing raid, and we needed somewhere to stay. At first, my father booked us into two rooms in the Regent Palace Hotel next to Piccadilly Circus. The hotel's huge basement served as an air raid shelter. My father Sol was an East End boy, and he had kept contact with his classmate Sammy Fisher, born Samuel Fishtenberg, later Lord Fisher of Camden. Sammy was the administrator of a Talmud Torah off Commercial Road, and during the war, he used to commute from Letchworth every day by train. Both his daughters were born in Letchworth.

'When Sammy learned that Sol's family had been bombed out of their home, he told him: 'Solly, you can't stay in a hotel with the kids. Come to Letchworth and I'll find you a couple of rooms. Then you can look around and find a house for yourself.' Sol wisely took Sammy's advice, and the family moved into two rooms at 114 Hallmead.

Murray's sister Frances Field (Cohen) remembers: 'We were one of the last Jewish families to arrive in Letchworth, which is why at first we had to share accommodation with a widow and her three children. It was a very tight squeeze. The bathroom upstairs had no basin – just a lavatory and a bath. Later, we moved to 9 Mullway.'

Murray remembers that the Scouts Hall in Icknield Way was used for *Yomtov* services, as well as for *Purim shpiels* and *Chanukah* parties. The hall above the Co-op shop in Eastcheap was used for weddings and for High Holidays. Murray earned pocket money from Abba Bornstein to cycle around to members of the Letchworth Hebrew Congregation, collecting membership fees of 1 shilling and 6d a week.

Murray and Frances's cousin Judith Lebrecht was from Leeds. Her mother had been ill for several years. Judith often visited Letchworth, and after her mother died, she came to live with the Cohens. Judith loved being in the countryside where there were open fields, and where even religious people went and sat outside the pub. Frances Israel (Richman) remembers: "I was told that a little girl – Judith Lebrecht – is coming to play with me. I thought that she spoke funny. I was too young to understand much about accents.'

Vivienne Alper (Gedalla) remembers as a 6-year-old how scared she was of the air-raid sirens, the searchlights in the night skies and the barrage balloons. "Eventually we arrived in Letchworth, where my parents rented the house at 77 Mullway. My father commuted to London every day by train. Although we were six children, my oldest brother was in the army, my two sisters were in Palestine, and my twin brothers who were seven years older than me, had been evacuated with their school. That left me alone every day in Letchworth with my mother.'

Many of Letchworth's Jewish evacuees were businesspeople and professionals who worked in offices, shops and warehouses in London. They continued to commute daily to their places of work to Finsbury Park (for Stamford Hill) and to Kings Cross (for the Hatton Garden diamond centre, the City and the East End). Derek Pollock remembers: 'A big attraction of Letchworth was undoubtedly its close proximity to London and the rail service that offered its passengers a daily return ticket to Kings Cross for only one shilling and eight pence.'

Morning services were held in the last carriage on the early train, also known as the Milk Train and nicknamed 'The Palestine Express.'

My mother remembers 'beards flying, *tallitot* swaying, and *tefillin* bobbing up and down.' On cold winter evenings, passengers returning by train from London sometimes had to navigate the snow, ice and fog – and the blackout – by forming a human chain from Letchworth station to Hallmead and Mullway.

Professor Ernst Sondheimer recalls: 'When a colleague was killed in an air raid, my father decided that we must leave London and we moved to Letchworth. My recollection is that we all – father, mother and two children – lived in one room at first and had to go through the kitchen to reach the only bathtub in the house. Somewhat better accommodation was found after a while. I was still at school in 1940 (in the sixth form) and travelled to London every morning by the workman's train, which left Letchworth at 6.33 and arrived at King's Cross at 7.58.'

Almost every house on the Aborn Estate had evacuees. Sometimes as many as ten people slept in a house, many on the floor. Frances Israel (Richman) looks back with incredulity at wartime Letchworth: 'I cannot believe how many evacuees crowded into the small houses in Hallmead and Mullway. I remember that the Persoffs at 41 Hallmead had an enormous number of lodgers, including Dayan Yehezkel Abramsky, the head of the London Beth Din, and his wife Rebbitzen Raizel.'

Mark and Sarah Persoff had six children: Avraham, David, Paselle (Passy), Zipporah (Zippy), Meir, and Menachem (who was born after the family returned to London). Zippy Rosenblatt (Persoff) recalls: 'The Abramskys were advised to evacuate to Letchworth for safety reasons. While they were waiting for their home to be ready, they stayed within the elastic walls of our tiny home. The Dayan was particularly fussy about the kashrut of his food and would only eat what Rebbitzen Raizel had prepared for him. Our flexible home also managed to accommodate our elderly dressmaker aunt, Miriam Zimmerman. Her unmarried journalist daughter Golda later boarded with the Richman family and joined the men on their daily trek by train. As Golda used to say, no one knew whether they'd find their office had been bombed during the night.'

Deborah Emanuel (Broch) recalls: 'Elderly people came from London to visit their families who had relocated to Letchworth and it was so exciting when my parents hosted them and I had to sleep on the floor on a mattress.'

The original Pied Piper operation primarily involved the evacuation of school-age children. But Pied Piper also included the evacuation of thousands of pregnant women who had to move to rural areas to await the arrival of their babies. These women were expected to give birth in hastily amassed maternity 'hospitals,' and to stay at their countryside billets for the remainder of the war.

As Joe Richman's daughter Frances Israel (Richman) says, 'My father had heard reports of the shambolic evacuation of pregnant women, some of whom ended up in the wrong places, while others had to hitchhike home with babes in their arms. My father was determined that my mother should not suffer this fate. He did not want her to end up in some random destination like John O'Groats.'

Joe's friendship with Abba Bornstein helped him to choose the self-evacuation option, and he and his wife were swiftly installed in 23 Hallmead in Letchworth. Their daughter Frances was born in the St Catherine's nursing home on Spring Road.

The evacuation of so many Jews to Letchworth in such a short period stretched the resources of the town's municipal authorities: billeting arrangements, overcrowding, the strain on public services, the requisitioning of properties, and food provision. In September 1940, Dr Isidore Epstein's contacts with the Board of Deputies of British Jews led to Miss B Fleishman being appointed as official liaison officer between the Jewish community and all the organisations in Letchworth that dealt with the Jewish evacuees. Miss Fleishman worked with the billeting officers, with ministers of churches, and with the Women's Volunteer Service.

On Chanuka 1940, the Jewish community in Letchworth organised a party for all Jewish evacuees, to which their non-Jewish fellow evacuees were also invited. 200 evacuees sat down at tables beautifully decorated and with lighted candles. A high tea was served, the children received sweets, the women received handkerchiefs, and men received cigarettes. The local Church of England minister, Rev Thatcher, spoke.

For all the days of Pesach 1941, an energetic canteen committee provided over 200 Jewish evacuees with kosher food in St Francis' College. Dr Epstein led a *seder* for adult evacuees and Rev Rosenberg led a children's *seder* on the first night. On the second *seder*, Dr Bernard

Homa led the proceedings for the adults, and Dr Weinstock for the children.

The autumn of 1940 saw a further wave of evacuation. Like Operation Pied Piper, this evacuation too was chaotic and confusing. Ariel Broch's mother Ella was the older sister of Judith Grunfeld, headmistress of the Jewish Secondary School evacuated to Shefford. Ariel's father was Rabbi Isi Broch. After Kristallnacht, Judith and Dayan Grunfeld sponsored the Brochs' entry to Britain, and Rabbi Broch worked as warden at the Jewish Secondary School.

When Rabbi Broch was interned on the Isle of Man in May 1940, Ella was left to fend for herself and her two youngest children. Together with other orthodox Jewish mothers and children, Ella was hurriedly put on a bus and driven for hours along unfamiliar country roads. Eventually, the evacuees disembarked in Letchworth and were led into the hall of St Francis' convent school.

To their consternation, the Jewish matrons discovered a large portrait of the Virgin Mary gazing down benevolently on them from the wall. When the Belgian nuns did not understand – or did not want to understand – what the problem was, the women took matters into their own hands and turned the portrait to face the wall.

The next day, the billeting officer handed Ella Broch and her children into the care of Mrs Morris, who took in refugees as her contribution to the war effort. Mrs Morris owned a large country house. Her husband, who ran a private company in Letchworth, was on active duty overseas. Ariel takes up the story:

'My mother had no real idea of her own whereabouts. She had no idea of her relative distance from her older children. All she had was a piece of paper given to her when she left London on which was written the cryptic words: "Ariel in Clifton, Naomi and Esther in Shefford". She had no idea where Letchworth was, never mind Clifton and Shefford'.

'Mrs Morris spread out a local map, and showed my mother that Clifton and Shefford were practically within walking distance of Letchworth. The very next day, Mrs Morris drove my mother to the Shefford billeting officer, where she was reunited with the rest of her children. She was soon allocated a house in Mullway. All her children – including me – left the Jewish Secondary School in Shefford and we began our schooling in Letchworth.'

According to Esther Herskovics (Munk), the Sassoon family was instrumental in saving her parents, Rabbi Leo and Hanny Munk and family from Nazi Germany. 'I arrived in England in January 1939 with my parents, followed shortly thereafter by my brother Willy, who had been on a Hachshara Kibbutz in Holland. In May 1940, my father and Willy were sent to the Isle of Man because they were "dangerous enemy aliens." This left my mother and me behind in our apartment in Lordship Park, N16.'

With Rabbi Broch incarcerated on the Isle of Man, and Ella Broch alone in Letchworth looking after five young children and pregnant with number six, Hanny Munk and her daughter Esther moved to Letchworth to help Ella Broch when she gave birth. They rented a small room from the Wahrhaftig family. After the Munk and Broch menfolk were released from internment, the Munk family stayed in Letchworth until Rabbi Munk took up a rabbinical position in Maidenhead.

On a BBC website, Byl Richards describes that Mr and Mrs Hackenbroch from London were compulsorily billeted with his family. 'They were a pleasant orthodox Jewish couple, both practising dentists, refugees from Germany; they travelled to London daily. We were bemused that they were not allowed to do anything on their Sabbath, could not touch money or even switch lights on or off. Mrs Hackenbroch told us that Jewish wives must always have a complete layette ready in case they became the mother of the Messiah!'

Until I read this quote from Byl Richards, I had never heard of this phenomenon. Sheila Kritzler (Oster), who was the target of open antisemitism, enlightened me. 'I was in the playground of my Letchworth school one day when one of the girls came up to me and hissed, "Jew-girl." I was 10 or 11 at the time, and this perplexed me. I said to the girl: "You don't know me. Why on earth would you want to insult me?" "Because," explained my gentile tormentor, "you don't believe that the messiah has come. What's more, you people believe that one of you will give birth to the messiah."'

One Letchworth family had expected to receive two little Cockney child evacuees, but instead received two teenage Jewish girls. Inga was from Berlin and London-born Doris from a Polish family. The Letchworth host family felt bad that a German girl and a girl with Polish roots had to share a bed. Like many English families, they made the mistake of thinking that because Germany had invaded Poland, this would be an issue. The host families found it hard to grasp that the two Jewish girls would naturally cling together.

Doris' family owned a skirt factory in London, and they visited her regularly in Letchworth. One weekend, Doris' 18-year-old brother Maxi cycled from London to visit his sister. The following weekend, Doris' mother arrived with a new skirt for the teenage daughter of the host family. Her parents asked how she knew the right size? Doris' mother gave the immortal reply that would become a catchphrase in the household for many years to come: 'Well, our Maxi looked her over.'

Helen Bornstein married Rev Lewis Rosenberg in 1937, and the couple were evacuated to Letchworth in 1939. Rev Rosenberg was involved in Jewish evacuee children's education, helped by Helen, who overcame rationing restrictions by growing her own vegetables and by home baking.

According to the minutes of the Letchworth Hebrew Congregation, several government hospitals were set up in the vicinity of Letchworth 'to receive patients injured in the bombing raids over Hackney and the East End. As many as 100 Jewish patients were at one time in these hospitals. A number of volunteers from the Letchworth Jewish community regularly visited these patients, giving comfort, assistance and advice to their unfortunate brothers and sisters.' Reverend Rosenberg supervised visitation activities, and he personally handled all the burial arrangements in the sad event that patients in these hospitals died. The Rosenbergs left Letchworth in 1943 when Rev Rosenberg was appointed leader of the Staines Jewish community, a post he would hold for the next thirty-six years.

The Freudmann family, diamond merchants from Belgium, arrived relatively late in Letchworth, after a tortuous journey that began on 10 May 1940, when the Germans invaded Belgium, France and Holland. The Freudmanns reached Glasgow, and travelled by train to London where they stayed with their cousin Sam Sebba in Totteridge. When a German bomb fell in the garden, it was time to leave.

As Mickey Freudmann describes: 'First we self-evacuated together with the Sebbas to a village called Newnham in Hertfordshire where we lived in the squire's house while the squire himself was serving in the army. We finally arrived in Letchworth in May 1942. For the next four years, we lived at various addresses. First, we rented a house with a garden at 1 Baldock Road, and then rented a house at "Corrie Wood", Hitchin Road, which had a huge garden and a locked hut with a very large miniature railway inside. We could only peer at it from the outside.

'Next, we moved to Rowan Crescent for a short while, and then to Kingsley House on Hitchin Road. Throughout our four years in Letchworth, my grandfather and parents worried about two of my father's brothers and their families who were trapped in German-occupied France. There was some irregular contact via the Red Cross, and my father tried desperately to help his brothers reach a neutral country. One brother was finally caught and murdered at Majdanek. My grandfather died about a year after we arrived in Letchworth, in 1943.'

The Freudmanns knew the Lunzers from before the war, and in Letchworth the two families lived quite close to one another, on the Sassoon side of the town. Mickey recalls: 'The Lunzers' eldest son Hugo served in the British Army and acted like a typical pukka British officer type. The Lunzers' daughter Erica served in the Auxiliary Territorial Service. My brother David often ran away from home, saying he was going to London. Invariably, we would get a message from the Lunzers that he was in their house.'

Another family that self-evacuated to Letchworth was the Grodzinskis under the matriarch Bertha, widow of Abie. As we will see in the next chapter, the family had been in Letchworth during the First World War – and now they returned to the garden city. Bertha's eldest children, Harry and Ruby, had taken over the reins of the family bakery business in 1930.

Frances Field (Cohen) remembers the wedding of Harry Grodzinski and Rita Kornbluth (Keva's sister) in the Grodzinski garden in August 1941. The wedding was featured on the front page of the local paper as the first Jewish wedding in Letchworth. According to Harry's son Johnny, when Harry and Rita's oldest son was born in Letchworth, his parents named him David in honour of David Sassoon, of Sassoon Library fame.

There is an interesting postscript to this Letchworth Grodzinski wedding. The *chuppah* ceremony was conducted by Rabbi Horowitz, who also wrote the *ketuba* – the marriage contract. Twenty-seven years later, when Shulamith, the daughter of Adi and Amelia Schischa was marrying Hanoch Landau in Letchworth – the last Jewish wedding to be held in the town – Adi asked to examine the Grozinski *ketuba* to make sure that he correctly spelled Letchworth in Hebrew lettering in Shulamith's *ketuba*.

Henry Ehrenreich was a Jewish Kindertransport child who arrived in June 1939 from Frankfurt where his father Nathan had been a prominent musician. In Operation Pied Piper, Henry was evacuated to Letchworth, where the billeting officer placed him with a German-speaking family that harboured Nazi sympathies and made Henry's life a misery. Luckily, his mother Frieda escaped from Germany on one of the last flights before war broke out. She reclaimed a desolate Henry and in December 1939 they flew to New York where they were reunited with Henry's father.

Not all the Jewish evacuees in Letchworth openly identified as Jews or were associated with the mainstream Jewish community. Sometimes, despite the best efforts of billeting officers and Jewish liaison officers, children fell through the gaps. Marian Leitner arrived in England from Prague with the Winton Kindertransport, and lived with a Letchworth family until the end of the war. She seems to have had no contact with the Jewish community. She worked in the renowned Marmet baby-carriage factory and later married a local man.

There were also Jewish families who deliberately sought no connection with the Jewish community. Moira Roth, her mother Eve Shannon and their friend Rose Hacker (nee Goldbloom), the English-born socialist feminist, inhabited their own eco-system. One refugee that Eve took in was Hans Redlich, a Jewish musicologist and conductor from Vienna, whose father was the last Minister of Justice in the Austro-Hungarian Empire. Eve and Rose became lifelong friends, and 'shared a passion for social change, rooted in a progressive Jewish background of community service and radical thought.' At the age of 100, Rose would achieve global fame as the 'oldest newspaper columnist in the business,' when she worked for the *Camden New Journal*.

As recently as 2014, some of the Letchworth host families were still trying to track down Jewish Vaccies who had been billeted with them seventy years earlier. One internet post read: 'Hello, I am looking for information for Stella Finkelstein who was an evacuee. Stella stayed at

The Freudmann Family

my mother's home in Letchworth. Mom remembers her being a year or two older than she was so I am guessing she was born around 1933-1935. Any ideas where I can look? Thank you! Janice (USA).'

Letchworth at war

'Sometimes when the Moaning Minnie air raid sirens sounded at night, we all trooped downstairs to the hall corridor and put saucepans on our heads, as officially advised!'

BYL RICHARDS

Vivienne Alpert (Gedalla) was quick to discover the advantages of living in Letchworth after escaping the Blitz in London. 'It had been nice living opposite Victoria Park in London, but it wasn't like living in the Letchworth countryside. Part of my route to school took me through fields. On the other side of the fence at the bottom of our garden there was a field. Sometimes my friends and I climbed over the fence and ran across the field to reach the road at the other side. I would often stand at the bottom of the garden and marvel at the beautiful sunsets.

'Letchworth was also a gift to children like me who had come from London. There were so many other Jewish families in Hallmead and later in Mullway, many of them with children, and we got to know most of them. There were the Lehmanns and the Cohens, the Bornsteins and the Persoffs, the Fishers and the Sterns, and others. Two of my best friends, with whom I played regularly, were Shifra and Judith Lehmann.

'Later in our stay, Rabbi Dr Isidore Epstein and his wife took up residence in a house in Mullway a few doors away from ours. I still have a book on my shelves, given to me for my 12th birthday, inscribed: "With love and best wishes to Vivienne from the Epstein family."'

Letchworth was not untouched by the Second World War. Twenty-eight high explosive bombs and 376 incendiary bombs rained down on the town, fortunately with no civilian deaths. Local Letchworth boy,

Group of children on Norton Common

Tom Walker, remembers: 'During wartime, we were continually woken up by the rumble of army convoys, lorries and tanks passing by, squadrons of British, American and German aircraft overhead both day and night, and the air-raid sirens. I can recollect seeing the German planes with their black crosses on their wings and swastika on the tail fins as they went over. Occasionally, an enemy plane that had been shot down would be put on show in the town centre. There were also ack-ack units and searchlight batteries scattered over the fields around Letchworth.'

Mickey Freudmann also enjoyed a front-seat view of military convoys: 'The place where we lived in Letchworth was on a fairly central axis of military movement. Around 1943/44, military traffic became quite frequent with huge American and British military convoys moving along the main Letchworth—Hitchin road. I also remember huge ammunition dumps along the roadsides in preparation for the invasion of Europe. I remember seeing German and Italian prisoners of war who worked in the surrounding fields. They had large round yellow or red patches on their uniforms to show that they were POWs.'

Frances Richman in her pram in Hallmead

Mickey recalls that from the time of the Normandy landings in 1944, his family had a large map of the war on the wall next to the kitchen. 'The map was issued by the *Daily Telegraph*, and every day we followed the progress of the war, putting pins on the progress on the different fronts. We also listened with great excitement and emotion to Prime Minister Winston Churchill's inspiring speeches.'

Byl Richards recalls that during air raid drills, when the Moaning Minnie air raid sirens sounded at night, everyone trooped downstairs to the hall corridor and put saucepans on their heads, as officially advised. Although Moaning Minnies originally referred to the screaming noise of a German weapon, it came to refer to the long, loud sound that warned people that enemy planes were about to drop bombs.

Zippy Rosenblatt (Persoff) remembers the disgusting, choking, rubbery smell of gas masks. 'Another memory is of playing in the street, bouncing pink balloons, and hearing the distinctive, threatening sound of an air raid warning. I ran indoors, terrified and screaming. There must have been several bomb shelters scattered around Letchworth, but I do not recall ever having to hunker down in one.'

Every day, as it got dark, Letchworth families had to put blackout curtains on the windows so that no lights would shine. People walked around with gas mask cases bouncing on their backs. Ariel Broch remembers the first school air-raid-warning exercise: 'The whole junior school spent some hours in the dugout shelter, singing songs and chewing special off-the-ration sweets. That was the only time our class went down into the school shelter. After the first heavy rain, it became completely waterlogged and was rendered useless.'

Letchworth held a War Weapons Week. As part of a Wings for Victory campaign, Letchworth organised a street collection to purchase a Spitfire. Henry Pollock, who had two sons in the armed forces during the war, organised the Jewish community branch of the Spitfire Fund. The Wings for Victory campaign successfully met its £5,000 target, and Letchworth proudly purchased a Spitfire in May 1940.

One day, as Dodi Gurwicz was on his way home from school, the siren sounded: 'I watched a dogfight between a Spitfire and a Luftwaffe fighter plane. I saw that the German plane had been hit – it was flying so low that I could see the markings on the plane. The German machine gunner shot at us and the children around me scattered. Miraculously, no one was hurt. We saw the German plane crash nearby.'

Ariel Broch reports on the same incident. 'One day, a solitary airplane with the German Cross insignia flew overhead, causing all the children to run for cover. I stumbled into a large, covered hole in the ground containing a sack and a stool. I convinced myself that I had discovered a spy's hideout.'

One Shabbat in August 1944, Mickey Freudmann was walking to *shul* with his father and his brother David. They witnessed a large formation of US Air Force Flying Fortresses on their way from their East Anglia bases to bomb the U-Boat pens in Brest, France. Suddenly, two of the mighty bombers collided and came spiralling down to earth near Weston: Says Mickey, 'It was very frightening and I remembered it all my life. Mickey's brother David describes the same incident: 'Looking up, we saw burning debris falling, we couldn't tell how many of the planes had collided, but it was the most horrific sight I had ever seen.

Even now, almost seventy years later, I can still hear the noise and see the falling burning pieces.'

Ariel recalls: 'Whenever I was home at one o'clock in the afternoon, there had to be absolute silence in the house for the one-o'clock news. No interruptions were allowed.' Frances Israel (Richman) also recalls the sacredness of the one o'clock news. 'I might have been too young to understand what war was, but we all knew that when Workers' Playtime on the radio finished, the pips heralded the one-o'clock news. We all knew that no one was allowed to make a sound.'

The biggest employer in Letchworth was British Tabulating Machine Company, later International Computers and Tabulators (ICT) and later still International Computers Limited (ICL). This is where the 'Bombes' were produced - the top-secret decoding machines that were used to break the code of the German Enigma machine in Bletchley Park and other secret locations.

If the Germans had known about the critical role of British Tabulating Machine Company to the war effort, the Luftwaffe may have diverted more bombing raids to the various company sites situated around Letchworth. But since none of the hundreds of employees knew what the 'Bombes' were designed for, it was hardly likely that the Germans would find out. It was not until the 1970s, when the story of Enigma started to come out, that people in Letchworth realised what British Tabulating Machine Company had been producing.

Secrecy shrouded the activities of municipal vehicle manufacturers Shelvoke & Drewry, which before the war had specialised in producing dustcarts. During the war, their production lines were converted to the Welfreighter miniature submarine developed by Britain's Special Operations Executive (SOE). It is only in recent years that official files detailing the existence of this project have been declassified. During the war, local residents were blissfully unaware that miniature submarines were being built in a Letchworth factory.

Another industry in Letchworth that contributed significantly to the war effort was Irving Airchutes, the largest parachute manufacturer in the world. Its parachutes saved hundreds and thousands of servicemen. The company was founded by movie stuntman Leslie L. Irving. He did not invent the parachute, but he developed the manual ripcord. When the RAF ordered Irving parachutes for all its airmen, Irving moved to Letchworth in 1926 and opened Irving Airchutes.

From 1919, the iconic Spirella factory – the UK branch of the American Spirella Corset Company, known locally as Castle Corset, was the largest employer in Letchworth. Spirella employed thousands of women who used stout laces to produce foundation garments. Workers rallied to the cry of 'Pull yourselves together, girls'. During the Second World War, Spirella converted its production lines to make parachutes for Irving Airchutes. Mickey Freudmann had reason to remember his neighbour Irving: 'He used to drive around in a big American car.'

Spirella Factory near Letchworth Rail Station

Because Mickey Freudmann's father was a foreign national, he had to receive a special permit to travel to and from London where he had his office in Hatton Garden, the diamond merchants' quarter. He needed a special permit to return after curfew hours, as there were restrictions on the movements of aliens after certain hours.

While living in Letchworth, my mother Chava Fachler (Becker) had moved from her job in the Houndsditch Warehouse to an office job with the Hechalutz movement and the Brit Chaluzim Datiim (Bachad) in Bloomsbury House. Her bosses, Erich Duschinsky and Aryeh Handler, looked after all the young people that Bachad and Youth Aliyah had brought to Britain with the Kindertransport.

One of these youngsters was Eli Fachler, who had been a pupil at the Whittingehame Farm School in Scotland, and was now a member of the tiny Hardmead Bachad kibbutz near Bedford. When Chava was asked to organise a summer camp for Rabbi Schonfeld's Adass-affiliated Ben Zackai Youth Group in Stoke Newington in 1941, Handler suggested that she check out Hardmead, which consisted of a house in the middle of fields, with no gas and no running water. One of the members was Chava's schoolfriend from Frankfurt, Betty Einhorn, who informed Chava that a strapping lad called Eli Fachler had joined the kibbutz two days earlier.

With so many male agricultural workers in the armed forces, women were needed to provide a new rural workforce. The British Ministry of Agriculture had no objection if Jewish refugee youngsters wanted to play at being kibbutzniks, so long as they fulfilled their land work quotas. Soon after arranging the summer camp at Hardmead, Chava and her fellow Letchworth friend Hanna Lehmann, received their call-up papers, since both were British subjects. By joining the Hachshara Kibbutz Movement, they could become Land Girls, officially the Women's Land Army (WLA). Hanna became a Land Girl in Bromsgrove near Birmingham. Chava became a Land Girl in Hardmead, arriving there in September 1941.

My father Eli was a "friendly alien", with Polish nationality. After refusing to serve with the Free Polish Army, he joined the British army in March 1944. In December 1944, while Eli was still a soldier, he and my mother Chava underwent a civil marriage ceremony in Folkestone, followed by a religious wedding on their Buckingham kibbutz. Eli managed to get home to Letchworth most weekends.

Two young men in Letchworth remarked on how proud they felt when they saw Eli in army uniform during the war. Murray Cohen: 'When Eli came home to Letchworth on leave, he made sure to strut around in his army uniform with his sergeant stripes, to show the local residents that Jews were also fighting in the war.' Sammy Hollander: 'I recall Eli in his sergeant's uniform at Rabbi Horowitz's shul.' It was only when I read these comments that I realized that Eli was probably the only visible Jewish member of His Majesty's armed forces in Letchworth.

During my research for my Letchworth talk, I came across the curious fact that Abraham (Abie) Betzalel Grodzinski died in Letchworth in 1918. I could not understand what Abie was doing in Letchworth in the First World War, over two decades before the Grodzinski family evacuated to Letchworth in the Second World War. I assumed that maybe Abie died in Letchworth because he was in a sanitorium there after contracting Spanish Flu.

Abie's grandson Johnny Grodzinski put me right: 'In 1888, my great-grandparents Harris and Judith Grodzinski, bakers by trade, arrived from Vilnius to the East End of London. There they hired kosher ovens and began a business that would grow from a trading barrow to a full-scale bakery. The business was managed by my grandfather Abie, who inherited the bakery at eighteen on his father's untimely death.

"There was a Jewish community in Letchworth in the First World War, and my grandparents and their children evacuated there from the East End of London to avoid German bombing.' In other words, Letchworth was already a sanctuary for the Grodzinskis and other Jewish families during the First World War.

Another Jew in Letchworth during the First World War was Alec Edward Cowan (originally Elias Cohen), who was brought to the UK by his cousins, the Goide family. Alec is described in census records as a cinema proprietor in Letchworth before the First World War. Does that mean that he owned or managed the Palace Cinema? Alec's son Theo was born in Letchworth in 1917. Did he have a *brit* in Letchworth? Was there a regular *minyan* in Letchworth during the First World War? If so, where was it held? Was Alec Cowan a synagogue goer? I do not know the answers to these questions, but the Cowan and Grodzinski families definitely knew one another.

There might have been an added reason why the Grodzinskis moved to Letchworth in the First World War. The war created a wave of intense anti-German revulsion in England, and German individuals – or people with German-sounding names - were being attacked. Abie may have correctly surmised that Letchworth people would be more tolerant.

Another explanation for the presence of a Jewish community in Letchworth in the First World War is that Britain took in over a quarter of a million Belgian refugees – including 15,000 Russian-born Belgian Jews. Letchworth became one of the key centres for Belgian refugees. Abie Grodzinski may have learned that some Antwerp Jews had formed a Jewish community in Letchworth.

Three of the Belgian refugees who arrived in Letchworth in 1914 from Antwerp were Jaques Kryn, a diamond merchant; his brother, Georges; and a colleague, Raoul Lahy. Together, they formed the Kryn and Lahy (K&L) Metal Works in Dunhams Lane, in March 1915. Many Belgian refugees who had fled to the Netherlands were invited to relocate to the UK to prop up faltering munitions factories. K&L was one of the factories that were almost entirely run and staffed by Belgians.

The K&L factory produced weapons and munitions for the war effort. By the end of 1916, the 2,000 Belgian refugees made up a quarter of the population of Letchworth. This led to a lack of housing, with some of the refugees living in empty factories and shops, and with two or even three families crammed into small cottages. Eventually new houses were built for the refugees in the Westbury area which was nicknamed 'Little Antwerp'.

The K&L foundry was itself acquired in 1928 by another Jewish-owned business – the steel foundry division of George Cohen & Sons. In the Second World War, the K&L foundry was a frequent Luftwaffe target, after the company converted its production lines, and was once again making munitions, including special mobile cranes that were used on D-Day. Berlin-born Hans Peter Jost was one of the Jewish employees at the K&L foundry in Letchworth between 1944 and 1945.

As a child, I spent hours playing with my favourite toy, an eighteen-inch Triang working model of a Jones Mobile Crane KL44. I always knew that Jones Cranes were manufactured in Letchworth, but what I have only now discovered is that Jones Cranes was a K&L brand. So in effect, my favourite toy crane had a double Jewish pedigree!

Two Parallel Congregations

'Members are informed that these collections are not authorised by the Committee and that none of the proceeds have been handed over to the Congregation Funds.'

ACTING TREASURER KIVA KORNBLUTH AND
HON SEC JOE RICHMAN

The Letchworth Hebrew Congregation was officially constituted at a general meeting held at the Howard Hall on Sunday 10 November 1940. In the minutes of the first meeting of the newly elected general committee at the house of Mr Lunzer, with Kiva Kornbluth in the chair, Rabbi Dr Isidore Epstein was unanimously elected chairman. The three Vice-Chairmen, each of whom would act as Wardens at their respective synagogues, were Sali Bornstein, H. M. Lunzer, and J. Stern. The Treasurer was Kiva Kornbluth, and the Hon Secretary was Joe Richman.

Between 1935 and 1952, including his Letchworth years, the distinguished Lithuanian-born Rabbi Epstein undertook the monumental task of translating the *Babylonian Talmud* into English. He would later become principal of Jews' College. Joe Richman was a senior member of British Mizrachi, and spent his wartime service as a fire watcher in London. He was also a hospital visitor – hence his unofficial title of Reverend – and he also gave barmitzvah lessons. Joe was a gifted *Ba'al Tefilla* who led the High Holiday services. Yossel Schischa recalls that his mother Amelia Schischa (Winegarten) always used superlatives to praise Joe's melodic voice.

Efraim Halevy recalls: 'Despite the fact that a real congregation came into being in Letchworth, I was too young to recollect an organized communal framework. The highlight of the year was the High Holidays, when all the Jews of Letchworth met in a big hall near the town centre for prayers. It was quite a long walk from Hallmead, but all of us were there. My father Elazar Halevy was the *Shacharit chazan*, the *Ba'al Koreh* and the *Ba'al Tokea* – his black *shofar* is constantly next to me on a bookshelf. *Mussaf*, *Kol Nidre* and *Neilah* were led by Joe Richman, who possessed a great tenor voice whose notes still linger in my 87-year-old ears.'

Joe Richman's daughter Frances Israel (Richman) describes the Halevys as the most Zionist family in Letchworth. During the Second World War, Elazar Halevy was entrusted to run the national Chief Rabbi's Passover Committee for Evacuees. He commuted daily from Letchworth to London during the Blitz, often staying overnight in the East End with his parents.

The formation of the Letchworth Hebrew Congregation was followed by the formation of several sub-committees. There was a Mikveh sub-committee, and an Education sub-committee. Shloime (Sali) Bornstein, chairman of the Shechita sub-committee, liaised with the Food Office, the department of the Ministry of Food that looked after the nation's rationing. There was a Visitation sub-committee, a Chevra Kadisha sub-committee, and a Membership sub-committee. There was a Housing sub-committee and a Social & Literary sub-committee. Kiva Kornbluth was chair of the Hospitality sub-committee that looked after Jewish members of His Majesty's armed forces stationed in the area.

The Minutes Book of the Letchworth Hebrew Congregation gives us a glimpse of the kind of issues faced by the Jews of Letchworth – at an organizational level, at a committee level, at a religious level, and at an interpersonal level. We also see how scrupulous the committee was in holding regular meetings, and even in faithfully recording unpleasant interpersonal problems.

A wide range of issues was handled by the committee. For example, Mr Lunzer was asked to exercise his authority so as to improve the decorum at the Howard Hall services. One Chanukkah, the committee agreed to spend 28/6d for sweets for the children of the Hallmead classes. The committee agreed to spend £3 7/6 for linoleum and a door mat at 40 Hallmead. The committee noted that an excellent report of

Howard Hall

the Congregation's activities had appeared in the *Jewish Chronicle*. Mr Persoff reported that members of the Stevenage Congregation had visited the Letchworth Social section and presented a Talkie Film Show.

The committee learned that on *Succot*, *Succahs* would be open to members of the Congregation by permission of the various hosts, with the committee providing the refreshments. The *succahs* were at 'Chilliswood' Broadway; 51 Bedford Road; 22 Bedford Road; 36 Hall Mead; 62 Mullway and 87 Mullway.

At the first meeting of the Letchworth Hebrew Congregation on 10 November 1940, Abba Bornstein was invited to accept the position of Hon President with a seat on all the committees. The committee decided to explore the nature of the relations between the community and Rabbi Horowitz.

One issue that exercised the committee was *schechitah*. On 17 November 1940, the committee learned that without the permission or knowledge of any responsible member of the committee, Jewish poultry was being sold in a Letchworth fish shop, and described as being under the supervision of the Board of Shechitah. A week later, Sigi Stern was authorised to act as the only kosher poultry purveyor in Letchworth, under the supervision of Rabbi Horowitz.

Rabbi Binyaminson was appointed *shochet*, and it was agreed to display the following text: 'Mr S Stern is the only authorised Kosher Butcher in Letchworth, appointed by the above congregation. Poultry, sold here by him, is under the rabbinical supervision of Rabbi J Horowitz, with the approval of the London Beth-Din.' In February 1941, the committee heard that 'Mr Stern was contravening the terms of his license.'

'Unique in the history of Letchworth,' is how Letchworth's local newspaper *The Citizen* trumpeted Chief Rabbi Hertz's successful pastoral visit to Letchworth at the end of March 1941. The congregation had the distinction of being the first of the evacuation areas that the Chief Rabbi visited.

At the *Shabbat* morning prayers that weekend, the Chief Rabbi preached to a crowded congregation in the Howard Hall. The next day, Sunday, over 400 people attended a reception in the Broadway cinema (which also sometimes served as a synagogue) in Chief Rabbi Hertz's honour. The chairman of Letchworth council stressed the bond of fellowship and goodwill that characterised interdenominational relationships. The chief rabbi, who stayed for the weekend as a guest of David and Selina Sassoon, expressed gratitude for the kindness shown to the Jewish evacuees by everyone in Letchworth. Another headline in *The Citizen* read: 'Jews and Non-Jews Meet Chief Rabbi in Letchworth.'

Membership of Letchworth Hebrew Congregation soon grew from fifty to ninety. Collection of weekly contributions was entrusted to the Lehmann brothers, J Ullman, Joe Pollock, and the Weinstock and Joseph boys. Eventually, the congregation adopted Sammy Fisher's suggestion to hire David Kaplin as the paid collector, and membership grew to 150.

By 5 April 1941, there was widespread talk of a breakaway congregation. In the minutes of a general meeting of the Letchworth Hebrew Congregation in May 1941, Elazar Halevy railed against 'those who have consistently sought to set at nought all constructive efforts of the committee.' He accused the naysayers of 'attempting to disrupt the congregation, of bringing discredit to the committee, and of sowing

The Synagogue and Yeshiva at 38 and 40 Hallmead

seeds of *sinat chinam* (groundless hatred) and *chilul hashem* (acting immorally.)'

In the same 1941 minutes, Sammy Fisher is thanked for securing a duplicating machine, and Hannah Lehmann is thanked for her clerical help. The tensions and fissures within the community are clear from Mr M Saunders' proposed vote of no confidence in the executive and committee.

There is an old joke about the Jew who was shipwrecked and lived on an uninhabited island for several years. When he was eventually found, his rescuers noticed that he had built two synagogues. Asked why, he pointed at one of the synagogues, and said: 'That's a synagogue I will never step foot in!'

Despite – or maybe because of – Isidore Epstein's world-famous stature as an English-language Hebrew scholar, there were those in the Letchworth Jewish community for whom he was not '*frum*' enough. As Murray Cohen puts it: 'Rabbi Epstein was regarded as being very English – not a proper rabbi.'

Dodi Gurwicz put it more bluntly: 'Rabbi Epstein's minyan was considered "semi-Reform."' Yossel Schischa describes Rabbi Epstein's minyan as 'a more English-style congregation.' Rabbi Epstein's daughter, Helen Botschko, describes her father's community as 'more United Synagogue style.'

The Letchworth Hebrew Congregation convened a special committee meeting to consider what action to take as a result of a leaflet circulated in the name of the Wardens, in which Rabbi Horowitz was described as Rabbi of Letchworth and District. Sali Bornstein was censured for attending a meeting at which he recorded his vote accepting Rabbi Horowitz as rabbi of Letchworth.

The committee decided to present Rabbi Horowitz with the following memorandum: 'You are aware of a printed notice circulated to members of the community, and affixed to the doors of the Synagogue at 40, Hallmead and Howard Hall, containing statements with some material parts of which are not true, and were put with the intention of causing internal strife in the Community. We do not suggest that you have instigated this circular. Yet you have not so far publicly issued any disclaimer. A disclaimer must be issued, and we suggest that this shall be done by you using a formula agreeable to yourself and to the Committee, or if you prefer, the Committee will issue one of its own accord.'

The committee unanimously approved a motion by Sammy Fisher placing on record its approval of the manner with which the Chairman had conducted the negotiations relating to the appointment of Rabbi Horowitz. On 28 May 1941, the Chairman welcomed Sol Cohen's offer to seek to improve communal differences. On 23 June 1941, the committee rejected the dissenting group's grievances, including a demand that all committee proceedings be conducted in Yiddish.

A letter, in English and Yiddish, sent in August 1941 and signed by the Letchworth Hebrew Congregation's acting treasurer Kiva Kornbluth and Hon Sec Joe Richman, was the tipping point: 'A report has reached the committee that collections have been made at weekday services at the Synagogue of 40 Hallmead. Members are informed that these collections are not authorised by the Committee and that none of the proceeds have been handed over to the Congregation Funds.'

The sharply worded letter continues: 'You are further informed that some members of the group who had been responsible for the disgraceful scenes at the General Meeting of last May, forcibly seized the Collector's Book from the Collector and extracted private information concerning payments of members, including yours, due to the congregation.'

The committee voted unanimously that Mr Sali Bornstein's association with the dissident group was incompatible with the loyalty to the committee. The chairman read a letter signed by Rabbi Binjaminson and Abba Bornstein to the effect that unless their demands were satisfied within 7 days, they would take steps to establish a new *Kehillah*. The Secretary was authorised to write to Mr. Ullman stating that the committee were quite agreeable for any points in dispute to be settled by arbitration.

On 4 September 1941, Mr Persoff said that he very much regretted the splitting of the Talmud Torah. Whatever quarrels there were in the community, the children should never be brought into it, and he felt that this split would be detrimental to the children's education. Sammy Fisher suggested that the dispute about the Talmud Torah and 40 Hallmead should be submitted to the London *Beth Din* for settlement. Dr Epstein said that if the other side was willing, arbitration would be the best course.

However, the split was already a fait accompli. On 8 September 1941, Dr Epstein informed the committee of his conversation with Rabbi Horowitz and said that although there were now two congregations, unity and cooperation were possible, especially insofar as the Talmud Torah was concerned. Intense formal and informal negotiations over the following days failed to prevent the final split. Dr Epstein's daughter Helen Botschko thinks that the split between the two congregations 'was a bit of a joke.'

On 20 September 1941, Dr Epstein reported that the newly-formed Yeshurun Congregation had turned down all proposals from the Letchworth Hebrew Congregation. In November 1941, Sammy Fisher proposed that the strongest action be taken to recover all unpaid fees due to the Letchworth Hebrew Congregation from the butcher, Sigi Stern, even if it meant summoning him to the London *Beth Din*.

The Letchworth Hebrew Congregation continued to arrange functions. In September 1941, an anniversary Intercession Service was held in accordance with the wishes of King George VI to observe a day of national prayer. In 1942, the following report was issued by the Letchworth Hebrew Congregation:

'After more than two years of existence, we are glad to take this opportunity of enumerating some of the activities and the work carried out by the Letchworth Hebrew Congregation.

Synagogue: Services on Sabbaths and Festivals are held at Howard Hall, 51 Bedford Road and 52 Mullway. Daily services are held at 42, Mullway and "Chilliswood", The Broadway. Many distinguished preachers have spoken at these services. A record is being prepared of the Yahrzeits to be observed by members and their wives who will be informed as they occur.

Classes: Talmud Torah Classes are functioning daily in the Hall Mead / Mullway area, also in the town. All children are welcome and information may be obtained from the Honorary Secretary of the Education Committee, Rev. L. Rosenberg, 87, Mullway. The classes meet immediately after school and tea and biscuits are provided the pupils before the lessons commence. Nearly ninety children now attend the classes. In addition, over 100 children are attending the religion classes organised and maintained by the Congregation in the day schools.

Liaison Officer: Mrs. P. Joseph has been appointed Liaison Officer and Government Helper. All evacuated Jewish people are invited to discuss their problems with her. Her address is: 26, Sollershott West.

Ladies Guild: The Ladies Guild under the auspices of the Letchworth Hebrew Congregation has now been re-organised and a programme of important work has commenced. After a few weeks, the membership has reached nearly 80. The minimum contribution is 3d per week. The Ladies are not only concerning themselves with congregational matters, but are taking part also in local and National efforts. A Hospitality and Visitation Committee has been formed to entertain members of the Forces visiting Letchworth and to visit Jewish patients in hospital. Enquiries should be addressed to: Mrs. F. Kirsch, Joint Hon. Secretary, "Oakwood", The Broadway.

Jewish Social Society: This Society has been formed for the youth of Letchworth. Many functions are already taking place and circles are taking place every Friday evening at different addresses. A full programme is being arranged for the future. All young Jewish people are invited to communicate with: Mick Abrahams, Esq., "Maison Stanley" the Wynd; or Harry Grodzinski, Esq., 29, Sollershott East. [The reference to Mick Abrahams is somewhat confusing. Harry (Henry) Abrahams had an upholstery workshop in The Wynd next to Stern the kosher butcher. While Harry attended synagogue on the High Holidays, he was not an active member of the community, and would definitely not have been involved in any Jewish Social Society. Harry's son Moich has no knowledge of any Mick Abrahams.]

The Letchworth Hebrew Congregation itself now consists of nearly 170 members. It has been responsible for providing facilities for the purchase of kosher meat in the town and last Passover was responsible for providing a Pesach Canteen for the children and adults.

We are also happy to inform you that the Congregation has succeeded in securing the services of Rabbi A. Singer (Rev. of Philpot Street Gt. Synagogue, London) as Education Supervisor. His task will be to organise the various educational activities of the Congregation and particularly to arrange for Shiurim and opportunities for study for adults. Rabbi Singer already conducts a Shiur at "Chilliswood," The Broadway, every Sunday evening (by courtesy of Mr. and Mrs. H.M. Lunzer). Apart from his educational work among adults, he takes a class in Gemara for advanced boys. He will address the Congregation on frequent occasions at the Howard Hall.

If you are a member of the Letchworth Hebrew Congregation, you will no doubt be gratified at the progress we have made and I am sure you will be pleased that as a result of your membership, so much has already been achieved.

If however you are not yet a member, we invite your cooperation with us in our work. Our aim is to get every Jewish resident in Letchworth to belong to the congregation and thus enable it to extend its activities. The Letchworth Hebrew Congregation has already established cordial relations with the civic authorities and a united effort will help us to enhance the good name of Letchworth Jewry.

If you are not a member of the Letchworth Hebrew Congregation, you will be receiving a visit shortly from the Secretary Dr. B. Heinemann. He will be able to amplify the information in this letter and to give you any further details you may require. I hope you will consider it your duty to join us, when arrangements will be made for the collector to call upon you regularly,

Yours very sincerely,
I. EPSTEIN – PRESIDENT H.M. LUNZER – CHAIRMAN
K. KORNBLUTH – TREASURER J. RICHMAN - HON. SEC.

Meanwhile, Rabbi Yosef Yona Horowitz agreed to become the spiritual leader of the breakaway Yeshurun congregation. He was officially inducted by Dayan Abramsky on 6 September 1941, two weeks before Rosh Hashana, at Station Place above Messrs Simmons Estate Office.

In a letter to Jewish families, D Lichtig, chairman of Adass Yeshurun, wrote: 'You have no doubt heard that the above Kehilla has been formed with the support of the most prominent members of the community.' This first formal invitation to join the breakaway Yeshurun congregation is signed by the chairman, the vice-chairman I Schwab, the treasurer S Hanstater, and the joint Hon. Secretaries, Sol Cohen and A Winegarten.

Rabbi Horowitz was arrested in Frankfurt following Kristallnacht in November 1938, and reached London with the help of Abba Bornstein. According to Murray Cohen, Nazi thugs had ripped off half of Rabbi Horowitz's beard, and for several years it did not grow back properly.

Rabbi Horowitz was president of World Aguda, and my father Eli told me that it was in this capacity that Rabbi Horowitz wrote to Pope Pius XII ("Hitler's Pope," as John Cornwell described him) from Letchworth, asking him to intercede on behalf of the Jewish victims of Nazi genocide. The ice-cold answer that Rabbi Horowitz received from the Vatican, according to my father, was that basically the Jews deserved what was happening because they rejected Jesus. I have no independent corroboration for this story.

In November 1941, a temporary committee announced the formation of a Yeshurun Ladies Guild. To mark its establishment, Rabbi Horowitz delivered a lecture on 'The ethics of Jewish family life.' Communications from the committee always indicated whether Rabbi Horowitz's lectures were in English or Yiddish.

By December 1941, the newly formed Talmud Torah put on an ambitious Chanuka programme including two Hebrew plays, *The Angels with Abraham* and *The Brothers with Joseph*. There was also an English play, *The Chanuka Lights*.

In late December 1941, the congregation hosted a guest speaker, no stranger to Letchworth, Rabbi Dr Solomon Schonfeld, who spoke on 'Ortho-practice, Orthodoxy and Judaism.' In July 1943, Rabbi Sassoon chaired a public meeting of an organisation called the Old Yishuv War Fund. The topic was 'To answer the call of the Old Yishuv in Eretz Israel.' The three guest speakers were Rabbi Horowitz, Rabbi Schonfeld and Rabbi A Rappaport. I have not found any other reference to the Old Yishuv War Fund, presumably it was an offshoot of Agudat Israel.

The Rosh Hakohol (equivalent to president) of the Yeshurun congregation was Rabbi Yerachmiel Binyaminson, a prominent follower of the Lubavicher Rebbe. Known as the Zhlobiner Rav, he had escaped to England in 1935.

Here is Ariel Broch's description of the Zhlobiner Rav's home near the top of Mullway. 'The front door opened onto a narrow hallway leading to a double room taken up almost entirely by a huge table. The Zhlobiner Rav would sit all day every day (except *Shabbat*) draped in his *tallit* and *tefillin*, studying the holy texts. On *Shabbat*, this double room would serve as a *shul* to accommodate up to thirty men for prayer services. On *Shabbat* afternoons, many people attended the traditional third meal, *Shalosh Seudos*, which included *challah*, salt herring, and bottles of soft drink. The Rav had a very gentle demeanour, and he would deliver his learned discourse, speaking softly in Yiddish.'

The Zhlobiner Rav's daughter-in-law, Zlate Binyaminson, relates a story about the many American and Canadian Jewish soldiers who used to come from London to the Binyaminsons for Shabbat. 'Even though there were not enough places for them, they were always warmly welcomed and apparently the visitors slept on some sort of straw matting. One day, a soldier from New York asked the Rabbi, "Where are you going to sleep?" The rabbi replied, "I am the boss!" The rabbi's wife Hannah had her own room. Out of curiosity, the soldier wanted to see where in fact the Rabbi did sleep. He kept himself awake and watched as the rabbi walked up and down the hallway with a *Gemara* in his hand till the morning.'

When Topsy Lunzer married the Zlobiner Rav's nephew David Benjamin, Topsy's grandmother Celine told David a story. One warm summer day, Celine was in the Lunzer home on Broadway, when she received news belatedly that her mother, Deena Eisenmann, had died of typhus in Bergen Belsen. Later that day there was a knock on Celine's front door. The Zlobiner Rav was standing there. He had walked from his home in Mullway. He told Celine that he had a feeling that all was not well in the family. She told him of the news she had received a short time earlier. He was her first comforter.

The Zlobiner Rav's great-niece Ruth Marriott says that although the rav was sickly, he would not accept money from anyone. On Purim, he accepted a little food but no charity. When Abba Bornstein felt that the Rav was in need of new clothes, he arranged for his tailor to make a suit for him, but to only charge ten per cent of the cost. The tailor spun a yarn about the hard times and his need to do a little work, so could he please make the suit? Naturally, Abba paid the rest.

In the last year of the war, when London was attacked by flying bombs, Rebekah Weisman, the great-niece of the Zlobiner Rav's wife Hannah, was dispatched to Letchworth to stay with her great-aunt and uncle. Hannah was a very fussy eater and lived on a diet of rye bread, cheese, tomatoes and milk. Ariel Broch recalls that Hannah appeared to sit all day in her kitchen, shaking a jar of milk in order to make butter.

Notwithstanding that two separate congregations now existed in Letchworth, there was a certain degree of goodwill and cooperation between them. Yossel Schischa offers an interesting perspective: 'On matters that were very important to both congregations – the Talmud Torah, the *mikve* and the cooperation in procuring kosher food – they definitely worked together. One example of this cooperation came in March 1942, when a circular announced the formation of the Letchworth Joint Passover Committee, including both the Letchworth Hebrew Congregation and the Hebrew Congregation Yeshurun. This joint committee made sure that unaccompanied children and adults who were unable to make their own Pesach arrangements could celebrate the festival properly. The circular stated: 'In the case of children, it is highly desirable that provision should be made for them to sleep over at least for the *sedarim* evenings.'

According to Topsy Benjamin (Lunzer), there was no women's mikve in the early days in Letchworth, and women had to travel up to London. Murray Cohen reports: 'After the Letchworth Council turned down an initial request to build a mikve, my late father, Sol Cohen, was asked to plead the case for a mikve. He approached the Council, and was successful.' Subscriptions for the mikve were initially slow, but eventually it was fully subscribed. The mikve was situated adjacent to 2 Cross Street, facing Norton Common.

According to Yossel Shischa, 'The house belonged to Sholom Hanstater, a wholesale grocer in London's East End. He was married to one of Rabbi Horowitz's daughters. Mr Hanstater allowed the *Kehilla* to build a mikve in his garden. It was a small single storey structure, adjacent to the house.' Sylvia Moise (Hanstater) remembers that her grandparents, parents, uncles, aunts and cousins all lived in the one bungalow, known as Nook Cottage.

When Yeshurun Congregation was first established, congregants were informed that 'the mikve is in the course of construction and will shortly be completed.' The official consecration of the mikve took place in November 1942, with an opening ceremony conducted by Mr Hanstater. At the end of the war, Hanstater wanted to return to London, and a difference of opinion arose between him and the *Kehilla* regarding the status of the mikve. According to Yossel Schischa: 'The disagreement was settled without going to arbitration in the London *Beth Din*. The *Kehilla* bought the property at a figure considerably lower than market value.'

Vivienne Alper (Gedalla) comments on women in the community: 'Although the Letchworth community was orthodox, women did not go to *shul,* except for Rosh Hashanah and Yom Kippur when we attended an overflow service.'

Between November 1941 and September 1943, there is a gap in the Minutes Book of the Letchworth Hebrew Congregation. Yossel Schischa claims that although Rabbi Horowitz was de jure the rabbi of only the Yeshurun congregation, he seems to have been accepted as the de facto rabbi of the whole town.

On 8 September 1943, Dr Epstein informed the committee that he and his family would be returning to London soon after the holidays. On 18 October 1943, a special meeting considered the situation arising out of Dr Epstein's imminent departure. Sammy Fischer reported that once the Yeshurun Congregation learned of Dr Epstein's departure, they were eager to come to an understanding with the Letchworth Hebrew Congregation.

On 27 October 1943, the Hon Secretary read a letter from the Yeshurun Congregation asking that five representatives from each congregation meet in order to negotiate a reunification. The split between the two Letchworth congregations was approaching its end.

In February 1944, just thirty months after the Yeshurun Congregation broke away from the Letchworth Hebrew Congregation, a 'complete unification of the two congregations' was announced. As part of the memorandum of understanding, the English name of the unified congregation would be Letchworth Hebrew Congregation, and the Hebrew name would be Kahal Adass Yeshurun.

It was agreed that 'Rabbi Horowitz shall be the Rav of the new Congregation,' and that he would serve as 'the Av Beth Din, as well as the spiritual, religious and educational authority.' Rabbi Horowitz 'would hold the office of chairman of the Education Sub-Committee,' and he would have 'the right of veto on all decisions of the Congregation.' A sub-committee was appointed to draft a unified constitution.

The first president after the amalgamation was the Zhlobiner Rav. The first chairman was Yankel Hollander, and the first secretary was B Heinemann. In the immediate post-war period, between December 1945 and April 1946, the amalgamated congregation advertised two lecture series featuring Rabbi Horowitz, Rabbi Solomon Sassoon, Dr B Heinemann, Rabbi Leib Gurwicz, Adi Schischa, Sigi Stern and Noach Kaplin.

Rabbi Horowitz giving a shiur

But even this new amalgamated arrangement did not last very long. Families continued to leave Letchworth, culminating in the departure in 1950 of Rabbi Horowitz to the USA. The significantly smaller community appointed Reb Oosher Feuchtwanger as Letchworth's communal rabbi, a post he held for the next twenty years.

The End of the War

'The instinct to be frugal was so ingrained that even in later years of plenty, we could not bear to see food thrown away.'

ARIEL BROCH

Rationing is a constant theme running through the memories of those who lived in Letchworth during the war. Zippy Rosenblatt (Persoff) remembers: 'We learned early on that our "sweets" were very much limited, and housewives had to scratch together ingredients for cakes and treats.'

For Ariel Broch, going shopping with ration books was part of the wartime daily routine. 'One of the most lasting effects on many of my generation was the rationing which was imposed on most food staples and clothing. Everyone was very careful in the handling of rationed items, making sure that everything was fairly shared. A fresh banana or a piece of chocolate would be carefully divided into equal parts and everyone would slowly and lovingly let a portion melt in their mouth. The instinct to be frugal was so ingrained that even in later years of plenty, we could not bear to see food thrown away.'

Efraim Halevy remembers the twin perils of rationing and kashrut. 'Maintaining kashrut in Letchworth was no easy task – there were little to no kosher groceries to the best of my recollection. Food rationing, including eggs, was a serious problem. As we approached *Pesach*, the few eggs that were sold were preserved with a nasty smelling liquid named Oat Egg. We discovered that using this on *Seder Night* was perilous.'

Frances Israel (Richman) remembers accompanying her mother before *Pesach* on a quest to persuade local farmers to part with some hard-to-find fresh eggs. One day, Mrs Richman, with Frances in tow, found a farmer who agreed to sell them some eggs. As they left the farm, Frances was told: 'When we get to the next farmer, don't tell him that we already secured some eggs.' As soon as they reached the next farm, Frances blurted out: 'The other farmer was very nice and he gave us some eggs.'

Zippy Rosenblatt (Persoff) also remembers egg quests with her mother. 'We went to a nearby farm to get eggs, a rare commodity during the war, and maybe we collected apples too. Many families like the Kents kept chickens in their back gardens.'

Vivienne Alper (Gedalla)'s parents kept chickens in a run in their Mullway garden: 'Rhode Island Reds, if I remember correctly. We always had fresh eggs, and therefore we never had to resort to dried eggs as many people did during the war. If any chicken stopped laying, the *shochet* arrived to slaughter it, which was horrible! I also remember accompanying my mother to a nearby farm to buy day-old chicks, which we kept in an open box in the kitchen until they were ready to join the others in the garden.'

Mickey Freudmann's family also raised chickens, and also ate chickens when the *shochet* came round: 'There was extreme rationing, and I still have some ration stamps both from Belgium and England. No civilians had private cars as there were severe restrictions on petrol. Many people used bicycles, and of course the train. It was a great thrill for us when we occasionally travelled by train to London. I remember how excited I was to go with my mother to London and shop in Baker Street.'

Mickey had another good reason to remember rationing: 'A second cousin working on an American Air Force base not far from Letchworth taught me to swim at the Letchworth swimming pool. He had a brother who was a major in the US army, and a first cousin who had also escaped from Belgium in 1940, and was serving in US Military Intelligence. They all came to visit us during the war. There was a very nutritious reason for looking forward to their visits – they brought us all kinds of goodies from the American PX stores which one could only dream of in the austerity of wartime England.

'The only manufactured clothes available, called "utility" clothes, were of very poor quality. We received parcels from an aunt and uncle in Canada. I remember how excited my brother David and I were when they sent us suits with knickerbocker trousers, and how we proudly wore them on *Shabbat*.'

On Dodi Gurwicz's visits to the Sassoons on *Shabbat* for *seuda shlishit*, he could not understand how – rationing notwithstanding – they served roast duck on huge platters. In fact, chicken and duck were not rationed.

In the early 1950s, my father Eli built a chicken hutch in the back garden of our 79 Hallmead home. My cousin Dovzi Lopian remembers crawling into the hutch to extricate eggs. I remember that the very first time our hens laid eggs, they didn't know what they were, so they pecked and pecked until they broke the yolks.

There were strategic advantages for orthodox Jewish families in maintaining cordial relations with their non-Jewish neighbours. One, it was very useful to have a neighbour who was willing to serve as a *Shabbos Goy*. Two, as Frances Israel (Richman) remembers, 'Jewish families could swap their bacon rations for coffee or other items. All the Jewish children used to flock to the home of Ray Kornbluth to enjoy a treat - peppermint ice cream. To this day, I don't know how she got the ingredients during rationing.'

Ray's son Jonathan tells the story of going to a local greengrocer before *Rosh Hashana* in order to buy a new fruit that would enable the family to make the *Shehecheyanu* blessing. The fruit they wanted was figs. After telling the Kornbluths that he had no figs, the greengrocer asked why they wanted this particular fruit. The Kornbluths patiently explained about the need for a new fruit on the Jewish festival. When the greengrocer learned that the Jewish holiday of Chanukah was approaching, he remembered that his Jewish customers buy figs for their holidays. He brought in a consignment of figs. The poor guy could not understand why not a single Jewish customer asked for figs for Chanukah.

Efraim Halevy recalls the unique Jewish humour produced by the war scarcities. 'An oft repeated joke concerned cases of tinned pilchards, a substitute for impossible-to-obtain sardines. The story was that these boxes were passed from family to family. One day somebody was brave enough to open one of the tins, only to find that the pilchards were inedible. When the recipient complained, he was told that the function of the tins was to serve as presents in the absence of anything else. An example of wartime humour – Letchworth Jewish style.'

My father Eli remembers that as designated farm workers, he and his fellow kibbutzniks 'received double rations of cheese and meat. We baked our own *challot* and cakes, and the girls did a splendid job in the kitchen under the supervision of Mrs Epstein, and later Keva Kornbluth.' Both the latter lived in Letchworth during the war.

My own early years in the immediate post-war period in Letchworth were very much in the shadow of the rationing book. Until my barmitzvah, apart from my Carmel College school uniform, I did not own any item of clothing that was bought new – everything was a hand-me-down from the Broch family.

Betzalel (Sigi) Stern, his wife Blanca and family arrived in Stamford Hill from Vienna just before the Second World War, and were part of the wave of Jewish families that made Letchworth their home. As Ariel Broch explains, 'The Sterns had three children, whose ages intertwined nicely with the Broch children. Martha was in my class, and Kitty was best friend with my sister Hannah. David was a little younger than Hannah, but was accepted as part of the gang, his cap always slightly awry, and one sock hanging down. Our mothers became good friends.'

After canvassing Letchworth Jewish families door-to-door early in the war to ascertain the demand for kosher meat, Stern collected orders from each household. He travelled to London to procure the requested meat cuts, and then delivered them from his home. This developed into a kosher meat and delicatessen business, originally under the supervision of the London Board of Shechita.

When Rabbi Solomon Schonfeld's father, Rabbi Avigdor, had founded the Union of Orthodox Hebrew Congregations in the nineteen-twenties, Kedassia was the organisation's kashruth arm. In order to separate the Kedassia shechita out of the monopoly of the London Shechita Board, Rabbi Solomon Schonfeld created the Letchworth Shechita Board. This was never actually an official part of the Letchworth Jewish community, but was tailored specifically for Stern.

Stern's Letchworth shop was first located at the bottom of Station Road, and then moved to The Wynd, where poultry was slaughtered. Reb Nachman Dachs was the *Shochet*, and Rabbi Binyominson was the *Bodek* (inspector.)

Parents and Children 1949

Jenny Todd (Thompson) writes in a Letchworth memories website: 'My dad's butcher shop was in the Wynd, which was a fascinating place. Just up the road from my dad's shop was the Kosher abattoir where each Monday the Rabbi would visit, donned in his robes and Wellingtons to kill the chickens etc. I remember as a kid jumping over the blood which would run down the road after the slaughter! Next door to the abattoir was Mr Abrahams' upholstery business. The Wynd was a community on its own.'

There was a bacon factory on Works Road at the northern end of Letchworth's industrial area, owned by a multiple butcher shop chain called Gunners. The Gunners abattoir's main function was the killing and processing of pigs, but they also slaughtered and processed cattle, lamb and calves. Stern managed to persuade Gunners to make available facilities for *schechita* for one or two hours every week. Benny Winegarten always thought it very incongruous that the Kedassia Shechita began its life in the Letchworth Bacon Factory.

An employee of Davis Precision Tools at the bottom of Works Road

The Abrahams' upholstery shop in the Wynd

who worked opposite the bacon factory, sometimes looked out of the window in the lunch break. 'You would see a little team of Jewish gentlemen in their black hats and their long black coats. They had come to slaughter the animals in their kosher way.'

Zippy Rosenblatt (Persoff) remembers VE (Victory in Europe) Day: "On Hallmead, and everywhere, residents brought out covered tables loaded with food and joined them edge to edge on the grass verges. Bunting was strung above on poles and trees, and the crowds joyously celebrated. A similar scene was re-enacted in Kingsbury for the Queen's 25th Anniversary, and I was transported back again to Hallmead in 1945.'

Frances Israel (Richman) remembers that on VE Day, the children danced around the maypole at the top of Mullway. 'I don't think anyone explained to us exactly what was going on. I did not really understand why we were dancing, I just remember that I really enjoyed myself.'

Ariel Broch remembers how the Letchworth Jewish Community joined their non-Jewish neighbours in celebrating VE Day in May 1945. 'There was no school, no homework, and for once even the Talmud classes were not allowed to interfere with the festivities. Every street had its party with tables and chairs set out in the middle of the road. There was bunting and flags, music and dancing. Light refreshments and soft drinks provided by street committees were consumed in large quantities.

'Naturally, there were separate tables containing kosher cakes. There were boisterous toss-up football matches – street versus street. Everybody mixed and mingled. Even the Jewish residents who usually kept themselves to themselves, now celebrated with their neighbours. I treasured my souvenir mug with a silhouette of the King and Queen.'

Murray Cohen remembers Jews inviting their Jewish friends to join them in drinking a *L"Chaim*. A lot of the drink was supplied by Yossele Horowitz (no relation of Rabbi Horowitz) who had a winery in the East End.

Neither of my parents were at home in Letchworth for VE Day. Chava was on study leave from her kibbutz, and was attending the Bachad seminary in Manchester. She recalls her experiences that day: "I danced the *hora* along with thousands of others in Manchester. The joy was indescribable. The whole of Manchester seemed to be out in the streets."

On VE Day, Eli travelled from Kempston to London to stay with his friend Sigi Feld. As Eli wrote in *The Vow*: "Sigi was by now a captain in the army. We celebrated together with a few hundred thousand others in Trafalgar Square and in front of Buckingham Palace." Unbeknownst to Eli, at least three other Letchworth residents celebrated in Central London. Brothers David and Mickey Freudmann travelled up from Letchworth by train with their father to join the jubilant crowds in Trafalgar Square.

A more sombre aspect of VE Day and the end of the war in Europe was that the rumours of the atrocities that the Nazis had perpetrated were now proved true. News of the Shoah had started reaching the Letchworth Jewish community during the war, but the non-Jewish community had heard very little. In *Letchworth Remembered* we read the memories of one St Francis' College student: 'On VE Day, a bunch of boarders went to the Broadway Cinema and saw a crazy Hollywood musical. On the newsreel we saw the horrific film of the prisoners in Belsen and Buchenwald – the two camps that the British Army had recently liberated.'

One of the first dividends of the end of the war was that regular postal services could resume. Frances Israel (Richman) has a powerful memory of the first parcels that arrived after the war. 'Sammy Fisher's daughter Marilyn received a walking and talking doll from a relative in the USA. For weeks, Marilyn was by far the most popular girl in Letchworth.'

VE Day was the signal for many Jewish families that had sought shelter from the Blitz in Letchworth, to plan their return to London or elsewhere. One by one, families left Letchworth. Vivienne Alper (Gedalla) recalls: 'People began to pack their bags. We must have gone promptly too, as I managed to have a month or so in the lowest class of my new school in Clapton. I found London grim and grey. I missed Letchworth and its greenness and its freedom and all my friends.'

I was born prematurely on Monday morning, 14 January 1946. When my mother Chava arrived at the Maternity Hospital in Hitchin to give birth to me, she asked Mrs Blanca Stern – who was just getting into a waiting car carrying her new baby, David – if she would inform Sam and Melanie Becker that they were about to become grandparents.

Derek Pollock arrived back in Letchworth in 1946 after seven years of army service in the Near East. He found Letchworth a rather strange environment, especially in contrast to the hustle and bustle of Cairo. 'It was to experience a new facet of life with the need to resume oneself to the realities of life with family and community, apart from the need to earn a living and find one's feet in what had become a strange new world.'

When Murray Cohen finished Letchworth Grammar School in 1947, he joined the army. At one point it seemed that he was going to be sent to the Far East, but eventually he remained in Britain. By the time Murray was demobbed, his parents had decided it was time to leave Letchworth and buy a house in London's Stamford Hill.

After their wedding, my aunt Marian Becker and my uncle Yankel Lopian (Aku Aku) first lived at 79 Hallmead with my grandfather and parents, before renting a small flat, also in Hallmead. In March 1948, Marian gave birth to their first son, my first cousin, Dovid Zvi. I was two when I attended his *brit*, and my articulation was quite indistinct. I asked my mother: 'Wassis name?' 'Dovid Zvi', she told me. 'Ah, Dovzi' I said. As Marian wrote to her former nanny Anna in Germany: 'I think of you so often, I wish you could just see my little Dovzi – the name is really David Zvi, but Yanky could not pronounce it properly, and I think this name will now stick!'

Dovzi's *Pidyan Haben* took place at 79 Hallmead, attended by his two grandfathers, Reb Elyah Lapian and Sam Becker. Another guest was Sam Becker's cousin the Poneveczer Rav, who said that he badly needed a haircut. Since it was Sunday, and shops were closed, Yankel gave him a haircut in our front room. A few months after Dovzi was born, Yankel passed his exams with flying colours, did his articles, and accepted a position with an accountancy firm in Manchester.

By 1950/51, the *Jewish Year Book* estimated the Jewish population of Letchworth to be 150. Here is the entry:

- *Letchworth Hebrew Congregation (Kahal Adass Yeshurun) (affiliated Federation of Synagogues), 40 Hall Mead, and Scouts Hall, Icknield Way*
- *Rabbi: Rabbi O. Feuchtwanger*
- *Reverend: Rev Shloime Stern*
- *Joint Treasurers: Shloime Bornstein and Shloime Stern*
- *Honorary Secretary: O Pressburger, 2 Cross Street*
- *Talmud Torah (All enquiries to the Secretary). Headmaster: Rabbi Solomon David Sassoon*
- *Mikveh (Ritual Bath), 2 Cross Street. Tel: 30. All enquiries to Mrs Shloime Stern*
- *Mizrachi Society. Chairman: Moishe Bornstein*
- *Agudas Yisroel Group. Chairman: Shloime Stern*

We see from the last two entries that the community had a Zionist society (Mizrachi) and a non-Zionist (some would say anti-Zionist) society, (Agudas Yisroel). By the end of the 1950s, with the departure of the Bornsteins and the Sterns back to London, most of the office holders mentioned in the 1950/51 *Jewish Year Book* had left Letchworth.

The entire Letchworth Jewish community used to pray in the Scouts Hall for the High Holidays, Sukkot and Simchat Torah. Haki Sassoon

Cross Street

remembers that in the name of communal solidarity, the Ashkenazi community one year invited the entire Sassoon household to join them in Scouts Hall. Chacham Yosef Doury, the private tutor of the Sassoon children, was shocked that the kiddush on Simchat Torah was held before the Torah readings. He could not help but notice the negative effect that the schnapps had on some of the worshippers. He informed Rabbi Sassoon that he would rather pray alone at home than be subjected to this experience again. Haki reports that the combined Simchat Torah service was not continued.

I remember turning up at Scouts Hall on one of the festivals, only to discover that there had been a mix-up, and another organisation was using the hall. Herman Schwab loudly led the negotiations. I do not remember the outcome. Did we pray that day in the Scouts Hall or did we find some alternative? Pamela Tendell also remembers the Scouts Hall: 'On special occasions, we were treated to parties at Scouts Hall in

Icknield Way. It was at a Purim Party that I met my dearest friend Carole Zetmar, with whom I am still in daily contact.'

By the time my father Eli started work at Stern's in 1947 after he was demobbed from the army, he was already the father of two boys – me and David. Sigi Stern's daughter Martha would later become Eli's Sunday morning tennis partner, and in the early 1950s, I accompanied my father to Martha's wedding to Zalman Marguiles.

Another employee at Stern's was Vienna-born Master Butcher Ossy Pressburger, who had arrived in Letchworth with his wife Gisa and their daughter Monica (Suzanne) in 1950. Ossy had served in the Pioneer Corps. His Viennese fiancée Gisela (Gisa) Spitzer obtained a British permit to work as a domestic servant, and was employed by the well-known children's author, Enid Blyton.

The Pressburgers rented the Cross Street cottage that housed the mikve. Suzanne Freedman (Pressburger) remembers having to explain to neighbours and classmates that the mikve was the 'Jewish Bathroom.' As a youngster of about 9 years old, I remember being asked to walk to Cross Street to turn on the hot water in the mikve, without actually knowing what it was or who it was for. Ossy took on the secretaryship of the Letchworth Hebrew Congregation, aided by Gisa. The books were audited by treasurer Sali Bornstein.

Not far from Letchworth was the Luton Jewish community, where Reverend Harry Ritvo had served as the spiritual leader for almost a quarter of a century. After the Second World War, the community converted a building in Bury Park into a synagogue, and in May 1952, the Luton Synagogue was consecrated by Chief Rabbi Dr Israel Brodie.

The Luton Hebrew Congregation had grown to some two thousand souls during the war, but was now reduced to about 200 members. Several of Stern's Luton customers had privately urged my father Eli to open a butcher shop in Luton. At first, Ritvo, whose responsibilities included shechita, had advised against such a move, on the grounds that the community was contracting and had no real future.

The British government's announcement that meat rationing would end in July 1954 had two immediate effects for the Letchworth Jewish community. Sigi Stern moved his business to Upper Clapton in London. The firm formally changed its name to Stern & Grunbaum, putting the seal on what had been the de facto partnership between Stern and

Moishe Chaim Grunbaum. Stern & Grunbaum continued to supply Letchworth customers after the move to London.

The second impact of the imminent end of rationing is that a panicked Rev Ritvo changed his mind, and pressed Eli to open a kosher butcher shop in Luton. Needing a Master Butcher, Eli invited Ossy Pressburger to join him as a partner in Home Counties Kosher Supplies Ltd, trading as Luton Kosher Foods. The Bornstein brothers, Sali and Moishe, advised Ossy to join Eli.

An unhappy Sigi Stern appealed to Rabbi Solomon Schonfeld to intervene. Some wild accusations were bandied around, but after studying the facts, Schonfeld apologised to Eli for having been dragged into the argument. Schonfeld wished Eli good luck with his new business, and for the rest of his life, he referred to my father as 'my Luton butcher.'

When my father Eli required working capital for his new Luton business in 1954, it was provided by his neighbour Shloime Stern. Letchworth's communal rabbi, Rabbi Feuchtwanger, issued and endorsed a kashrut licence and certificate for the Luton shop, and the other licensing authority was the Luton Shechita Board. When all the Shechita Boards in Britain formed the National Shechita Council, Eli became a founder member as representative for Letchworth.

Three other Letchworth-based former Stern employees joined the new Luton business: Ivan Prunic, a non-Jewish Yugoslav sausage-maker; Albert Johnsone; and Ferdinant (Ferdi) Steinshreiber. When Ferdi and his wife Jolan Leni and daughter Kitty first arrived in Letchworth from Hungary in around 1947, they lived with the Abrahams family. It helped that Mrs Abrahams spoke Hungarian. Moich Abrahams remembers: 'The Steinschreibers lived in our very large unusual room which was directly over The Arcade. I think it was one of the largest rooms in Letchworth, apart from the Sassoons. They stayed with us for about a year.' A few months after joining Luton Kosher, Ferdi left Letchworth to open his own kosher butcher shop in Glasgow.

A curious report headlined 'Mikve Decision Defered' appeared in the *Jewish Chronicle* in 1958, about the question of a mikve for Luton that came before Luton Town Council. The report continued: 'The Council's Parks Committee had received representatives of the Luton and Letchworth Mikve Board, asking for space in the proposed new

The Abrahams Family

public baths building. It was decided to defer the decision until the next meeting of the Council.' I recall my father mentioning this proposed Luton mikve at the time. Yossel Schischa speculates that Reverend Ritvo of the Luton Hebrew Congregation may have wanted to bolster his case by enlisting the support of Rabbi Feuchtwanger and Rabbi Sassoon on behalf of a non-existent 'Luton and Letchworth Mikve Board.'

In June 1960, the Letchworth community's Hon Secretary Walter Gottfried sent out a letter that recognised the changes that had taken place in the community, and invited discussion on the future: 'A new stage has been reached in the development of our community. We are endeavouring to consolidate and further to develop communal, social and educational facilities to benefit all Jewish residents in this district, and we feel sure to have your wholehearted support.'

In 1962, Hon Sec Laurence Hack invited members of the community to comment on a proposed constitution: 'During the lifetime of our Community, no set of rules has been available to guide Committees in their duties. It is felt that numerous points of administration should be covered by a set of rules agreeable to the Community.'

> **LETCHWORTH JEWISH LADIES' GUILD**
>
> *cordially invite you to a*
>
> ## Purim Party
>
> SUNDAY, 13TH MARCH, 1960, at 3.30 p.m.
>
> **WILBURY SCHOOL**
> BEDFORD ROAD, LETCHWORTH
>
> *REFRESHMENTS*
>
> CHILDREN'S FANCY DRESS PARADE : FILM SHOW
> ETC.
>
> ADMISSION 2/6   CHILDREN 1/6
>
> TOMBOLA IN AID OF WORLD REFUGEE YEAR

Flyer for Purim Party 1960

During the 1960s, while Reb Oosher Feuchtwanger continued to serve as the spiritual head of the Letchworth Jewish Community, the president of the community was his brother-in-law, Rabbi Solomon Sassoon.

The David Sassoon Library

*'Shal Naalecha me'al raglecha.' (Put off thy shoes
from off thy feet, for the place whereon thou standest
is holy ground.)*

EXODUS, CHAPTER 3, VERSE 5

One of the most prominent wartime residents of Letchworth Garden City was not a person at all. It was a library – the Sassoon Library – the same library that Philippa Parker had contacted me about. Curated by David Sassoon and regarded as one of the world's biggest private libraries of rare Jewish manuscripts, the Sassoon Library was housed in Letchworth between 1940 and 1970.

David Sassoon was a descendant of the eighteenth-century patriarch of the Sassoon dynasty, Sheikh Sassoon ben Salech, the president (nasi) of the Baghdad Jewish community. Sheikh Sassoon's grandson Abdulla, later Albert Sassoon, settled in London, and was made a baronet in 1890. Albert's granddaughter was Flora (Farha), about whom historian Cecil Roth wrote, 'She walked like a queen, talked like a sage and entertained like an Oriental potentate.'

17-year-old Flora made a big impression on her grandfather Albert's Hebraist and Talmud scholar half-brother Solomon when they first met. He was impressed with her linguistic skills as well as with her prowess in Bible and Talmud. Albert and Solomon had built schools for Baghdadi Jewish children in Bombay (today Mumbai.) One of those children was my son's father-in-law David Ness, who attended a Sassoon school until he made Aliyah at the age of eight in the early 1950s.

Solomon and Flora married. After Solomon died, Flora became a businesswoman, philanthropist, famed hostess and Jewish scholar, first in India and then in England. She took on many public religious roles that were unusual for an Orthodox woman of her time. Pleas for funds used to come addressed to 'Flora Sassoon, England', and she would respond by hand on the day that the letters arrived. Flora was a fervent Zionist, and was a strong supporter of the 1917 Balfour Declaration. She visited Jerusalem with her son David in 1925.

Wherever she travelled, her entourage included a *Shochet* and a *Minyan*. When Flora died in London in 1936, the Chief Rabbi of British Mandatory Palestine, Isaac Herzog, eulogized her as 'a living well of Torah, of piety, of wisdom, of goodness and charity, of the staunchest loyalty to tradition, and out of her wonderful well Israel could draw in abundance noble incentives and lofty inspiration.'

When Flora and Solomon's son David was 8 years old, he astonished his parents by trading his toy kite for a rare printed book containing an Arabic translation of the *Book of Ruth* that was written for Baghdadi Jews who lived in India. That trade was to be the first item in David's lifelong pursuit of collecting Jewish books and manuscripts. David always claimed that he assembled his library because he wanted to observe the *mitzvah* of writing or acquiring a Sefer Torah by extending the *mitzvah* to include all religious literature.

By age eight, David knew by heart the prayers for the entire liturgical year and practically the entire Hebrew Bible. He received his general education at a local Anglican institution, St. Peter's High School. Later, instead of being educated at Eton like several of his Sassoon cousins, David was sent to a *yeshiva* in North London.

David learned the family business from his mother when she served as chairwoman of several Bombay enterprises such as the Sassoon Spinning and Weaving Company. In 1901, Flora and her two children moved to London. In 1912, David married Selina (Sarah Ziskha) Prins, scion of two famous Ashkenazic families from Holland and Germany. Selina's father Moshe Meir ben Rabbi Eliezer Liepman Prins, a diamond merchant from Amsterdam, owned a magnificent library. Selina was the granddaughter of Rabbi Marcus Lehman, the renowned Talmudic scholar who was the first Orthodox Jewish novelist of Jewish-themed writing. David and Selina lived in a stylish and spacious Mayfair home. Their two children were Flora (Farha), born in 1914; and Solomon (Suliman), born in 1915.

David Sassoon was highly esteemed. Rabbi Chaim Oizer Grodzinski, recognized as the leading *posek* and spiritual guide of his generation, addressed him as 'The Prince (Nagid) David Sassoon.' In his search for manuscripts and old books, David travelled extensively to Yemen, Germany, Italy, Syria, China and the Himalayas. He would purchase items from the noted bookseller Rabbi David Frankel and from the famous Orientalist Silvestre de Sacy.

David spent ten years negotiating to buy the *Farchi Bible*, a beautifully calligraphed and illuminated 1383 bible which contained over 1,000 pages and more than 350 illustrations. He purchased several manuscripts that had been discovered in the Cairo Geniza.

David served as treasurer of the Etz Chaim Yeshiva in London. He supported a charity established to aid the Lubavitcher Rebbe during his hospitalization in Paris in 1937; he was a member of the Commission for Kashruth in London; and he was an elder of the Bevis Marks Synagogue. In April 1938, worried about the safety of his library following the Austrian Anschluss, David confided to his diary:

'Last night, I removed some manuscripts and printed books from their home of many years and with great care wrapped them in paper in order to send them for safekeeping in a more secure place. This afternoon, my son Silman, may God protect and keep him, and I took the packages and began to place them on the inner seat of a taxi. Later, my righteous duchess [Selina], may God protect and keep her, and I went to a place called Winchester House Safe Deposit, on [Old] Broad Street, and with a broken heart and crushed spirit, we stored the books in an ironclad room.'

Although David Sassoon retrieved the volumes from Winchester House in March 1939, his concerns for their safety were well founded. The Sassoon residence in Bruton Street was bombed in 1940 during the Blitz and almost all the windows were shattered. According to David Sassoon's grandson Haki, it was the Lunzers who persuaded David and Selina to join them in Letchworth.

In October 1940, the Sassoon retinue – including the cat Mrs Peters – arrived in Letchworth. That first night, they had nowhere to live, so they decamped in the office of a Letchworth estate agents and in the railway station. The next day, they purchased the house at 15 Sollershott East.

Sassoon House

Between 1912 and the move to Letchworth in 1940, the Sassoon Library grew from 500 manuscripts to 1,300. Just as the Sassoons had a private synagogue in their Mayfair home before the war, they continued this custom after the move to Letchworth, where David Sassoon lived out his final two years.

Norman Oster was ten when he first visited the Sassoon home in Sollershott East in early 1942. He remembers a little old lady whom he mistook for Rabbi Sassoon's mother Selina, but who was probably Nanny. Norman was impressed with the sheer number of books in the house: 'We had a lot of books in London, but I had never seen so many books in glass cabinets before. While I was there, I heard Rabbi Sassoon say to a visitor, "I am just the custodian of the books." I had never heard the word custodian, but from my Latin lessons I knew that custos meant guardian.'

Cambridge student Charles Heller was fascinated to see what was on the book-lined shelves where the services were held at the Sassoons in the 1960s: 'I have never forgotten the bound volumes of the Jewish newspaper from Shanghai, which included a *dvar Torah* in which the editor referred to "The Rev Dr Solomon Isaacson". It eventually hit me that he was referring to the medieval commentator Rashi – Rabbi Solomon the son of Isaac. Another volume that fascinated me was the *Diwan Daoud* - the catalogue of the books in the Sassoon library. How wonderful it must be to have all the books you own listed in such a fine volume.'

In a 1966 article in *Jewish Life Magazine*, entitled 'The Sassoon Treasures,' Rabbi Dr Zvi M Rabinowicz describes the Sassoon Library in Letchworth as the world's greatest private collection of priceless Torah scrolls, incunabula, manuscripts and unpublished writings covering a period of nearly a thousand years. Rabbi Rabinowicz stated that when he visited the Sassoon Library, he was reminded of Exodus chapter 3, verse 5: '*Shal Naaleicha me'al raglecha* - Put off thy shoes from off thy feet for the place whereon thou standest is holy ground.'

This sense of awe was shared by so many others who visited the Sassoon Library. Rabbi Norman Solomon recalls that in the 1950s, he held enlightening discussions with Rabbi Sassoon about the family's invaluable collection of manuscripts, including the famous autograph of Rambam's commentary on the Mishna: 'A facsimile of the manuscript was published at that time with Rabbi Sassoon's Introduction, in which he demonstrated its authenticity on the basis of a novel analysis of Rambam's "fast" and "slow" styles of handwriting.'

One day during my teens, Rabbi Sassoon showed me what I thought was a relatively small Torah scroll. Sephardi Torah scrolls are read with the scroll standing vertically in a case, unlike Ashkenazi scrolls that are read horizontally on a flat surface. But when Rabbi Sassoon opened the scroll, I saw that although it was handwritten on parchment, it was not a Torah scroll – it didn't have the distinctive cursive writing.

When I asked Rabbi Sassoon what I was looking at, he replied: 'It's a handwritten work by the Rambam.' Naturally, I was very familiar with Maimonides, the 12th century Jewish commentator and philosopher, and I hope I looked suitably impressed. 'No, you don't understand', said Rabbi Sassoon. 'Maimonides wrote this scroll in his own hand!'

Five years after Rabbi Sassoon and family left Letchworth for Jerusalem in 1970, the Maimonides scroll made headlines. Israel's

Education Minister and the Hebrew University of Jerusalem tried to raise the millions of pounds required to purchase the entire rare Sassoon Library. Part of the library was being auctioned by Rabbi Sassoon and his sister Flora Feuchtwanger (Sassoon) to pay for death duties in Britain.

The issue was raised in the Knesset, where calls were made for the state to buy the Sassoon collection. Knesset Speaker Yisrael Yeshayahu and members of Knesset met with Rabbi Sassoon in an effort to persuade him not to sell it abroad. No one – including Rabbi Sassoon himself – wanted the collection to end up in non-Israeli hands. There was general relief when anonymous buyers donated the collection to the Jewish National and University Library in Jerusalem.

If I felt privileged to be shown the Maimonides scroll, my schoolfriend David Alexander was positively bowled over when he was 15 years old: 'Our family were frequent visitors to Letchworth, always staying with the Fachlers. Naturally, we attended Shabbat and *Yom Tov* prayers at the Sassoons. On one occasion, when my father Yisrael had already acquired the status of honoured guest in the Sassoon family home, I tagged along when Rabbi Sassoon invited him for a private viewing of the 12th century Maimonides *Mishne Torah* manuscript.

'My father approached the large, heavy scroll with awe and reverence, and soon the two adults – Rabbi Sassoon and my father – were leaning forward and reading the sacred text in unison. I can honestly say that I can never ever remember seeing my father so emotional and so excited. I wasn't invited to approach, let alone touch, smell or read the *Mishne Torah*. Yet many years later, my heart skipped a beat when I read that it was being sold at auction. "I know this *Mishne Torah*," I exclaimed to my astonished wife. "I've seen it. Up close. Well, almost up close. And I will never forget the emotional impact it had on my father."'

Another visitor with his parents to the Sassoons in the 1960s was David Dangoor, a classmate and good friend of my brother Mordechai. David has an impeccable Baghdadi pedigree. His father was the philanthropist, Sir Naim Eliahou Dangoor. His grandfather was Eliahou Dangoor, the world's largest printer of Arabic books. And his great-grandfather was Hakham Ezra Reuben Dangoor, the Chief Rabbi of

Baghdad. David himself is vice-president of the World Organisation of Jews from Iraq (WOJI).

As David says, 'My father and Rabbi Sassoon were both learned and both very interested in similar matters, including Jewish history in Iraq, the evolution of the Hebrew language in recent times, and genealogy, which they discussed eagerly. I remember a discussion I had with Rabbi Sassoon himself about memory, and how and why we forget. His answer was that our memory had to attenuate gradually or our brains would find it difficult to focus on the here and now. Today, sixty years later, neuroscience has reinforced this kind of idea with evidence of perception problems among those unusual people with near absolute recall. I often think about that discussion we had.'

Sometime in the late 1960s, before the Sassoons left for Israel, and before the digital era, Rabbi Sassoon looked for a professional photographer to photograph precious pages of manuscripts from his father's Library. Rabbi Sassoon must have known that many of these manuscripts were destined for auction.

Moich Abrahams takes up the story. 'My brother Bernie ran away from home when he was 17 or 18 years old. He joined the RAF, where he studied photography. When our dad died in 1961, Bernie ran the upholstery business for a couple of years before he opened his own photographic studio in The Wynd. Rabbi Sassoon entrusted Bernie with the job of photographing the manuscripts. Bernie spent several weeks working on this major assignment.'

Jewish bibliophiles seem to sprout like mushrooms in England. In addition to the Sassoon Library, there was the major collection of Elkan Nathan Adler. Indeed, David Sassoon was known as 'the Elkan Adler of the Sephardim.' Another major collector was Moses Gaster, the *Chacham* of the Spanish and Portuguese Congregation in London, whose collection included thousands of Hebrew, Samaritan and Slavonic documents.

Yet another in the pantheon of great Hebrew book collectors of the twentieth century was Jack Lunzer, an industrial diamond merchant who was related to the Sassoons and whose mother Celine and brother Henry lived in Letchworth. Together with his wife Ruth Zippel, the Italian-born daughter of a Polish merchant who had a collection of a thousand volumes, mainly Hebrew books printed in Italy in the sixteenth century, Jack created the Valmadonna Trust Library. Jack supervised the acquisition of 13,000 books and manuscripts, and acquired parts of the Sassoon Library.

I find it remarkable that two of the world's greatest private collectors of rare and early Hebrew books – David Sassoon and Jack Lunzer – had such a strong Letchworth connection.

Rabbi Solomon (Suliman) and Alice Sassoon

'Do half a cup of tea.'

DAVID ALEXANDER'S
mishearing of Selina Sassoon's invitation to have a cup of tea.

It is difficult to think of a family that made a bigger impact on the Letchworth Jewish community than the Sassoon/Feuchtwanger household. David Sassoon, doubtlessly replicating the regal way he saw his mother Flora being treated, used to refer to his wife Selina as 'my righteous duchess'. Generations of visitors to the Sassoon home, first in London and then in Letchworth, experienced a genuine regal aura that surrounded Selina. My mother Chava Fachler (Becker) always said: 'We did not need to meet real royalty – we met Selina Sassoon.'

The *Kibbud Em* – honouring your mother – displayed by Rabbi Solomon Sassoon to the family matriarch (whom everyone called 'Old Mrs Sassoon' to distinguish her from Rabbi Sassoon's wife Alice) made an indelible impression on all visitors. Judith Lebrecht remembers Shabbat afternoon tea at the Sassoon's, with Selina Sassoon sitting at the top of the table on a big throne-like chair, being treated like a queen.

Moich Abrahams remembers Selina in the Sukkah, pouring tea with a very, very shaky hand. Esther Sitzman (Schwab) describes her impressions of the Sassoons thus: 'They were like a royal court, although they themselves lived with great simplicity. There were servants, there was a constant flow of guests and there was the library. I was too small to appreciate the historic implications of what was going on. When you went there you sensed you were in a different world.' Ann Ruth Cohn (Grunfeld) was struck by the extraordinary respect that Rabbi Sassoon showed to his mother. 'Rabbi Suleiman, who was perhaps in his mid-forties, asking his mother Selina, like a small respectful boy, "Imi, may I please open the window?" I was greatly impressed by this chivalrous respect and honour for his mother, and I have never ever forgotten it.'

Ann Ruth says that the Sassoons home combined true gentility, refinement, Torah, and much scholarship. She remembers the exquisite garden, which was a delight to wander through. 'We were served elegant China tea in fragile ornamental dishes and thinly sliced cucumber sandwiches and delicious cake which made us feel very spoiled and important. We met Alice Sassoon, the daughter-in-law of the house, and her husband Rabbi Suleiman Sassoon, when they were quite young. Father usually discussed *halachah*, *Torah*, Jewish history and politics with Rabbi Sassoon, while we played outside with the sleepy old tortoise that inhabited the garden.'

Not all young visitors to the Sassoon household on Sollershott East shared the awe. Frances Israel (Richman) retains memories of a different kind: 'I was petrified when my father used to take me with him when he went to talk to Rabbi Sassoon. The grandeur of the house and the people overwhelmed me.'

Mickey Freudmann's grandfather Joseph used to study with Rabbi Sassoon every day. 'When my grandfather died in 1943, Rabbi Sassoon delivered the eulogy, and wrote the words on his gravestone in Edmonton Cemetery. For me, Rabbi Sassoon was an incredibly distinguished and colourful personality.

'There was a beautiful *Aron Kodesh* (the ark that holds the Torah scrolls) in the room where we *davened*. I once visited the Museum of the Jews of Babylon in Or Yehuda, Israel. When our guide mentioned Rabbi Sassoon, I told her that I had known him when I was a boy in Letchworth. She was absolutely thrilled. She then said to me, "I have a surprise for you", and took me to another part of the museum. There in front of me was the original Sassoon *Aron Kodesh*.'

Mickey remembers that when Selina Sassoon entered the room, her son Rabbi Sassoon would stand-up, and only sat down again when she was seated. As a 10-year-old, I once received a severe reprimand from Rabbi Sassoon because I failed to stand up when my father Eli entered the room. Margalit Fachler (Cohen) had never in her life seen anything like the respect paid to Selina Sassoon, who was already quite frail. 'She always had such a regal smile. No one ever turned their back to her, and her family addressed her in the third person.'

Head teacher of the Letchworth cheder 'Miss Portal' (Mrs Mimy Sandhouse) remembers the uniqueness of Shabbat at the Sassoons: 'We all naturally stood up when Rabbi Sassoon's mother – otherwise known as the Queen – entered the dining room. We were very fond of her, and we loved to hear her true stories which kept us all spellbound. I still have her beautiful and extremely neat hand-written note she had sent me to thank me for the job I was doing with the children.'

Stella Cuckier (Bornstein) recalls that on Sundays, Selina Sassoon used to have guests to afternoon tea. Even though her hand shook, she insisted on pouring the tea herself. Ruth Keller (Kirsch) remembers

Cheder Pupils, 1990

Selina sitting at the head of the table, with her daughter and daughter-in-law helping to serve the guests.

Ralph Berisch used to take walks on Shabbat with Selina. She explained to him that Letchworth had different trees in every street, and she shared with him the names of all the trees. She discussed with Ralph the Mishna in *Pirkei Avot* about breaking off from Torah study. 'You should be studying, but if not, then you should show admiration and appreciation of nature and God's world.'

According to Derek Pollock, the sense of holiness that emanated from the Sassoon home in Sollershott East was to reach into the hearts of so many of the younger generation. 'That sense of piety and holiness has turned so many of our children into the role models seen in today's Jewish communities.'

In the early 1930s, Rabbi Sassoon's father David had been recommended by Dayan Shmuel Yitzchak Hillman, great-grandfather of the current Israeli president Isaac Herzog, to hire Rabbi Eliyahu Eliezer Dessler, newly arrived in England, as a private tutor for his son Solomon. When Solomon's elder sister Flora (known as Baby Flora to distinguish her from her grandmother Flora), complained that it was unfair for her to be excluded from these lessons, Rabbi Dessler taught them both. This arrangement lasted some 15 years, first in London, and later in Letchworth.

In 1941, Rabbi Dessler responded favourably to a proposal to establish a *Kollel* for advanced learning in Gateshead for married post-yeshiva students. Many of the founders of the Kollel were living in Letchworth at the time: Rabbi Elyah Lopian, his son-in-law Rabbi Leib Gurwicz, his son Rabbi Chaim Shmuel Lopian, and Rabbi Binjaminson (Zhlobiner Rav).

For several years, Rabbi Dessler's weekly travel schedule involved spending Shabbat in Gateshead and then travelling south to the Sassoons in Letchworth, before visiting other communities. He would prepare his lessons on the train. Mickey Freudmann's father helped support the Kollel. Rabbi Dessler used to visit the Freudmann family home in Letchworth.

In 1948, Rabbi Dessler left Gateshead to become the *mashgiach* – spiritual director - at the Ponevezh Yeshiva in Bnei Brak, Israel, which had a strong Letchworth connection. The yeshiva's founder, Rabbi Yosef

Rabbi Sassoon in the garden of 15 Sollershott East

Kahanaman, the Ponevezher Rav, was a frequent visitor to Letchworth between 1945 and the late 1960s. He was a cousin of my grandfather, Sam Becker, and he attended many Fachler and Lopian family celebrations in Letchworth – including my cousin Dovzi Lopian's *pidyan haben*, my barmitzvah and my brother Meir's *brit*.

Through his lessons with Rabbi Dessler, Rabbi Sassoon became an accomplished Yiddish speaker. Rabbi Sassoon's niece Mozelle Gubbay (Feuchtwanger) relates this delightful anecdote: 'Rabbi Sassoon was walking through Dalston, south of Stoke Newington, during the Second World War when he was stopped by an elderly Charedi Jew who started talking to him in Yiddish. Rabbi Sassoon replied politely in fluent Yiddish. "Oh, wonderful," said the old man, "You are from the same Polish *stetl* as I'm from." The man was trying to trace family from his hometown. Rabbi Sassoon was obliged to tell the disappointed Polack how sorry he was, but that he had never in his life stepped foot in Poland.'

London-born Rabbi Sassoon spoke English to his Dutch mother, and Arabic and Hebrew to his father. Rabbi Sassoon's son Haki remembers growing up speaking the dialect of Arabic used by Baghdadi Jews. 'Our house was very Indian,' he says. When I once asked Rabbi Sassoon where and when he learned to read and write English, he gave me the surprising answer: 'I studied the advertisements on the London Underground on my way to my Hebrew tutor.' Rabbi Sassoon must have been a quick learner because he also told me that by the age of 18, he had read the complete works of Freud.

Rabbi Sassoon received semicha in 1936, and had his own private students in their Bruton Street home. One student was Chaim Miller, who would later spend the war years in Letchworth. Another young boy tutored by Rabbi Sassoon in London was Jack Lunzer, whose family would later live in Letchworth. Zippy Rosenblatt (Persoff) remembers that her two older brothers attended Rabbi Sassoon's Sunday morning *shiur* in Letchworth during the war.

Leon Paget (born Pfingst): 'When my father was released from internment, I regularly accompanied him to the Sephardi services at the Sassoons. I marvelled at the magnificently plated boxes containing the Torah scrolls. Many a time after we had put our coats on and were leaving, Rabbi Sassoon would send his Indian servant to fetch us back for a sumptuous lunch – a *mitzvah* for which we were always very grateful.'

In 1932, David Sassoon had started working on the manuscript of *A History of the Jews in Baghdad*, but he died in Letchworth in 1942 before completing the manuscript. His son Rabbi Solomon Sassoon took on the task of completing the book, but he had difficulty with his father's handwriting. Looking for someone to help him decipher and type up the manuscript, he found my grandmother Melanie Becker, newly arrived in Letchworth. Melanie died in 1947, and when Rabbi Sassoon finally published his father's book in 1949, he generously thanked Melanie.

Rabbi Sassoon had an aunt, Rachel, who was his father David's older sister. Rachel married David Elias Ezra, and the Ezras were famous for their philanthropic activities. David Ezra was named Sheriff of Calcutta in 1926, and was knighted by King George V in 1927. Sir David died in 1947. In 1950, there was great excitement in the Letchworth Jewish community when Lady Rachel Ezra came to the town to visit her sister-in-law Selina, her nephew Rabbi Sassoon, and her niece Flora Feuchtwanger (Sassoon).

Moich Abrahams says about Rabbi Sassoon: 'He had this knack of treating everybody the same, giving each person that special attention that only an enlightened person can do. Even before my barmitzvah in 1954 in Hallmead, which was officiated by Rabbi Sassoon, I used to visit the Sassoon home regularly with our lodger, Mr Walter Gottfried. We often came on Friday night for the Sabbath service and were invited to stay for the Sabbath meal. Everyone was assigned a place to sit, and I remember often being placed next to Rabbi Sassoon. We would discuss topics like mathematical puzzles. The Sassoon boys, David and Haki, helped to serve and pass the *challah* around to the guests. The family of Cochin Jewish cooks stood at the room entrance as the first blessings were said.

'Rabbi Sassoon was a great advocate of proving scientifically the Divine origin of the Torah. He explained to me the theories about the numerical patterns in the Torah. He gave me examples of hidden patterns, words which occurred in a unique way. This prompted me to ask him how many times the word 'Love' appears in the Torah. In the mid-1950s, there were no computers for this kind of research. Sure enough, Rabbi Sassoon later wrote to me that he had found that it occurred 22 times. This was highly significant, since the Torah is written with 22 symbols.'

In addition to all his other activities, Rabbi Sassoon kept abreast of what was happening in the wider Anglo-Jewish community. The early 1950s saw anti-Shechita campaigns being initiated in European countries with unfortunate frequency. In 1954, a bill was introduced in the House of Commons, calling for the repeal of the provision exempting Jewish and Muslim slaughter in the Slaughter of Animals Act of 1933.

In order to increase support for this bill, the Council of Justice to Animals and the Humane Slaughter Association of England distributed anti-Shechita propaganda throughout England, and asked Urban and District Councils to pass resolutions in support of the bill. 549 councils did so. Repeated attempts were made to outlaw Shechita in Parliament.

Without waiting for the Chief Rabbi's office to respond to the new threat against Shechita, without waiting for the Board of Deputies to act, and without asking anyone's permission, Rabbi Sassoon in Letchworth took the initiative. At his own expense, he wrote and published *A Critical Study of Electrical Stunning and the Jewish Method of Slaughter (Shechita)*. He then printed the booklet, and distributed it – all at his own expense – to every single Member of Parliament and every single urban and district councillor in the UK. His initiative succeeded – and the anti-Shechita campaign fizzled out. Rabbi Sassoon's booklet was reprinted eight times between 1955 and 1956.

In March 1960, the *Belfast Jewish Record* reported on a rabbinical conference convened by Chief Rabbi Brodie in Westcliff-on-Sea. 'In contrast to these purely talmudical proceedings, there was the unexpected appearance of Rabbi S D Sassoon of Letchworth, a son of the late and scholarly David Sassoon, who in fluent and polished Hebrew gave a report on the latest research in disciplines affecting Shechita and its defence against hostile criticisms and attacks.

'The young rabbi, who holds no official position and who is today the leading expert on the scientific aspects of Shechita, carries out his worldwide investigations and publishes the results entirely at his own expense. It was fascinating to learn from this modest and undemonstrative speaker to what extent the latest medical and veterinary researches not only confirm, but really reveal the divinely inspired insights which lie behind the rabbinic laws of Shechita.'

Other books that Rabbi Sassoon wrote include *Moshav Zekenim* (1959), a commentary of the Tosafists on the Pentateuch from a manuscript in his collection; Abraham ben Maimon's commentary on Genesis and Exodus, from a Bodleian manuscript (1965); an elegant facsimile edition of the Mishnah commentary of Maimonides (3 volumes, 1956–1966); and *The Spiritual Heritage of the Sephardim* (1957).

Rabbi Sassoon was a great believer in dream interpretation. Carol Eini (Roth) remembers: 'Rabbi Sassoon told me that I should take note of my dreams. He said that dreams dreamt on Friday night had deeper meaning, and that dreams dreamt on Friday night in Eretz Yisrael had even deeper meaning.'

I heard the following story about *sha'atnez* – the biblical prohibition of cloth containing a mixture of wool and linen, from Rabbi Sassoon himself: 'For years, I had all my suits made by a Jewish tailor who lived in Letchworth. One night, I had a dream, in which my father appeared to me. "Silman, you need to check your suits for *sha'atnez*." "But Abui," I answered him in my dream, "all my suits are made by my reliable

Jewish tailor in Letchworth." When I woke from my dream, just to be sure, I sent all my suits to the *sha'atnez* laboratory in London to be tested. Lo and behold, there was *sha'atnez* in every suit.'

In 1995, Moich Abrahams' 89-year-old mother Margaret fell and broke her arm. Moich visited her regularly in Lister Hospital, Stevenage. 'She had been in hospital about two weeks when I had a dream that was so vivid and unusual that I wrote it down as soon as I awoke. I dreamt that I was with the late Rabbi Sassoon and we each held a glass of wine. He and I then toasted, clinked glasses, and said *L'Chaim*. That very day, I drove to my mother in hospital, and excitedly told her my dream. About a week later, my mother unexpectedly passed away. I have always interpreted that dream as being a sort of message from Rabbi Sassoon about the nature of Life and Death.'

Rabbi Sassoon was the founder/president of Eastern Community synagogues in Golders Green and Stamford Hill. When Israel's Ashkenazi Chief Rabbi, Yitzchak Halevi Herzog, died in 1959, the search for a successor dragged on for five years. In 1964, Israeli politician Moshe Chaim Shapira of the National Religious Party had the novel idea of inviting Letchworth-based Rabbi Sassoon to become the first-ever joint Ashkenazi and Sephardi chief rabbi of Israel.

There was certainly a logic behind this suggestion. With his Ashkenazi mother and Sephardi father, the Yiddish-speaking Rabbi Sassoon was uniquely qualified to fulfil this dual role. However, he rejected the feelers. As he said to me at the time, 'In Israel, they eat you up alive. I do not want to be swallowed up in politics and bureaucracy.' Efraim Halevy offers an alternative explanation for why Rabbi Sassoon declined to submit his candidacy: 'He said that he was too junior for the position.'

This was not the end of Rabbi Sassoon's involvement in chief rabbi politics. With Chief Rabbi Israel Brodie due to retire in 1965, rumours starting surfacing in autumn 1964 of a surprise candidate to succeed him: Rabbi Isaac Herzog's son Yaakov. Although Yaakov was an ordained rabbi, he enjoyed a career as a prominent civil servant. In November 1964, the *Jewish Chronicle* reported that Sir Isaac Wolfson had mentioned Herzog's name at a meeting of the selection committee.

The Sassoon and Herzog families were very close – Selina Sassoon and Sarah Herzog enjoyed a lengthy correspondence. In November

1964, Rabbi Sassoon helped persuade Yaakov to announce his candidacy. Sadly, Yaakov died before he could take up the post, which was eventually filled by Emanuel Jakobovits.

For generations of Letchworth children, the Sassoon *succah* was a place of wonder. It was sumptuously decorated, with pictures of famous rabbis on the walls. Gail Zivan Neriya (Vanger) remembers how the succah's special roof was closed on rainy days. Jean Shindler (Pollock) remembers how every Succot, Selina Sassoon would tell a story, 'The Cobbler and the Pebbles,' which Jean's grandmother Florrie had written as a poem.

Generations of Letchworth children in the 1950s and 1960s fondly recall that on *Chol Hamoed* Succot and other occasions during the year, the accordion-playing Rabbi Sender Dominitz would come with his family from London and entertain the children. Succah refreshments included Grodzinski's Swiss rolls and orange juice. Patricia Reifen (Hassan) remembers 'being served scrambled eggs on crackers' in the succah. Shulamith Landau (Schischa) remembers that every child came home from the Succah party with a gift.

For Shulamith, Simchat Torah at the Sassoons was a truly joyous and memorable occasion. 'I remember the exceptional way we celebrated, with so many beautiful upright Sephardi Torah scrolls, the solid silver breastplates and the gold bells.' For many, one of the highlights of Simchat Torah at the Sassoons was Chacham Yosef Doury's unique, playful and unforgettable rendering of the Alef Bet song. To our Ashkenazi ears, hearing the words pronounced "Aleph, Beth, Gimmel, Daled, Hey, Wow" sounded positively exotic.

Gail Zivan Neriya (Vanger): 'As children, we eagerly participated in the Simchat Torah dancing. We were given wooden sticks that held glittery flags with pop-up Torah scrolls. All this enthusiasm was ignited by Rabbi Sassoon and Avraham Gubbay who danced and chanted, jumping up and down until the floorboards shuddered on the women's side of the partition. There was great excitement as we danced in the street, singing at the top of our voices.'

One of Jean Shindler (Pollock)'s clearest childhood memories is dancing with the exquisite centuries-old *Sifrei Torah* brought out once a year and covered with sparkling silver: 'Simchat Torah was the only time in the year that I actually saw a Sefer Torah.'

One of the Simchat Torah traditions at the Sassoons was to throw sweets. It was no secret that Buby Bornstein had poor eyesight. His son Chaim tells the story: 'One year, during the dancing, in the excitement of the moment, my father accidentally threw a sweet that knocked over one of the beautiful – and very valuable - vases that the family had brought with them from India. The vase fell and shattered. Everyone fell quiet, and my father felt terrible. Mrs Selina Sassoon defused the embarrassing silence by telling my father not to worry, since she had another vase just like the broken one.'

Shulamith Landau (Schischa) remembers the annual Chanukah and Purim parties held in the Scouts Hall at which communal rabbi, Reb Oosher Feuchtwanger addressed the community. She also remembers her mother going to hear Reb Oosher's pre-Pesach talk to the ladies of the community. Shulamith recalls the excitement of burning the Haman effigy, and the fireworks exploding in the Sassoon garden.

Jean Shindler (Pollock) describes Purim at the Sassoons: 'It was like Guy Fawkes Night, the 5th of November. An effigy of Haman made by Rabbi Sassoon was burned on a bonfire, and then he would organise a firework display. I remember how we children wrote the name of Haman on the soles of our shoes – and would then rub our shoes on the ground every time Haman's name was mentioned.'

For Jean, the Sassoons brought a touch of exoticism to the Jewish festivals. 'It was at the Sassoons that many of us first came across the custom of the *Tu B'Shevat seuda*, a festive meal to celebrate the New Year for Trees." I attended several *Tu B'Shevat seudot* at the Sassoons, and I remember being amazed how they had managed to source mangos, papaya, lychees and other exotic fruits, long before these fruits became commonplace in Britain.

For many young girls attending the Shabbat morning prayers, the *mechitza* folding screen was a source of endless fascination. Gail Zivan Neriya (Vanger): 'I recall the living room where we learnt to *daven*, and where we peeked at guests through the *mechitza* and sang familiar liturgical melodies. I remember the panes of glass overlooking the garden where we secretly drew shapes when the windows steamed up. Jean Shindler (Pollock): 'The screen used as the mechitza was so high that we couldn't see over it.' Hazel Schwartz (Ward): 'I can still see the room and the divider to keep men away!' From the perspective of a young girl, it makes perfect sense that the function of the Sassoon *mechitza* was perceived as keeping men away.

Kerry Back lived next to the Feuchtwangers and the Sassoons, and especially remembers being allowed to sit in the library, only later realising that this was such an honour. 'We all lived as one. There was no difference between the different ethnic communities. When I grew up, and was asked, "Are you Ashkenazi or Sephardi?", I did not understand the question.'

Rabbi Sassoon loved chess, and Peter Roth remembers that he used to play blindfold chess with several of the Letchworth children simultaneously. Moich Abrahams remembers playing chess with Rabbi Sassoon on relaxing Shabbat afternoons, when the huge lounge had been rearranged after hosting the prayers in the morning.

During the week, there was a constant stream of visitors to the Sassoons. Some wanted to see the rare manuscripts in the Sassoon Library. Others came to Letchworth to seek advice from Rabbi Sassoon. Haki Sassoon says that he and his brother David were often allowed to remain in the room during intensely personal conversations between visitors and Rabbi Sassoon. If the visitors questioned the presence of David and Haki, Rabbi Sassoon would say: 'If you can trust me, you can trust my sons.' As Haki says, 'What was said in the room was never ever discussed again. We just knew that we would never be allowed to repeat anything.'

Other visitors to Rabbi Sassoon sought him out because of his reputation as a generous donor to charitable causes. As his son David recalls, many collectors found it worth their while to make the journey to Letchworth in order to enlist his father's aid for their particular worthy cause. Having come all the way from London, they were naturally invited to stay for a meal.

Eventually, Rabbi Sassoon bought a caravan which he parked at the back of no. 15 Sollershott East. He used the caravan to store boxes of books, but there was also a desk and chair. When he did not want to be interrupted by visitors or collectors, he would retire to the caravan, giving instructions to the household to say that he was in Scotland.

In 1969, the Lubavitcher Rebbe wrote to Rabbi Sassoon from New York, seeking financial aid for the Jews of Bombay:

Greetings and Blessings: It has been brought to my attention that the Jewish community in Bombay is facing a serious crisis. According to my information, which apparently comes from a reliable source, there are at present about 450 Baghdadi Jews there, whereas the Bnei Israel community numbers about a couple of thousand, spread over the whole of India.

Of the three existing Jewish schools, two are expected to close in May 1970, partly for lack of funds, and partly because the number of students has fallen. The largest Jewish school is the Jacob Sassoon School, where about 300 children, including some Bnei Israel, receive more or less free education and free meals; however, because of lack of funds, free meals might soon be stopped, while snacks will be given only to the poorer children.

Knowing of your keen personal interest in the Jewish community of India, especially Bombay, and of how much your ancestors have done to provide vital education and social services for our brethren there, I am confident that you will look into the present situation, and do all that you can, in the great tradition of your family.

Hoping this letter finds you in the best of health.

With blessings.

One of the children that Rabbi Sassoon and his brother-in-law Rabbi Feuchtwanger took an interest in was Ralph Berisch, later Rabbi Refoel Berisch. The Berisches were the only Jewish family in Weston, the village near Letchworth where the Bornstein brothers had their Tower Clothiers garment factory. Ralph's father had escaped from Germany to Scotland before the war. The Berisch home in Weston had no hot water, no heating, no radio, and an outside WC.

When Ralph was born in 1945, Rabbi Sassoon arranged for him to be circumcised by the Zlobiner Rav on Shabbat in Letchworth, with Sigi Stern as the *Sandek*, the person honoured with handing the baby to the *Mohel*. The Sassoons and Feuchtwangers embarked on what would become a long-term commitment to Ralph's spiritual and material welfare.

Ralph remembers that Flora Feuchtwanger knitted him a cardigan which he practically lived in. He was collected by Mr Woods' taxi three times a week for *cheder* with Mrs Rand, first in Baldock and then in

Letchworth. When Ralph reached the age of ten, the Sassoons put a bedroom at his disposal every Shabbat at 18 Sollershott East. He was personally tutored by Rabbi Sassoon, Rabbi Feuchtwanger, and later by Harry Leitner. The Sassoons and Feuchtwangers bought him clothes, gave him pocket money, and virtually adopted him.

Ralph witnessed first-hand the family's legendary hospitality. When the postman arrived each day, he would always be invited by Alice Sassoon or Flora Feuchtwanger to sit down for a cup of tea. Ralph remembers than when guests of the Sassoons arrived at Letchworth station, the taxi drivers knew exactly where to deposit them.

Rabbi Sassoon was the proud owner of a motorbike. According to Ralph, when Rabbi Sassoon was attending a wedding in London, he would ride his motorbike in his wedding clothes, with the box containing his top hat tied on behind him. I have a personal reason to remember this motorbike. I used to sit on the back, clinging on for dear life to Rabbi Sassoon – neither of us wearing crash helmets, of course – as we careened through the streets of Letchworth between Sollershott East and Hallmead in the short period when services continued in Hallmead.

After the motorbike, Rabbi Sassoon bought a Ford Zephyr. He told me that he was constantly being stopped for speeding on the A1 road between Letchworth and London.

Rabbi Sassoon and the community made a barmitzvah for Ralph in 1958. After morning prayers, there was a sit-down meal in the library. Ralph recalls: 'I received £5 from Rabbi Sassoon, and a watch from the community. Rabbi Feuchtwanger gave me the *Kitzur Shulchan Aruch* – the Code of Jewish Law, with a promise that if I learned a certain section by heart, I would receive £50. I would later claim my prize.'

After his barmitzvah, Ralph stayed with the Sassoons every Shabbat in the winter months. Rabbi Feuchtwanger would write a letter to Ralph's headmaster, explaining why Ralph had to leave school early on Friday afternoon. Ralph was also a frequent visitor to the Fachler family down the road in Sollershott East. He loved the informal atmosphere of a home that was so open. 'One never quite knew who was there.'

One of the regular visitors to the Sassoons was Aby Van Praagh, whose mother was an old friend of Selina Sassoon from their childhood days in Amsterdam. Aby took Ralph under his wing. He took him on his very first trip to London. They were studying together one day when Aby made an accurate prediction: 'One day, you will be able to take out any of the Hebrew books here, and be able to study on your own.'

In about 1960, Rabbi accordion-in-the-succah Dominitz started a boarding school in London. Aby asked Ralph's father for permission to send Ralph to the school, on the understanding that funding would be provided. Ralph was the first pupil. He later attended the Yesodey Hatorah school in London, followed by Gateshead Yeshiva where he was ordained as a rabbi. Ralph married Loli Levy from Gibraltar. Even after they were married, the couple would often spend Shabbat in Letchworth. When they returned to Gateshead on Sunday, Alice Sassoon would give them food for the journey, 'enough for a month,' says Ralph.

Rabbi Refoel Berisch channelled his Letchworth upbringing and experience into a career of encouraging and mentoring children who shared his own childhood background. I have often wondered whether Rabbi Sassoon and Reb Oosher Feuchtwanger had any premonition when Ralph was born that their concern for his welfare would be so richly repaid.

For the first fifteen years after the Sassoons moved to Letchworth, the family held a daily Sephardi minyan in their home, as they had done in their Mayfair home. Norman Solomon remembers: 'My wife and I often attended Shabbat services at the Sassoons. We relished the Baghdadi-*nusach* reading of Torah as well as the delicious kiddush which followed.' After the Hallmead *minyan* ended in 1958, both Yossel Schischa and I mastered the Baghdadi melodies for leading the services and reading from the Torah in the Sassoon *minyan*.

Moich Abrahams describes himself as 'probably not your typical Letchworth Jewish boy. 'Although my mother was a Chassidic lady, my father was not *frum*. Emotionally and intellectually, I was a very late developer. Despite the best efforts of Mrs Rand's private Hebrew introductory lessons in our home above the Arcade, in the centre of Letchworth, and despite Rabbi Feuchtwanger's *cheder* lessons in Hallmead, I struggled with my Hebrew reading.

'This made me quite frustrated and disillusioned with formal prayers. I disliked not understanding what I was saying when praying in Hebrew. In hindsight, if I had been a more mature and capable student of religious matters and the Hebrew language, I might have followed the path of Ralph Berisch.

'However, that was not my destiny. One day, when I was about fourteen or fifteen, I was in the Sassoon garden with Rabbi Sassoon, and I told him, "If I am going to pray, I need to know who or what I am praying to." Rabbi Sassoon answered me thus: "Imagine you are on a pathway towards the best that you can be. Have a dialogue with that one; use that as your form of prayer." His answer struck a strong chord with me. I found it very liberating. I have no doubt that it helped push me to whom I am today.'

Shulamith Landau (Schischa) remembers that Rabbi Sassoon 'shared his latest Torah insights with such thrill and excitement during a break in the Shabbos morning service.' Ruth Keller (Kirsch) remembers Rabbi Sassoon as 'a remarkable man and an original enlightened thinker who spoke at least six languages fluently and had a wide knowledge of science, nature and mathematics and, of course, Judaism.'

Robby Jaffey used to accompany his brother David to attend Shabbat morning services at the Sassoons. 'I remember that at the end of the service, there would be some argument about which melody to use for Adon Olam – the Sephardi or the Ashkenazi. As soon as the service ended, I rushed into the back room where we sat around the table. Goodies were piled on the table, including chocolates, cake and kiddush wine. After the food, we youngsters sat in a circle and one of the teens led the group. I don't remember much about the songs and stories, but I do remember the time my late brother Joel returned from Israel and entertained us on a Sunday with his guitar and sang Israeli songs.'

Many visitors to the Sassoon household over the years retained very positive recollections of the three generations of cooks – the dark-skinned Judah family from Cochin, in Kerala, India: Aharon, Meir Chay, and children Ruby and Ezra. For most newcomers to 15 Sollershott East, this was their first time they encountered black Jews.

Whenever a boy of my age was visiting the Sassoons on a Sunday, I would be invited to take him for a walk in Letchworth, presumably while his parents were sequestered with Rabbi Sassoon. This is how I first met Jonathan Bekhor, who later joined me in Carmel College.

Haki Sassoon describes some of the permanent or temporary members of the household, including Uncle Joe Gubbay, Rabbi Sassoon's and Flora Feuchtwanger's great uncle. Joe's London apartment got bombed in the war and he lost everything. He had gone to live with his brother, founder of Lauderdale Road Synagogue, but when his brother died, his widow demanded that Joe leave. He had nowhere to go, so he used to come every Shabbat to the Sassoons.

Other people who were part of the Sassoon household included Marta Rosenbaum, a nurse who had arrived in England from Germany in 1936. Marta took over from housekeeper Margaret Patten, when she got very old. A very important figure in the Sassoon household was Nanny, Miss Thompson, who had been with the Sassoons since before Rabbi Sassoon was born in 1915, and who helped raise two generations of Sassoon and Feuchtwanger children. Many of us still remember the reverence with which the entire family related to Nanny. On a more light-hearted note, some of us remember the phrases 'Nanny said I may' and 'Nanny didn't mean it' being used when David, Haki, Mozelle and Jacob used to argue with their parents.

Haki remembers the names of some Letchworth families – frequent or infrequent visitors to the Sassoons – that few others remember. The Hobbins family in Field Lane had a son and a daughter, and used to attend prayers at the Sassoons. Haki remembers two widows, Mrs Papp and Mrs Kowpie, who arrived from Hungary after the 1956 revolution.

A frequent visitor to the Sassoons in Letchworth was family friend Professor Abraham Fraenkel, a world-renowned German-born Israeli mathematician, Zionist leader, and the first Dean of Mathematics at the Hebrew University of Jerusalem.

Several members of Rabbi Sassoon's London community were frequent visitors in Letchworth. Eze Silas recalls spending memorable *Shabbatot* and *Yamim Tovim* with the Sassoon family at Sollershott East. 'The family's hospitality is legendary.' Other visitors included Benny Myers and his older brother Ellis, who was a High Court judge.

When people hear the name Dr Adler, there can be some confusion. In Golders Green, there was a Dr Adler who was a very popular GP. In Letchworth, Dr Adler referred to Dr Yoachim Adler, husband of Martha, Alice Sassoon's sister, frequent visitors to Letchworth on Shabbat and holidays. 'Our' Dr Adler was a Cohen, and he used to recite the priestly blessing in the Sassoon minyan in a rich Frankfurt Yekkish accent. On

Simchat Torah, it was always his role to announce the *Chatan Torah* and *Chatan Bereshit*. I can still hear his "*Amoud, amoud, amoud*" ringing in my ears.

Margalit Fachler (Cohen) had studied English in London in the early 1960s. By a strange coincidence, she even visited our Letchworth home before she and I met, in the company of Suzanne Freedman (Pressburger) from Letchworth, and my friend Ann Dawes (Rau) from London. In the summer of 1966, Margalit arrived in Letchworth from Tel Aviv as a young bride-to-be: 'I spent almost every weekend for the next five years in Letchworth. On my first Shabbat, a gift awaited me. It was an ornate jewellery box, a welcome gift from the Sassoons, into whose world I now entered for the first time.

'I regarded myself as a highly sophisticated Tel Aviv girl who had attended a religious high school. Nothing prepared me for the jaw-dropping world I discovered when I first encountered the Sassoon and Feuchtwanger household. I was overwhelmed by the aristocratic aura and other-worldliness of the family.'

Margalit and I were invited to a meal at the Sassoons. As a seasoned veteran of such occasions, I knew what to expect. I failed miserably to prepare Margalit, as she explains: 'Before I went for my first meal at the Sassoons, Yanky warned me: "There will be copious amounts of food, so pace yourself." When the food started to be served with great pomp and ceremony, I started counting the dishes. When I got to dish #10, I proudly turned to Yanky and said, "You see, I paced myself." Yanky gave a wry smile and said: "The main meal has not yet begun!"'

Shortly before the Sassoon / Feuchtwanger household moved to Jerusalem in 1970, Rabbi Sassoon asked me: 'Yanky, do you know what's been wrong with Ashkenazi rabbis for the past 200 years?' At the age of twenty-four, this question was above my paygrade. 'No,' I replied, 'please enlighten me.'

'For centuries,' Rabbi Sassoon explained, 'Ashkenazi rabbis have been so rigidly inward-looking that they have failed to find a shared common language with many members of their flocks, especially the younger generation. If someone was not fully observant, the Ashkenazi rabbis shunned them and wanted nothing more to do with them. But it's never been like that in our community. Sephardi rabbis accept and embrace everyone, regardless of their level of observance. Our rabbis prefer to emphasize communal unity and family ties rather than fanatic observance. Because we are not judgmental, our communities have always treated their rabbis with great respect.'

Rabbi Sassoon proceeded to give me an example. 'Last week, two non-orthodox brothers from the Baghdadi community in London came to Letchworth to ask me, as the rabbi of their community, to give them a blessing for their new joint business venture.' Rabbi Sassoon was referring to Baghdad-born and London-raised brothers Maurice and Charles Saatchi. Amid a huge blast of media publicity, they had joined forces to set up their own new advertising agency, Saatchi and Saatchi, which for a while would dominate the global advertising industry. Rabbi Sassoon knew full well that the brothers were not observant. Yet he found it totally natural that they would make the trip to Letchworth to receive a blessing from their rabbi.

Another pair of brothers, this time Letchworth brothers, had earlier been the beneficiaries of Rabbi Sassoon's tolerant attitude. When Peter and Stephen (Hans) Kirsch, the sons of Frederick and Liesl Kirsch, started attending Shabbat morning services at the Sassoon's, Rabbi Sassoon indicated to them that they should *duchen* – recite the traditional priestly blessings.

The Kirsch brothers were embarrassed by this request, and Stephen took Rabbi Sassoon aside. 'Rabbi Sassoon, you know that Peter and I are not Shabbat observant. You have probably guessed that after the Shabbat morning service, we drive to our glove factory. We don't feel comfortable giving the priestly blessing.' 'Are you sure you are genuine Cohens?' asked Rabbi Sassoon. 'Quite sure,' answered Stephen. 'Then you duchen!' replied Rabbi Sassoon. No further argument. No chastisement. No making them feel uncomfortable.

Yet another example of this more lenient approach is related by Rabbi Sassoon's son, Haki: 'In our Letchworth home, we had an *Eruv* – a ritual halachic enclosure that allows activities that are normally prohibited on Shabbat, specifically: carrying objects from a private domain to a semi-public domain – around our yard. We asked our teacher, Chacham Yosef Doury, a wise, learned and reliable rabbi, if we could ride our bicycles within the *Eruv* on Shabbat. He told us that it is permitted, providing we removed the horn and the batteries for the light before Shabbat. My father agreed with him, but he was concerned with the feelings of the Ashkenazi neighbours who might not understand. So we refrained from riding on Shabbat.'

Margalit Fachler (Cohen) recalls one of the more eccentric visitors to the Sassoon household: 'Who could ever forget Mr Lionel Mozes from Shanghai? He was constantly barging around the Sassoon house close to the time for prayers, calling out "Time, time!" He always reminded me of a Lewis Carroll character in *Alice Through the Looking Glass*.' Cambridge student Charles Heller uses almost identical language to describe Mr Mozes: 'Who can forget Mr Mozes rounding everyone up with his calls of *Minha! Minha!*'

As I was compiling the material for this book, it occurred to me that I was missing any substantial material on Rabbi Sassoon's wife Alice, even though she was a ubiquitous presence in our lives for so many years. All I knew was that her maiden name was Benjamin, that her sister Martha was married to Dr Adler, and that she was a refugee from Europe who had come to work in the Sassoon's Bruton Street home in London. I also knew that Alice and my mother Chava were constantly plotting and planning the eating and sleeping arrangements for the visiting Cambridge students.

I asked Alice's son Haki, a valuable source of information for this book, if he could fill in the missing details about his mother. Here is Haki's surprising response:

'If it were up to my mother, I would not be able to answer your question. As a young child and even as a young adult, every time I tried to push my mother about her family background or about my grandparents, she brushed my questions aside. She would always mutter something like: "Have you nothing else to do?" I simply could not pry any information out of her. She was a doer, always busy. She was not given to idle chat – and for her, details of her family history came under that category.

'I would have remained in total ignorance on this matter were it not for an elderly aunt who sat me down one day in her elegant Jerusalem apartment, while I was a yeshiva student in the city. She said to me: "Listen, there is something I need to tell you. I am not getting any younger, and I suspect that your mother, my niece Alice, has not told you anything about her life before she came to England. I feel that if I do not pass on this information to someone soon, no one will ever know the story."'

Here is what Haki gleaned from his aunt: 'My mother, Alice Benjamin, lived in Frankfurt before the war. Her sister Martha had moved with her first husband to Rotterdam in the Netherlands. On 9 November 1938, Kristallnacht, Alice's mother happened to be visiting Martha in Rotterdam. Alice was all alone in the Frankfurt apartment during the Kristallnacht ordeal, apart from her younger brother.

'The day after Kristallnacht, the Gestapo knocked on the door of the apartment in order to arrest the brother. Quick-thinking Alice had hidden him under the bed, and she turned on the waterworks. "Why have you come again," she shrieked. "You have already arrested him." In the absence of hand-held computers, the Gestapo had no way of checking Alice's claim, and they left.

'Alice got word to her mother to remain in Rotterdam, and she immediately dispatched her brother to join his sister and mother there. Alice gave her brother his passport, she gave him money and food, and she put him on a train to the Dutch border, relying on his ingenuity to find a way to get across.

'My mother Alice was once again alone in the apartment when the Gestapo returned. They had checked their records, and discovered of course that Alice's brother had not been previously arrested. This time, Alice was able to truthfully tell them that she did not know his whereabouts. The Gestapo believed her, but also relieved her of all the valuable silverware in the apartment. Her situation was desperate.'

In Rotterdam, meanwhile, Martha was a member of a benevolent club that helped the sick. Haki continues: 'Martha was friendly with Mrs Posen, the sister of my paternal grandmother Selina Sassoon in London. The Posens had lived for several generations in Frankfurt, where they owned a big silver shop. Mrs Posen's parents refused to avail of the opportunity of escaping, either to Palestine – on the grounds that they were anti-Zionists – or to England. Eventually, their silver shop was destroyed by the Nazis, and the Posens senior fled to Amsterdam.

'In London, my grandmother Selina and my grandfather David Sassoon had been helping Jewish refugees escape from Germany by guaranteeing the British government ten shillings per week so that the refugees would not be a burden on the state. Selina and David even secured premises next to their Bruton Street home to serve as a hostel for the female refugees they had sponsored.

'Mrs Posen wrote to her sister Selina asking for a favour: "Could the Sassoons please stand guarantee for a Miss Alice Benjamin?" The Sassoons agreed, and Alice arrived in England in June 1939, and moved into the hostel. At that time, my grandfather David Sassoon was looking for a secretary, and the very capable and highly organised Alice fit the bill.

'When the Sassoon household moved to Letchworth in 1940, Alice continued working for my grandfather, and travelled frequently to Letchworth. It was probably Rabbi Dessler, who was tutor to my father and my aunt Flora, who suggested the *shidduch* between my mother Alice Benjamin and my father Rabbi Solomon Sassoon.'

Mrs Posen's son Philip (Refoel) later married Thea Eisemann, a childhood friend of my mother Chava Fachler (Becker). Three of Thea and Refoel's daughters, Miriam, Naomi and Chana, were frequent visitors to Letchworth while they were attending, at different times, the Gateshead girls' seminary. Rabbi Sassoon was the matchmaker when Naomi Posen later married my late brother Marcus Mordechai.

When my first son Ashi was born in October 1967, Selina Sassoon was still alive, but already in her last few weeks. She told her daughter Flora Feuchtwanger (Sassoon) that she had had a dream that she was in the Posen silver shop in Frankfurt, choosing a gift for Ashi. Flora promptly travelled up to London to Mapping and Webb silversmiths and bought a silver spoon as a gift for Ashi, who spent every single Shabbat of his first four years in Letchworth before my parents left for London.

Rabbi Asher (Reb Oosher) and Flora Feuchtwanger

'Anything that can help Jewish young people connect more with their roots must be a good thing. Anything that helps bridge the gap between the frum and the secular must be a good thing.'

RABBI ASHER FEUCHTWANGER

When hundreds of Jewish families who had sought temporary residence in Letchworth returned to London at the end of the war, the drastically reduced Jewish community of 150 had to urgently restructure. The rabbi chosen to become the communal rabbi was Oscar (Asher) Feuchtwanger, fondly known to everyone as Reb Oosher.

Born in Antwerp, he was a gifted Talmud scholar whose mild manner hid a fierce brain. He arrived as a refugee to Britain in 1937. After the fall of France in 1940, the British Government responded to public panic over the 'enemy within' by temporarily interning tens of thousands of foreign nationals. The young rabbi who would later become the Letchworth community's spiritual leader, was interned on the Isle of Man. As if this were not enough, the British authorities decided to send him to Australia. Not because he had an urge to explore the outback, but because he was suspected of being a potential Nazi sympathiser. He found himself aboard an internment ship which has lent its name to one of the most notorious voyages in British maritime history.

On 10 June 1940, together with over 500 German Nazis and Italian Fascists, 2,000 Jewish internees – including Reb Oosher - boarded the HMT (Hired Military Transport) ship *Dunera* in Liverpool. With 7

Rabbi Feuchtwanger

officers and a crew of 309 poorly trained soldiers, nearly 3,000 men were crammed on to a vessel built to hold 1,600. The soldiers brutally searched and looted the Jewish internees' luggage. In scenes reminiscent of the worst excesses of the Nazis, passports, documents, *tallitot, tefillin* and prayer books were tossed into the sea. The ship's officers either stood by indifferently or actively participated. Less than twenty-four hours out of Liverpool, the *Dunera* was hit by a German torpedo, which miraculously failed to explode.

The 57-day voyage was a nightmare of inhuman conditions and brutal mistreatment, yet some internees were able to preserve some semblance of intellectual life onboard. Reb Oosher's daughter Mozelle Gubbay (Feuchtwanger) reports that her father told her that he spent most of his time studying.

'The Nazi Germans' behaviour was exemplary,' wrote the *Dunera's* captain in his report at the end of the voyage. 'They are a fine type, honest and straightforward, and extremely well-disciplined. The Jews can only be described as subversive liars, demanding and arrogant ... not to be trusted by deed or by word.' The captain was court-martialled. The maltreatment of prisoners earned the *Dunera* the label 'hellship.'

After being interned in Australia, Reb Oosher was one of the lucky *Dunera* passengers to obtain an immigration certificate for Mandatory Palestine. He is mentioned by name in the book *The Dunera Internees* by Benzion Patkin, for his role in diffusing a potential revolt during the 1941 voyage from Australia to Egypt. The spokesperson for the Jews on the voyage demanded that the orthodox Jews cut off their peyot and dress normally in the western style.

'Fortunately,' writes Patkin, 'an orthodox-religious Rabbi Feuchtwanger, also a member of the departing group, succeeded in persuading the young men to acquiesce. "Everybody," said Rabbi Feuchtwanger, "will be able to live and conduct his way of life according to his own wishes, after we have arrived in our own land."'

Once the internees arrived in Egypt, Reb Oosher intervened again when the group realised that their train from Kantara would arrive in Tel Aviv on Shabbat. Reb Oosher successfully persuaded the orthodox men that this was a case of *pikuach nefesh*, where saving a human life overrides everything else – even the Sabbath. From Palestine, Reb Oosher made his way back to London, where he resumed his studies with Rabbi Dessler.

The practical and sensitive attitude that Reb Oosher displayed during his Australian voyages would become his signature during his years as Letchworth's communal rabbi. In 1953, my five-year-old brother David did not survive tonsils surgery. Reb Oosher and Flora Feuchtwanger took the brave decision to send their children, Mozelle and Jacob, to have their tonsils out in the very same Letchworth Cottage Hospital where David had died.

With this incredibly noble gesture, Reb Oosher wanted to demonstrate to my parents, Eli and Chava, that they had not made a mistake in allowing David to undergo surgery. Mozelle Gubbay (Feuchtwanger) confirms that indeed she and her brother Jacob had their tonsils out in this period.

Another example of Reb Oosher's sensitivity was at my brother Chaim's barmitzvah in Letchworth in 1963. My mother Chava describes what happened: 'At the barmitzvah, Rabbi Feuchtwanger had given a little vote of thanks to us as host and hostess and then he finished his speech as follows: "Heartiest Mazal Tov to the whole Fachler family. We hope to see you all again, Please God, for the batmitzvah of their daughter Melanie." That was a real surprise, for until then there had never been a batmitzvah in Letchworth. Reb Oosher told me: "You had three barmitzvot in a row, how do you think Melanie feels to be left out?"' In February 1966, Melanie celebrated her batmitzvah. Thanks to Reb Oosher, Melanie had set a precedent in Letchworth.

There cannot be many batmitzvah girls who are immortalised in a poem that features in *The Golden Treasury of The Best Songs and Lyrical Poems in The English Language*. The poem, *On The Brink Of A Pit*, mentions Melanie by name, as well as Letchworth Garden City and my father Eli. The poem was written by the prolific poet and author, David Holbrook, whose daughter Kate was a friend and classmate of Melanie at Hitchin Girls Grammar School.

The blind Liverpool-born poet Kevin Morris has written an analysis of *On the Brink of a Pit*, in which Holbrook drives Kate from his home in the Hertfordshire village of Ashwell, to a party in Letchworth to celebrate her Jewish friend Melanie's batmitzvah. Morris says that this is a deeply shocking poem which never fails to move him, and is as relevant today as when it was written. With Kevin's permission, I am reproducing some of his comments.

> *The friendship between the 2 children is very close:*
> *'I took our child to her party, carrying a book-token*
> *Covered in child-gay seals, because they love one another'.*
> *And:*
> *'Melanie assured me with her guileless big blue eyes*
> *Her father would bring Kate home, fondly drew her into the house'.*
> *Here we have a beautiful picture of two children, one Jewish and the other non-Jewish who love one another and are unconcerned with racial or religious differences. This beautiful portrait is enhanced as the street is full of birdsong and: 'Warm sun honeyed the suburban gardens'.*
> *Yet the line: 'handsome women tapped over a few skeleton leaves on the muddy pavements', signifies that all is far from being right. Holbrook wants 'a thousand lives to worship what Melanie was', and the thought*

of the horrors of the mass extermination of Jews causes him to openly weep in the street, 'There being as much hate in garden cities as at Majdenek.'

Melanie remembers that even before the move from Hallmead to Sollershott, Reb Oosher was a regular at the kiddush at the home of Bertha and Sali Bornstein. 'Reb Oosher was our family's *posek* (scholar who makes halachic rulings), and both my parents treated him with utmost respect.'

Ann Ruth Cohn (Grunfeld) described Reb Oosher as a *Talmid Chacham* who enjoyed the company of her father, Dayan Grunfeld. Reb Oosher communicated with some of the leading scholars in the Jewish world, across the communal divide. In 1948, he consulted Zelig Reuven Bengis, Chief Rabbi of the *Eidah HaChareidith* in Jerusalem over some obstruse topics in Tractate *Bechoroth*.

However, the scholarly Reb Oosher was far from unwordly. Rabbi Norman Solomon said of him: "He was my regular teacher during my time in Letchworth, and I learned far more from him than just Talmud. On one occasion I called at his office and found him dictating a letter to his secretary. He indicated that I should stay and listen. The letter, addressed to the local Member of Parliament, strongly supported, in the name of Judaism, government proposals to abolish capital punishment. This was in the wake of the 1955 hanging of Ruth Ellis, the last woman to be hanged for murder in Britain.

'I asked Rabbi Feuchtwanger the question he was anticipating: "But surely the Holy Torah itself mandates the execution of murderers. How can you oppose it?" His enlightening reply was that although *halakha* did indeed in principle mandate capital punishment, its requirements for evidence were far more stringent than those of English law. The retention of capital punishment would inevitably result in the execution of individuals whom *halakha* would regard as not guilty. His response certainly opened my mind to a new way of thinking.'

In June 1956, Reb Oosher circulated a letter to the Jewish community in Letchworth extolling the virtues of keeping kosher. The letter ended thus: 'Any parent who may find it too difficult to prepare kosher midday meals for their children should contact us at their earliest so that if there is sufficient demand our Congregation may consider whether to send and distribute packed meals directly to the schools for the Jewish children.'

Before I left Letchworth for Carmel College in 1957, I used to cycle over to the Schischa home in Pasture Road where Yossel Schischa and myself used to study *Gemara* with Reb Oosher. Several years later, Reb Oosher helped Peter Roth study for, and pass, his 'O' Level Hebrew exam.

Neil Roland still has the book *The Jew And His Duties – The Essence of the Kitzur Shulhan Arukh*, accompanied by a business card from Reb Oosher. On the card, Reb Oosher had written: 'On behalf of Letchworth Hebrew Congregation to Dear Russell.' Neil explains: 'I thought at first that this was a barmitzvah present, but then I read: "On your leaving us". The book was given to Russell when he returned to Manchester, alone, aged fifteen, to attend Manchester Grammar, and to help Mother arrange for their new home.'

In 1964, Reb Oosher travelled from Letchworth to Manchester to attend Ruth Ward's wedding to her second husband Theo Roland. A cine film recording of the wedding, taken by Russell, can only be viewed back to front. Neil Roland explains: 'All the guests including a youthful looking Chava and Eli Fachler in mid-60s attire are seen walking backwards down the elegant front steps of the South Manchester Synagogue. As a child watching this scene, I had assumed that in days gone by, this is what Jewish people did at big events. Somehow, Chava and my mother, who are seen on the film talking to each other, were quite able to walk backward down a flight of stairs without ever looking behind them.'

David Alexander's description of Reb Oosher probably mirrors the impression of many of my generation: 'My memory of Rabbi Feuchtwanger during the three years that I was a frequent visitor to Letchworth is of a short, rotund elderly gentleman with a Yekkish-style short beard and a strong German accent. It is a shock for me to realise today that he was only in his early fifties at the time I knew him. It is also difficult to explain quite why he left such an impression on me.'

Moich Abrahams remembers that Reb Oosher walked around Letchworth wearing 'what seemed to be somewhat short trousers, that is, the trouser leg bottoms were several inches above his ankles. As a young lad, this amused me.'

When I was a 19-year-old yeshiva student in Israel in 1965, I bumped into Reb Oosher in a Tel Aviv synagogue. He told me that he was there to sit his exams to become a Dayan. He sailed through the exams, and had his Dayanut certificate signed by Israel's Ashkenazi Chief Rabbi Isser Yehuda Unterman, and the Sephardi Chief Rabbi Yitzchak Nissim. Despite his Dayanut qualifications, Reb Oosher chose not to practice as a Dayan in Israel, and he returned to Letchworth.

While he was sitting his Dayanut exams, Reb Oosher made a special effort to personally check on a former pupil of the Letchworth cheder. As Patricia Reifen (Hassan) explains: 'In 1964, the Jewish Agency sent me to Jerusalem to the Machon L'Madrichei Chutz La'Aretz – Institute for Youth Leaders from Abroad. Rabbi Feuchtwanger came to visit me to check if everything was alright."

I remember a conversation I had with Reb Oosher in Letchworth, well before the global 'Let my people go' campaign for Soviet Jewry. He made a prediction that at the time sounded fantastical. 'In our lifetime,' he assured me, 'I have no doubt that the doors of the Soviet Union will open and hundreds of thousands of Jews will come to Israel. What worries me is: How will Israel cope with so many youngsters whose Communist and atheist education will have left them bereft of Jewish and Zionist history?'

For Reb Oosher, it was not 'if,' it was 'when' the Jews of the Soviet Union would arrive in Israel. He clearly had a better grasp of global political trends than many professional pundits.

The swinging sixties may not have directly impacted on Reb Oosher – but they did not entirely pass him by either. After the Six Day War, a whole new phenomenon hit Jewish music – a fusion of pop music and Chassidic music. In the USA, the pioneers were The Rabbis' Sons. In Israel, a bunch of immigrant students from the UK under the leadership of Liverpool-born founder Martin Davidson, formed Avnei Hakotel, literally The Stones of the Western Wall.

In early 1970, I drove Reb Oosher from Letchworth to London to attend a boisterous Avnei Hakotel concert. He was probably the oldest member of the audience. Afterwards, I asked him what he thought. 'I enjoyed it,' he replied with a smile. 'Anything that can help Jewish young people connect more with their roots must be a good thing. Anything that helps bridge the gap between the *frum* and the secular must be a good thing.'

Professor Cyril Domb wrote an obituary for Reb Oosher in the *Jewish Chronicle*: 'Because of Rabbi Feuchtwanger's exceptional humility, many failed to appreciate the breadth and scope of his Torah learning. He struck a bond of sympathy with religious university students and young intellectuals. He was always ready to devote his time to *shiurim* and discussions with them, and many generations of Cambridge and London students are indebted to him for their first insight into Talmud and *halacha*. His biographical knowledge of Torah leaders was encyclopaedic. This is particularly reflected in his book *Righteous Lives*.'

Reb Oosher's wife Flora Feuchtwanger (Sassoon), the older sister of Rabbi Solomon Sasson, was a formidable character in her own right. Reb Oosher and Flora had corresponded through the Second World War. Their daughter Mozelle believes that the *shadchanit* was Reb Oosher's aunt, Mrs Rosenfelder.

Dr Judith Grunfeld, the headmistress of the Jewish Secondary School that was evacuated to Shefford, gave Flora this ringing endorsement: 'The secretary, who came to us as a voluntary helper from the neighbouring town of Letchworth, had chosen this work in our education centres as her part of the National Service which every British single young woman was obliged to give. She belonged to an old aristocratic family, and was the noblest of characters. I can recall many moments when her bearing and exemplary ways of patience were a great lesson to the children so entirely dependent on us for example and guidance during these years.'

Leon Paget describes the wedding of Reb Oosher and Flora in Letchworth a few days after *Tisha BeAv* 1945: 'A lush affair in those days was a reception after the wedding of Flora Sassoon, which extended to the lawn at Sollershott.' Because of the closeness of Dr Grunfeld and Flora, Ann Ruth Cohn (Grunfeld) was one of the bridesmaids. Recalling that the wedding was marked by 'wonderful Sephardi elegance', Ann Ruth wrote: 'I felt as if we had left England in the middle of the war and been magically transported to a fairy-tale island somewhere in the tropics. The ceremony took place on their beautiful grounds. I was allowed to stay at the Sassoons' overnight. Our bridesmaids' dresses were a fairy tale straight out of the Arabian Nights. Each bridesmaid received a tiny necklace of real pearls.'

Gail Zivan Neriya (Vanger) cherishes a particular memory that symbolizes the uniqueness of Flora's generosity of spirit. Before Gail became Shabbat-observant, she was getting out of the family car on Field Lane one Shabbat afternoon when she met Flora. Says Gail, 'She greeted me so warmly and naturally, with a lovely smile and a warm "Shabbat Shalom." I will never forget the feeling of not being judged and of not being made to feel embarrassed.'

All the girls who had interactions with Flora retain very positive memories of her. Gail remembers learning *Eshet Hayil* with her, and Ruth Keller (Kirsch) remembers Flora as being very knowledgeable. One of Sue Deutsch (Knight)'s first memories is being told by Flora that she could eat as much Swiss Maestrani chocolate as she wanted. Sue had never experienced such generosity.

As befits her name, Flora had a huge interest in flowers. Several of the girls who studied with her remember that she pressed dried flowers into her *Machzor*. Stella Cukier (Bornstein) recalls: 'After Yanky left Letchworth to attend Carmel College, I started lessons with Flora. She was very knowledgeable about flowers. I used to walk around the garden with her, and she explained the flowers to me. Flora taught me to do my nails and in general to look after myself. I found the three hours that I spent with her every week very exciting.'

In addition to collecting flowers, Flora also collected autographs of leading rabbis, Zionist leaders, writers, and others. Many of these autographs are reproduced in Reb Oosher's book, *Righteous Lives*.

When the Letchworth Talmud Torah closed in the late 1960s, Melanie studied with Flora in the Sassoon library. 'We had a syllabus from the London Board of Jewish Education that we followed, and Flora accompanied me to Woburn House in London to sit the exams. She taught me things that have remained embedded in my memory, and I was fascinated by her fabulous pronunciation. I was impressed that Flora was a student of Rabbi Dessler. She had an encyclopaedic knowledge of Judaism, and could effortlessly look things up in the Gemarrah. She was also a fabulous cook. For several days after the birth of my youngest brother Yossi in 1967, we received fried fish and trifle from the Sassoon kitchen.'

Margalit Fachler (Cohen) remains in awe of Flora's knowledge: 'Although I had a good grounding in Jewish studies from my religious high school in Tel Aviv, Flora Feuchtwanger was the first woman I ever met who had studied the Talmud. Today, this is no longer a novelty, but back then it was very new to me.'

One of the most popular frequent visitors to the Sassoon and Feuchtwanger household in Letchworth in the early 1960s, especially among the young adults, was Avraham Gubbay. The only son of a Baghdadi merchant family, he left Palestine as a baby because of Arab unrest. The family sailed via England to the US, aiming for Shanghai where they had relatives. America's entry into the Second World War in 1940 kept the Gubbays in New York, where Avraham attended a modern Orthodox high school in Manhattan, followed by Chicago University and several Ashkenazi yeshivot.

En route to Israel in 1962, Avraham stopped over in Letchworth to visit his cousin, Rabbi Sassoon, who advised him to continue his studies at Etz Chaim Yeshiva in London. Avraham spent almost every Shabbat in Letchworth, where he proved to be an accomplished *shaliach tzibur* leading the services. Daniel Ohana was one of several Etz Chaim Yeshiva students that Avraham used to invite to Letchworth for Shabbat. Daniel recalls: 'For those of us who came from overseas, the experience of being with the Sassoon and Fachler families reminded us of the warmth of home that we so missed.'

After being ordained as a rabbi in Jerusalem, Avraham married local Letchworth girl Mozelle, the daughter of Reb Oosher and Flora Feuchtwanger. The wedding was held in the Sassoon garden in Letchworth, and I came back from Israel to help organise the wedding.

Families Broch, Winegarten and Schischa

'Shisha mi yodea – Who knows six? Shisha ani yodea – I know six. Shisha lives in Pasture Road.'

FROM THE FACHLER PASSOVER SEDER

Ann Ruth Cohn (Grunfeld) describes her frequent bus trips to Letchworth: 'This beautiful garden city contained many entire Jewish families in evacuation. We enjoyed these visits immensely. There we would visit Mother's only sister, Mrs Ella Broch and her husband Rabbi I Broch in their neat little cottage in a street populated by many interesting Jewish families. Our six Broch cousins were gorgeous children who were physically unlike any of us – they had all inherited their father's blonde hair and dazzling blue eyes.'

In March 1941, Rabbi Broch was released from internment and the family reunification was complete. Because wartime Letchworth was top-heavy with rabbis, there were few vacant rabbinical positions in the town. Ariel Broch remembers:

'My father gave private lessons and occasionally taught in the Letchworth community's Hebrew classes. He reluctantly became a recipient of subsidies from the Jewish Relief Fund. Eventually, he found a position with the Mizrachi Federation as a representative and collector. For the next few years, he lived out of a suitcase. He would rarely be home in Letchworth except for weekends and *Chagim*.

'Dressed in a black jacket over a white shirt and dark tie, and pinstripe trousers, usually topped by a dark fur-collared overcoat, and of course his black Eden-hat covering his black velvet Yarmulke, he became a well-known figure at many railway stations, and even on remote Scottish roads, where he would hitch-hike to his next destination. Telephone books became his constant guides, as he looked for Jewish sounding names in out-of-the-way places. He slowly built up an itinerary – from Aberdeen to Land's End, and including Wales. He became an unofficial Visiting Rabbi for people who had no other contact with their co-religionists.'

On Sunday afternoons, Sigi Stern used to take his children on an outing, and always invited the Broch children to join them. In wartime, when petrol was only available for business purposes, very few people had a car. For Ariel, the trips in the Stern van were a real treat: 'The picnics had wonderful tasty fare that we Broch children could never afford at home.'

In the summer holidays, the Broch and Stern children formed a gang, including Ariel, his sister Hannah, her friends Sally Hollander and Kitty Stern, Kitty's younger brother David, and Ariel's friend Manny Koppel. 'We would roam the countryside by bike, go swimming or go to the pictures, or just play street cricket. We would pack a picnic and go to the local park, or take a twenty-mile cycle ride to Cambridge and punt on the river behind the colleges. We would cycle to Hitchin or Baldock to visit the fairs and markets, or watch a movie in the tiny 20-seat cinema in what was then the village of Stevenage. Grown-ups also were strangely absent from our world.'

The Beckers and Fachlers (Hallmead) and the Brochs (Mullway) lived back garden to back garden. In December 1944, Rabbi Broch officiated at the wedding of my parents Chava and Eli on their kibbutz in Buckinghamshire. My father Eli knew Rabbi Broch from Berlin. Deborah Broch recalls: 'We were forever in and out of one another's homes. We watched the Fachler boys – Yanky, David and Marcus – grow up, and we loved taking them for a walk to the Norton Common, as the local park was called.'

In 1950, Rabbi Broch accepted a rabbinical position in Germany. Ariel Broch explains: 'My father realised that if he wanted to gain a rabbinical position, it was imperative to learn English as quickly as possible. He was hampered by a lack of idiomatic language skills. When invited to audition for a rabbinical position, he would usually have his candidacy declined. He could therefore not find a salaried position in his field of expertise.' Rabbi Broch decided to leave Letchworth for Germany where he could use his rhetorical skills in his native tongue.

When the Brochs left their Mullway home for Germany, Sigi Stern's brother Shloime and family moved in. Shloime had lost his first wife and four of his children in the Shoah in Hungary. Only Shloime and two sons survived. While recuperating in Switzerland after the war, Shloime met and married a distant cousin, Malka, the sole survivor of her large family.

The same passage that linked the back gardens of the Fachler home in Hallmead and the Broch home in Mullway continued to see frequent two-way traffic between the Sterns and the Fachlers. My mother Chava was very fond of Malka – or Malkale as everyone called her. I was always impressed that Shloime and his son Brudie – both of whom were certified *mohalim* - would fly all over the world for the privilege of performing a *brit*.

When the Second World War broke out, several of watchmaker Meshulem Winegarten's eleven children had already left home in Stamford Hill. The oldest daughter Amelia kept house for her father. Although they had a bomb shelter, when the house opposite was bombed in 1940 and some of the residents killed, Mr Winegarten decided to move out of London. He first took his family to Bournemouth and then to Harrogate. He felt that Harrogate was too far from his London jewellery, watches and silver business that was run by some of his sons, including Moshe and Aharon (known to everyone as Boy).

Mr Winegarten finally arrived in Letchworth in 1941 with his elderly mother and the housekeeper, Chava Zalcman. Accompanying them were Amelia and assorted unmarried children including Benny. Mr Winegarten repaired watches that his sons brought from the shop in London. The family first moved into a rented house in Cashio Lane, Norton, a village very close to Letchworth. According to Shulamith Landau (Schischa), Amelia's daughter, the Norton home was like a kibbutz.

Adi (Abraham) Schischa arrived in Stamford Hill from Hungary in spring 1939. His mother was a sister of Sigi and Shloime Stern. One day in 1940, as Adi was walking down the street in London, a German bomber flew low over him with impunity, there being no anti-aircraft defences yet in the area. Adi ducked behind a fence to save himself, and decided that it was too dangerous to stay in Stamford Hill. He took the train from Finsbury Park to Letchworth to explore the religious enclave there, and spent the day on a fruitless search for lodgings.

Adi's son Yossel takes up the story: 'My father was on the point of giving up. He was already making his way back to the station, and had reached the railway bridge when he met an elderly Jewish matron. She was the mother of Moishe Saunders who was married to Abba Bornstein's sister Bertchen. Mrs Saunders senior told my father that she knew of a room at 41 Elderfield where someone had just moved out. My father rented the room, and purchased a small bookcase which would become the nucleus of what would become a very large library. I still have the bookcase.'

In Letchworth, Reb Chaim Nuta Katz introduced Adi to the Winegarten household in 1941, and Adi and Amelia were married in 1943. In 1948, Mr. Winegarten bought The Coppice in Garth Road, which would later be renamed Pasture Road. An important factor was that The Coppice had central heating, a relative rarity in Letchworth at the time.

Mr. Winegarten died soon after they moved, and when in 1949 Amelia gave birth to her third child (following Leah in 1945 and Yossel in 1947), the Schischas called her Shulamith, after Meshulem. Adi started a property business which was his prime source of income for the rest of his life. Adi also became an acclaimed historian and Judaica collector.

Another Winegarten daughter, Nina, married to Willy Neuberger, travelled up every day to London to work. On Sundays, she taught in the Letchworth Cheder where Rabbi Warhaftig was the headmaster. She remembers sitting in the small women's section of the synagogue at 40 Hallmead, where she also was taught by Reb Oosher Feuchtwanger.

On weekdays during the war, Benny Winegarten travelled to Schneider's Yeshiva in London. According to Benny, some families moved back to London in 1943 when things were quieter, only to return again because of the V2 menace.

Yossel Schischa's grandparents and uncle Dovid arrived in Letchworth from Hungary in 1948, and stayed until 1951-1952 when they left for the USA. Yossel's grandfather Reb Shimon Schischa was a very punctual man. 'He had a key to 40 Hallmead, and he was always the first to open the door every morning. I have happy memories of sitting next to him *davening* there.'

Yossel's sister Shulamith Landau (Schischa) remembers leading rabbis visiting Letchworth after the war. 'Visitors included the two roshei yeshiva of Gateshead, the brothers-in-law Reb Leib Gurwicz and Reb Leib Lopian, both of whom had lived in Letchworth during the war. One summer, Rabbi Avraham Gurwitz and his rebbitzen and their young family spent their holidays in the Fachler home while the Fachlers were away. When the two Kedassia *shochtim*, the Chabad Raskin cousins, came to Letchworth to slaughter meat on *Chol Hamoed Sukkot*, they used to have their lunch in our *sukkah*.'

The Schischa house on Pasture Road unwittingly lent itself to a piece of Fachler folklore. Seated around the Seder table, we used to sing: 'Shisha mi yodea – Who knows six? Shisha ani yodea – I know six.' But instead of continuing with the original *Haggadah* text, 'Shisha sidrei Mishna – Six [shisha] are the books of the Mishna', we always used to belt out: 'Shisha lives in Pasture Road.' In dozens of households around the world, that tradition persists to this day. Fachler children, grandchildren and great-grandchildren still sing 'Shisha lives in Pasture Road' on *Lel Haseder*, often without knowing why.

The Coppice, home of the Schischas

Hallmead and Mullway

'There was little to no daily traffic. The only memorable exception was the day in 1943 when my aunt Ray drove up in a roofless sports car driven by her fiancé, Harry. Almost all the street turned out to survey the car.'

EFRAIM HALEVY

Efraim Halevy recalls his life in Hallmead: 'Our family used to meet up with some of our neighbours, including Abba Bornstein and his five daughters. Abba's house was slightly bigger than all the others. My father knew Abba because they were both senior office holders in the religious Mizrachi Movement. Of all my early friends, I remember the Persoff family, who lived across the road at 41 Hallmead. I was also friendly with the Richman family at 23 Hallmead.'

According to Efraim, Hallmead was practically car-free. 'There was little to no daily traffic, certainly no private cars. From my perspective, the only memorable exception was the day in 1943 when my aunt Ray drove up in a roofless sports car driven by her fiancé, Harry. Almost all the street turned out to survey the car. The wedding took place in our front garden. All the Jews in Hallmead, and not a few non-Jewish neighbours, came to watch the ceremony. When the married couple drove away after the festivities, calm was restored, allowing us children to resume playing hopscotch undisturbed in the middle of the road, which had become our daily sportsground.'

This scene was to be replicated in Hallmead ten years later in 1954 when a large British Road Services lorry disturbed the peace of Hallmead and pulled up outside no 79. With swarms of children watching in anticipation, a brand-new red bicycle emerged from the lorry, a gift to me from my Uncle Yankel Lopian (Aku Aku) in

Manchester. The neighbourhood kids cheered as my father Eli sat his oldest son on the bike. He held the saddle and said cheerily, 'Don't worry, I'm holding you.' Two seconds later, he let go, and I did not notice as I sailed proudly down a traffic-free Hallmead. It was as easy as riding a bike.

Efraim's family left Letchworth after D-Day in June 1944, and returned to West Hampstead. 'Many of my close friendships established in Letchworth lasted long after our family departed for Palestine in 1948. The nearest I have been to Letchworth since I left is when I was invited to Cambridge to talk about my time as head of the Mossad. I noticed a signpost for Letchworth, and memories came flooding back.'

Rabbi Wahrhaftig's daughter *Rebbitzen* Miriam Lieberman recalls living in Hallmead: 'I attended the local primary school, Westbury. We had cheder after school from 4-5 pm where my father taught. Nobody had much money for extras or special treats, but we did make good friends. I have stayed friends with Rabbi Horowitz's daughter Judy Zimmerman (Horowitz) for over eighty years. Our next-door neighbours at 79 Hallmead were the Rottenbergs. We returned to London in 1945 when I was eleven.'

Miriam's mention of the Rottenbergs reminds me that as a child, all sorts of industrial trade catalogues would arrive at our home, addressed to the Rottenbergs. I would pore over them with great interest, not understanding a word.

Zippy Rosenblatt (Persoff): 'It was only natural that my Letchworth playmates were the children of the many Hapoel Mizrachi friends of my parents who all lived close by. June Kent's Mullway back garden abutted our Hallmead back garden. It was easy to visit her by just crossing over the thin wire that separated the two yards. However, I did not dare do this when the Kents' ferocious cockerel was stalking the grounds! I spent many happy hours playing with Frances, daughter of Joe and Sarah Richman, and Chana, daughter of Abba and Hella Bornstein.'

Although Frances Israel (Richman) enjoyed her years in Hallmead, life was not without antisemitic incidents. 'A few doors from us lived a non-Jewish family. Their son was forever baiting me with calls of "Dirty Jew." I remember complaining to my teacher that I was not dirty. My father Joe tried unsuccessfully to have the family leave their Hallmead home.'

Frances remembers outings to the Broadway cinema to watch musical films starring Judy Garland: *Easter Parade* and *The Wizard of Oz*. Ruth Ann Cohn (Grunfeld) also has memories of going to the cinema: 'We greatly enjoyed the antics of Charlie Chaplin as well as the unforgettable antics of Laurel and Hardy. We were enthralled by such epics as *the Thief of Baghdad* and *The Wizard of Oz*.'

The Gedalla family, including six children, moved to Letchworth after the Blitz, and rented 77 Mullway. Mr Gedalla commuted every day to London where he was the manager of the Machzike Hadass *Shul* in Brick Lane. Vivienne Alper (Gedalla) recalls: 'In Mullway, the children would all play together. I was friendly with the Lehmann girls and the Persoff family. I remember being impressed when Hannah Lehmann went to Palestine on an illegal boat.'

The flat where the Becker/Fachler family lived at the bottom of Hallmead could barely accommodate my grandparents, Sam and Melanie Becker; my parents Chava and Eli; and my two aunts, Marian Becker and Miriam Fachler. With my mother pregnant with her first child (me), the family looked for larger accommodation. My grandparents approached Abba Bornstein, but he told them that he did not have anything available. My father Eli was deputised to try his luck with Abba.

Eli describes what happened next: 'I told Abba that I wanted to rent one of his houses when it became empty. I deliberately wore my army uniform. He was quite proud of me, the model of a *chalutz* (pioneer). Normally one had to pay key money to get one of Abba's empty properties. This could not be done openly, as it was not strictly legal, but Abba claimed it was his only source of income from his properties. The amount of rent he received was government controlled and did not – he claimed – cover the expenses of repairs, maintenance, and management. I had no funds at all, never mind paying key money. Abba knew my financial situation, and although he cried that he was losing over £100, he still let me have 79 Hallmead. We all moved in. The house was in my name, and my in-laws paid the rent.'

Hallmead was rapidly becoming predominantly non-Jewish, as families left Letchworth and retuned to London or to other destinations further afield. Our new home at no. 79 Hallmead was a terraced house, with a front and back garden, a living room and kitchen downstairs,

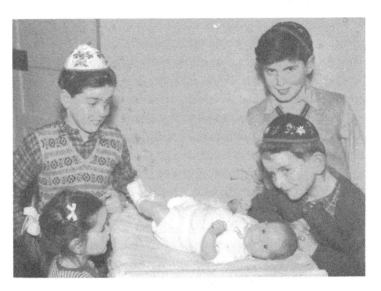

The 5 Fachler Children: Hallmead, 1958

with three bedrooms and a bathroom/toilet upstairs. I was one of the first post-war babies born in Letchworth. Because I was premature, the *Mohel*, Dayan Baumgarten, performed the brit on my *Pidyan Ha'Ben* on the thirtieth day after my birth. The Cohen was Mr Taviansky. I was named Yaakov, after my grandfather Sam's father Yaakov Becker. Yaakov soon became Yankel, then Yankele, and within a very short time, I was Yanky.

Our Hallmead home had an open coal fire in the living room, and the upstairs rooms were heated with an electric heater. Coal had to carried in every morning from the coalshed. By 1951, as the mother of four boys, Chava was well and truly established as a Hallmead matron.

Chava's sister Marian Becker met the youngest son of Reb Elya Lopian, Yankel, at a Torah Ve'avoda function in Letchworth. Shortly before their wedding, my grandmother Melanie Becker passed away on my first birthday. The funeral was in the Adass Cemetery, Enfield. Mr Schwab organised the official documents with the Registrar.

As a young child, I always referred to my Uncle Yankel Lopian as 'Aku Aku.' Rebekah Weisman, who lived for a while in Letchworth with her great-aunt Hannah, the wife of the Zlobiner Rav, had another name for Yankel. 'Letchworth was a delightful, close-knit community. Myriads of young men visited the house. I made friends with quite a few of them. One of them, Jacob, had read Dickens and I called him 'Classical Jack.' Classical Jack was my Aku Aku.

My father's sister Miriam was next to leave the nest. She married Joel Litke, a German-born yeshiva student who was interned as an enemy alien in 1940, first on the Isle of Man and then in Canada. He had completed his *Semicha* and had been offered a position as communal rabbi in Guelph, Ontario. Miriam and Joel married, and moved to Canada in 1948.

When King George VI died in February 1952, his coffin was brought on the Royal Train from Sandringham to London via Cambridge. This meant that the train passed slowly through Letchworth. Many people stood on the bank overlooking the railway line to see the coffin surrounded by guardsmen. I accompanied my mother Chava, who had been very fond of the king. We caught a view of the royal train as it passed under the railway bridge near Letchworth Station.

Between the death of King George and the coronation of his daughter Elizabeth, there was the Great Smog of London, which lasted from Friday 5 December to Tuesday 9 December 1952. The reason I remember it is because of the stories told by dozens of people arriving in Letchworth who told us how bad the smog was. Phrases like 'You couldn't see your hand in front of your face' excited my young imagination.

The coronation of Queen Elizabeth II took place on Tuesday 2 June 1953. For the first time in British history, ordinary people could watch a monarch's coronation in their own homes, after it was announced that the crowning of the Queen would be televised. Since we did not have a television, I watched the coronation at the home of Sali and Bertha Bornstein. Mozelle Gubbay (Feuchtwanger) remembers going to watch the coronation at the Kaffells. Because of the *mitzvah* of celebrating royal occasions, the Schischas rented a TV especially for the coronation.

There were street parties all over Britain, including Hallmead. The whole street came and sat at tables on the grass island. The coronation was also filmed in colour. The first time I consciously remember going to the Broadway Cinema was in the company of hundreds of other schoolchildren from several Letchworth schools when we went to watch the edited film of the coronation in colour.

Coronation street party, Hallmead 1953

Apart from the van that my father drove when he worked for Stern, I don't think we had our own car until the early fifties. Our car was a Morris Major – my father called it Moishe Major – also known as the Morris Oxford Six that had a starting crank handle. There were still relatively few cars in Hallmead.

For me, Hallmead was a complete eco-system. It was where we lived, where Sali and Bertha Bornstein lived, where my friend Geoffrey Woollard lived, and where the synagogue and cheder were located at no. forty. My day started when I heard my wake-up beep from Moishe Bornstein's Hudson outside my window as he drove to no. forty. I joined him there for the morning prayers before returning home for my porridge breakfast. Then on to Wilbury School. Then back for lunch. Then back to school. Then to afternoon cheder at 40 Hallmead. And finally home to no. seventy nine. From the age of five, I walked everywhere unaccompanied.

Sammy Hollander remarks that Jewish orthodox practices could create obstacles to 'fraternization' with the locals. 'I do not, for example, recall ever visiting the homes of my non-Jewish schoolfriends, primary or secondary.' Throughout my Hallmead days, my non-Jewish schoolfriend, Geoffrey Woollard, and I were in and out of each other's homes. Geoffrey's mother knew that she could not give me any food.

Geoff himself has an interesting perspective: 'Although I was surrounded by Jews, I had little contact with them other than you and your family who were happy to accept me as a friend.'

In the audience of my 2017 talk in Letchworth about Jewish Letchworth were two 'boys' (in their early seventies) who remembered me from Hallmead. In the Q&A, one of them very gingerly alluded to antisemitism when he asked whether I remembered being 'the subject of any ridicule' when I lived in Letchworth. I answered that personally I had not, but that I knew others who had. He explained apologetically that kids simply picked stuff like antisemitic slurs from home, and that no harm was ever meant.

My main problem with Hallmead was dogs. Throughout my childhood, I never got used to them. I did not know a single Jewish family with a dog until I moved to Israel. I was always afraid of Hallmead's canine population, as well as their cousins in neighbouring streets.

In times of tragedy, the small Letchworth Jewish community really pulled together. When my younger brother David died in 1953, it was Herman Schwab who arranged for the inquest to be held early the next morning at the Hitchin Coroner's Court. When I returned to school, I informed my teacher Mary Stanfield that David was now an angel in heaven. It may have been our neighbour Mrs Preston who put this idea into my head. When my grandfather Sam Becker died in 1955 in our 79 Hallmead home, the community once again rallied round. I remember the shiva.

I remember that several retired Jewish workers from the Bornstein factory in Weston lived in Hallmead and Mullway. On Purim, my mother used to send me to deliver *Mishloach Manot* to Mrs Dinkle and Mrs Kay, and probably some others whose names I do not remember.

In my earlier years in Hallmead, the milk was delivered on an electric milk float – until the exciting (for me) Co-op mobile shop started visiting Hallmead. I remember 'Fish Bob' parking his small van outside our house, opening the back doors, and selling his fresh wares. Another noteworthy weekly event was the coalmen carrying their heavy sacks of coal and depositing them in the special coal bunker.

Tom Baker remembers that Puffed Wheat was produced at Letchworth's vegetarian Golden Block margarine factory, next to

Irvings. 'About every half hour, having reached a certain temperature, the wheat exploded. Hearing it from the goods yard, it sounded as though it was being done in a big tin can.'

In 1956, when I was ten, thanks to my father's acquaintance with Mr May, the manager of Golden Block, I earned lucrative pocket money by supervising the Kosher-for-Passover margarine at the factory. As each box of margarine came off the Golden Block production line, I sealed it with a kosher stamp. Delivery trucks took the boxes from Letchworth for distribution to Jewish shops around Britain. I'm not certain that my employment was strictly legal. I was underage, and probably not eligible to stamp the boxes. I hope I was not responsible for the factory going into liquidation in 1960.

My Hallmead bedroom window looked out on to the street. On weekends, I used to hear our next-door neighbour, Mr Hobbs from 81 as he returned home late at night from one of the pubs that surrounded Letchworth. He would sing so loudly that the entire street could hear him. This was my very first encounter with someone who was the worse for drink.

Letchworth had one main shopping district, consisting of Leys Avenue and Station Road and the streets around them. Frances Israel (Richman) remembers the thrill of being able to touch the merchandise in Woolworth, unlike other shops where the merchandise was behind a counter. Carol Eini (Roth) remembers my mother Chava taking her to Spinks haberdashery and ladies' clothes to buy a blouse for her birthday.

Jean Shindler (Pollock): 'I remember a weekly walk with my parents, partly sitting on my father's shoulders, to the Letchworth Arcade where both Anna and I bought a chocolate bar by putting a three pence coin in the sweet machine. I remember splashing about in the paddling pool in Howard Park, and later having swimming lessons in Letchworth's municipal pool.'

As a child, I loved the Letchworth shops. I remember the art deco Dickinson and Adams car showroom. I was always intrigued by the name 'The Country Gentlemen's Association' in Icknield Way, and I never knew it was an insurance company. I remember shoe shops: Bustins, Freeman Hardy and Willis, and Clarks. There was Underwoods hardware, The Scotch Wool Shop, and the Co-Op on Eastcheap which had a pneumatic cash transfer system. I was excited when the first self-service supermarkets opened. I knew a few people in town who I would greet by name, like Mr Abrahams in the Wynd and Mr Smith in Boots – he was the father of my Catholic classmate Geraldine.

One day, a large sack of wooden bricks of all shapes and size arrived in our Hallmead home, a gift from the Sassoons. These bricks gave me and my younger siblings years of fun. We used to buy Dinky Toys and Matchbox toy cars at Munts on Eastcheap. There was a Hobby Shop where I bought balsa wood kits for making planes, and I used to buy Airfix plastic kits for the planes, trains and cars that I assembled.

On the entertainment front, there was the occasional funfair that visited Letchworth, and of course there were the two cinemas. Many of the films that I enjoyed at the Broadway during the 1950s and early 1960s were patriotic war films: *Reach for the Sky*, the story of Douglas Bader; *The Dam Busters*; and *Bridge over the River Kwai*. Another film that stands out in my memory is *A Night to Remember* about the sinking of the Titanic.

Eleven years after the end of the Second World War, international events impacted once more on Letchworth. In 1956, tens of thousands of refugees escaped from Hungary during the unsuccessful uprising that was brutally put down by Soviet forces. I recall that some Hungarian Jewish refugees appeared in Letchworth, but did not stay too long.

Carol Eini (Roth) remembers: 'At the beginning of 1957, every Sunday, a rather sad and serious Hungarian man in his 40s used to come for tea at our house. I have no idea how he got to Letchworth or who else in the Jewish community hosted refugees. I don't remember his name.'

In *Letchworth Remembered*, an unnamed English teacher describes his experiences: 'Nine Jewish Hungarian refugee children came to Letchworth and were supported by the local Jewish community. The local council gave them a council house in Bursland and this became a Yeshivah – a traditional orthodox Jewish school. The children were intelligent and tremendously hard working, starting at eight in the morning and continuing until five in the afternoon.

'Then, in the evening, I took them for a couple of hours to teach them in such a way that their English could be acceptable under the requirements of the Education Act. They spoke neither English nor German just as I lacked Yiddish or Hebrew, so it was an interesting early experience of Multicultural Education. Within nine months they all spoke English and went off to the United States.'

A somewhat different memory of the Hungarian refugees in Letchworth is recorded by another English teacher: 'In 1957, amongst those refugees were a lot of Hungarian Jewish children – orthodox Jews – and they founded an orthodox school in Monklands. They got me to teach them in the evening so that they would get by in the school. They spoke no English. They were very bright children. It was all very low-key.' So, was it Bursland, Monklands, or both?

Haki Sassoon remembers that Rabbi Sassoon and Reb Oosher Feuchtwanger had dealings with half a dozen university-age Hungarian refugees, and that Reb Oosher followed their progress after their short stay in Letchworth.

When Moich Abrahams was 13 or 14, he was employed as a burial society collector. 'I would go to 79 Hallmead where the Fachlers lived, and Mrs Fachler would give me a list. I then rode around Letchworth, collecting money from Jewish families for the burial society. I was the proud OFFICIAL burial society money collector. At the end of my rounds, I would take the money collected back to Mrs Fachler. When I gave up this job, my brother Lenny followed in my footsteps.'

On 15 April 1905, a passenger train from London pulled into the world's first Garden City. Letchworth was now firmly on the map. In the early years of the Letchworth Jewish community, most people – residents and visitors alike – reached the town by rail. There were few bus connections, and relatively few people had cars. A few miles from Letchworth, at Icklesworth, was another rail track, not the London-Cambridge line. Together with my cousin Dovzi Lopian, I used to join other train spotters. It was on the Icklesworth track in July 1938, that the A4 class locomotive Mallard had reached a speed of 126 mph to set a new steam locomotive world speed record – which still stands today.

The last *simcha* to be celebrated in Hallmead before the Fachlers moved to Sollershott East was my brother Meir's *brit* in February 1958. Because my mother's uncle, the Poneveczer Rav, was in England, he came to Letchworth and was Meir's *sandek*. As Yossel Schischa related to Meir many years later: 'My father suddenly burst into my room at home and said: "Quick, get ready, the Poneveczer Rav is in town, and I want him to give you a blessing."'

The Tendells were the last Jewish family in Hallmead. As Pamela Tendell recalls: 'After I left school in 1958, I joined the Luton Jewish Youth Club where I met my husband just a year later. As each of the four Tendell children got married, we left Letchworth. Our parents joined us in London in 1974." When Wallie and Amy Tendell left, they had been living in Hallmead for almost 30 years.

Schooldays in Letchworth

'I want to go to Palestine to help establish a Jewish State.'

ARIEL BROCH
at his Letchworth Grammar School entrance interview

Wilbury Junior School

Efraim Halevy retains highly negative memories of Wilbury Junior School in wartime: 'I was the only Jew in my class. All the teachers were non-Jewish spinsters – almost all the men had been called up to serve in the armed forces. I spent four gruelling years there, and hated every minute. I had a clear feeling that these two ladies had little to no sympathies for "the Jews."'

In 1951, my mother Chava Fachler (Becker) accompanied me to my first day at Wilbury Infants, located in the church hall of St Thomas Anglican Church on Bedford Road. I was puzzled that some children were crying. Before I shooed my mother back home, I asked her why they were crying. I found her answer – 'Because they don't want to go to school' even more perplexing. How could any child not want to start the big adventure that was school?

Ten years after Efraim's torrid time at Wilbury, my own memories of the school are much more positive. I liked my teachers and I liked the headmaster, Mr Smith.

My first teacher at Wilbury Infants was Mrs Mary Stanfield. Even though like any normal six-year-old, I was in love with her, I realised from the way my parents spoke about her that something was amiss. The something was that her husband, Mr Stanfield, was the Jewish Bernie Steinfeld. This was my very first introduction to a mixed marriage, and Mary was the first non-Jewish spouse of a Jew that I ever met. I seem to remember that Bernie's father also lived in Letchworth.

As an Orthodox child, I was allowed to keep my school-cap on all day at Wilbury. At home, naturally, I wore a yarmulke. One day, on my own initiative, I asked my headmaster Mr Smith whether I could wear my yarmulke at school. 'Of course', he replied, 'just bring a note from your parents.' My bemused parents gave their permission, and for the next fifteen years, any Jewish boy who wanted could wear a yarmulke instead of a school-cap in any school in Letchworth.

On a July morning in 1956, when I was ten, Mr Smith marched into our Wilbury classroom: 'Does anyone know what the news headlines are today?' he asked. As someone who routinely read the *News Chronicle* every morning before school, I was the only person in the class to raise his hand. 'Sir, Nasser grabbed the Suez Canal.' I remember being very impressed with the map of the Middle East that Mr Smith drew that day on the blackboard. In retrospect, he was probably an old school Imperialist who supported the later Anglo-French intervention.

As was usual in most schools in Britain, Wilbury's day started with morning assembly consisting of hymns and New Testament readings. As the only Jewish child in the school, I sat outside the assembly hall, together with my classmate Geraldine Smith, the only Catholic child at Wilbury. I had a crush on Jillian, the class beauty. Knowing that her being Church of England and my being Jewish was a problem, I used to fantasise that she confided in me that she used to secretly say 'Juz Crust' in the prayers.

I passed the eleven plus exam which would have entitled me to attend Letchworth Grammar School. However, my parents wanted me to have a Jewish secondary schooling, and they did not want me to commute every day from Letchworth by train to London, which Yossel Schischa did. In April 1957 I sat the scholarship entrance exam for Carmel College, Rabbi Kopul Rosen's Jewish boarding school in pastoral Berkshire on the banks of the River Thames. When I won a scholarship, I left Wilbury on a Friday afternoon in late April 1957, two weeks into the summer term – and started Carmel on the following Sunday.

Westbury JMI (Junior Mixed Infant School)

Dodi Gurwicz remembers his wartime schooldays. 'Before passing my eleven plus and joining the grammar school, I went to Westbury where

I experienced a lot of antisemitism from other children. They used to lie in wait for us on the way to school, and Charlie Rottenberg had to fight his way through.'

Zippy Rosenblatt (Persoff) encountered her first taste of antisemitism when attending Westbury: 'In the winter of 1944, when I was four and a half, it had been snowing and the local kids were taunting my sister Passy and me, 'You bloody Jews!' I stamped my little red Wellington-covered foot, and insisted, 'We're not!' Zippy also remembers the enormous size of the classes, maybe sixty children: 'The swollen size was no doubt due to accommodating the floods of evacuated children from across the country and even from abroad. There was no such thing as toys or bright posters. I remember we had to write or draw on individual slate boards. Paper was far too precious.

Here is the perspective of a local Letchworth boy at Westbury, Tom Walker: 'In due time I became a five-year-old, six days after war broke out. I started school at Westbury School. Miss Wade was the headmistress. Wartime was upon us, and air raid drills were a regular feature of our early school-days. When the sirens sounded, we would evacuate the classrooms and go into the underground shelters at the side of the playgrounds, good fun in summer but cold and dank in winter.'

Tom remembers the influx of Jewish children to Letchworth: 'We had evacuees from London who had been bombed out, and hosts of Jewish children too. When I first started at Westbury School, Jewish children were taught at school in the mornings and Gentiles in the afternoons and we would change over each week. The Rabbis were very much in evidence about the town. One I remember was from the rich Jewish family the Sassoons. One other such gentleman rejoiced under the name of Rabbi Farhtwanger, a name which us children took great amusement in repeating.'

Deborah Emanuel (Broch) attended Westbury before going to Pixmore Secondary. Deborah's brother Ariel was eight years old when he started at Westbury in late 1940. He was placed in the second bottom class with a Jewish boy called Jacob whom he knew from London.

Ariel describes his first day at Westbury: 'All the boys were rushing and jostling before grouping in two opposing corners of the playground, screaming on the tops of their voices, "All in for release!" Jacob and I just stood there trying to figure out what to do. It was obvious that there were two boy-gangs operating here, the bigger one collecting its members at the top corner of the playground. We tried to push our way in that direction, but were stopped by a tall youth. "We don't want any Jew-boys here!" he said. We walked desolately away and stood at the side to watch the proceedings.

'At a given signal the two gangs rushed at one another, and tried to take prisoners. If they touched an opposing boy twice on the shoulder, he became a prisoner, and was escorted to that gang's corner. To release him, the members of the other gang had to infiltrate by force, and pat the prisoner on the head and shout "Release", and he was freed.

'As we watched, a big red-headed boy called Dick came over to us and invited us to join his gang. We looked at each other at this sign of acceptance, and readily agreed. Afterwards we became the most daring and enthusiastic "Release" players, rushing into the opposing camp with such ferocious intent that it earned us the respect of the other boys. We never again heard the phrase "No Jew-boys here."'

Moishe (Maurice) Cohen, who later married fellow Letchworthian Judy Kornbluth, moved with his family to Mullway in the winter of 1939/40, when he was four years old. 'I started Westbury Junior School – where even my non-Jewish school friends called me Moishe – in September, 1940. The only other Jewish pupil in my class was Bernice Fisher, daughter of Sammy Fisher, and she and I regularly came first and second in our class. I'm not sure if there were older Jewish children in the school.'

My brother Chaim attended Westbury in the fifties, and my brother Meir went there in 1963. Earlier, my parents had enrolled Meir in a preschool in Letchworth. Meir somehow got it into his head that 'going to school' was a one-off event. After his first day, he point-blank refused to return to the pre-school. It did not help that on that first day, when the teacher called the roll, she called Meir by his birth certificate name, Malcolm. He responded by punching her.

Jean Schindler (Pollock): 'Westbury was only a few hundred yards from our house. Like many Jewish children in Letchworth in the 1960s, I was the only Jewish child in my class. This meant that I did not have to attend school assemblies. On one occasion, we had to go to the assembly for general notices, and I remember quietly saying the *Shema* prayer to myself while hymns were being sung.'

Robby Jaffey says that at Westbury, 'we were the chosen few of the Jewish faith. There was Meir Fachler, Jonathan Kirsch and me. I think that maybe Daniel Kirsch was there too. Every morning, there was a school assembly. Meir had got permission to be excused from participating, and the rest of us followed along. Thus from the age of six, we were all known to be Jews.'

My sister Melanie was also a pupil at Westbury. At the age of nine, in 1963, she wrote an essay called *My Music and Poetry Life*. Westbury entered Melanie's essay in a national children's literary competition run by the *Daily Mirror*. Letchworth's local newspaper, *The Citizen*, proudly reported that Melanie won a prize – the princely sum of £10 (worth about £180 today).

Grange School

Every school-day from when I was six years old, I would accompany my younger brother David to the bus stop outside the Wilbury Infants School in St Thomas church hall on Bedford Road where he caught the special school bus for the Grange School. I would then continue on to Wilbury Junior School about 250 yards up the road, and at the end of the school-day, I would return to the bus stop to wait for David and we would walk home together.

I found a letter from the Grange School's headmaster, Robert Unstead, that he wrote to my parents expressing the shock and sadness of all the staff at the school when David died suddenly in 1953. Unstead later became the most popular historian in the English-speaking world.

Gernon Lodge Preparatory School

Gernon Lodge has produced at least two distinguished professors: Sammy Hollander, and the (non-Jewish) Letchworth-born noted social sciences educator Professor Howard Glennerster of the London School of Economics. In 1995, Sammy wrote about his Gernon Lodge experience in his memoir, *The Literature of Political Economy*:

'The school was run by two liberated and progressive ladies. Those were splendid times, rather easy-going with much attention given to dramatics, Shakespeare in particular, music and exercise with emphasis on country dancing. I worshipped my teachers – a general trait that only ended when I became a teacher myself. There was no interfaith tension whatsoever; Jewish pupils simply left the room when "All things bright and beautiful ..." was sung each morning. It was sometimes dangerous for Jewish children to walk alone because of stone-throwing louts – for Letchworth is in a chalky area with many stones at hand – shouting: "Go back to Palestine!"' Murray Cohen, who did not go to Gernon Lodge but was also on the receiving end of the taunt 'Go back to where you came from,' later discovered that his tormenters were not referring to Palestine – they were referring to London.

Sammy also remembers his French teacher at Gernon Lodge, whom pupils addressed as 'Mademoiselle'. She seems to have been one of the Belgian refugees who arrived in Letchworth in the First World War. Other Jewish children who attended Gernon Lodge include Judy Kornbluth, Sally Hollander, Stella Cukier (Bornstein), Shulamith Landau (Schischa) and Jean Shindler (Pollock). Jean remembers the nature walks around Norton Common and collecting acorns and horse chestnuts to put on the nature table.

When Stella broke her ankle and her leg was in plaster, a boy at Gernon Lodge called her a dirty Jew. She kicked him with her plaster, which cured him of any further outbursts.

Letchworth Grammar School

'I want to go to Palestine to help establish a Jewish State.' This was the unexpected answer that Ariel Broch gave the headmaster of Letchworth Grammar School, Sydney Wilkinson, who had asked him during his entrance interview, 'What are your ambitions in life?' Ariel recalls the circumstances: 'My interview took place in 1943 when the Allies' war situation looked exceedingly precarious. The headmaster no doubt expected me to say something patriotic like, "My ambition is to join the Forces and beat the Axis." Nevertheless, I was accepted into Letchworth Grammar.'

Ariel recalls his first day at the school: 'Mason, the second-form bully, decided that I – little Ariel – would be his next target. I had all the necessary victim attributes. I didn't belong to any group or gang, I was probably short of friends, I looked a bit puny, my English was heavily accented, and – most importantly – I was a Jew boy. It started at the very first play break. I felt a push. I turned around to see Mason glaring at me.

'"What are you doing walking in front of me?" demanded Mason. "I didn't see you," I replied. "You will apologize on your knees," said Mason. A small crowd was gathering around us. I saw that it was hopeless to expect help from any of them. I stood my ground, my shaking voice belying my bravado. "Why?" I asked. "Are you a king or an idol or something?"

'Mason, who was a few inches taller than me and a lot heavier, gave me a shove. "Don't talk back to me," he said. "On your knees!" Mason gave me another push, harder this time, and pushed me right into the growing crowd. They pushed me right back into the middle of the circle. I had had enough. I let fly, throwing myself furiously at Mason. The onslaught caught him by surprise. I punched his face with all my might. Mason fell back into the crowd, but they pushed him back for further punishment. I went for his nose, and got in two big punches, causing blood to spurt out.

'Just then, as if by magic, the crowd melted away. Attracted by the commotion, Mr Wilkinson appeared. "What's your name?" he asked me. "Broch," I answered. "Come to my study, both of you," he instructed. We faced the headmaster. "I don't know what the fight was about," he said, "and I don't want to know. But I do want to know who started it." We both remained silent. "Very well," the headmaster said. "You will both stay in after school and write five hundred lines – I must not fight in school. Dismissed."

'Mason left to nurse his nose. Mr Wilkinson said: "Oh, Broch is it? Between you and me, I know who started it. Jolly good show! But officially you are reprimanded and will still have to write the lines. Take care." That was the last time I was bullied at school, and it was how I earned the nickname – "Four-foot-fist Broch."'

Ariel did not feel comfortable during morning assembly. Nor did Frances Field (Cohen): 'The Jewish children did not go into morning prayers, but stood in the corridor until the prayers were over. The Jewish pupils were then called in for the announcements. Because so many religious Jewish children did not go into the morning assembly, the non-religious Jewish children also didn't. I found it cringe-making when each day we marched in after the morning assembly.'

Frances explains that the classes at Letchworth Grammar School were mixed, 'but the boys sat on one side of the classroom and the girls on the other. There was very little chance of fraternising, because there were separate entrances to the school for boys and girls, and separate playgrounds. I used to cycle to school from our Mullway home.'

Zippy Rosenblatt (Persoff)'s two older brothers, Abraham and David, also enjoyed cycling to the grammar school from Hallmead: Zippy is convinced that one of the attractions of Letchworth was the healthy environment it provided. 'My two older brothers grew taller than the average Jewish lad. David always claimed this was due to their endless bike riding and the fresh air. In its publicity posters, Letchworth Garden City promoted itself under the slogan: "Health of the country, comforts of the town."'

One of the brightest of the Jewish boys at Letchworth Grammar during the war years was Jack Epstein, the son of Rabbi Isidore Epstein. According to Jack's sister Helen Botschko, 'Jack was an exceptional individual in his behaviour, character and way of talking.' It was probably these qualities that persuaded Wilkinson to make the astonishing comment: 'I made Jack Epstein head boy, even though he was a Jew.' Jack's best friend in Letchworth was another Jack – my uncle Jack Yankel Lopian.

Someone else who enjoyed cycling to the grammar school was Sheila Kritzler (Oster). She remembers hearing of Wilkinson's reputation as an antisemite. Her abiding memory of the grammar school was the valuable life's lesson she received from one of her teachers: 'Don't lift up your pen until you have read the whole question.'

Sylvia Moise (Hanstater) remembers hearing about Wilkinson's antisemitic remarks second-hand. She also has her own memories of antisemitic incidents. 'Although I was very little at the time, I do remember that on the way home from school one day, we were confronted by a line of children strung out along the road to try and stop us from passing, accompanied by references to our Jewishness. I don't recall that there was a huge amount of malice in the incident.'

Sammy Hollander describes his transition at age eleven to Letchworth Grammar School: 'The bullyboys (including a few of the staff) were more in evidence. But the standard of instruction was, on the whole, surprisingly good for so small a town. Physics was taught late on Friday afternoons and Jewish students were obliged to leave early in the winter months, generating an unholy muddle in my mind regarding the physical sciences. History, fortunately, was not taught on Friday, or I might not be writing this particular record.'

Murray Cohen was nearing his eleventh birthday when his family moved to Letchworth in 1941. 'At first, I was sent to Norton Rd Secondary School where the headmaster was a delightful man called Mr Hazeman. This was before the eleven plus exam, and quite soon, my father paid for me to attend the co-ed Letchworth Grammar School. As a member of the school rugby team, I never hesitated in giving a good whack to anyone making antisemitic remarks.

'I never really got on with Mr Wilkinson. He had a habit of frequently threatening us with expulsion. Each class appointed its own class monitor, who served as liaison with the headmaster. For some obscure reason, my classmates elected me. I must have been very free with my opinions, because two or three times, Wilkinson said to me: "If you tell me once more how to run my school, I will expel you."'

Murray describes a field next to the school playground containing a pile of coal and coke for the school boilers. 'The boys soon discovered that they could play football with round-shaped pieces of coke. This practice came to a halt when Douglas Bunyon was hit over the eye and had to be hospitalised. The following morning, at the assembly, Wilkinson threatened expulsion if anyone used coke for football again.'

Frances Field (Cohen) remembers that David Kaplin (the future Dayan Kaplin) was in her class. 'He was a genius, but he hardly participated in the lessons, preferring to sit right at the back of the class. The Kaplin family had lived near the London Docks, a frequent target of the Luftwaffe, and moved to Letchworth. David celebrated his barmitzvah while he was at Letchworth Grammar. He would later bemoan the fact that he was not able to have his own personal *tefillin* at the ceremony. However, he was compensated by the fact that his barmitzvah *pilpul* discourse was heard by both Rabbi Elyah Lopian and Dayan Yechezkel Abramsky.'

Frances remembers Wilkinson was very perplexed by the Jewish pupils: 'He pleaded with us to go on to university. He simply could not understand why such bright pupils were not interested in pursuing third level education.' Frances' cousin Judith Lebrecht had visited Letchworth several times before moving there permanently after the war to live with her uncle and aunt, Sol and Sadie Cohen. After attending Wilbury School, Judith went to Letchworth Grammar School. She remembers that there were still several Jewish pupils there, including the Stern sisters, Martha and Kitty.

Norman Arthur Routledge, later a distinguished professor of mathematics and friend of Alan Turin of Enigma fame, said about Letchworth Grammar: 'It was a lively school in which the staff were united in hatred of the headmaster!' Norman's mother panicked when war broke out, and she arrived on the doorstep of her sister in Letchworth with her five children. In Letchworth, Norman met and befriended the Jewish Viennese composer and musicologist, Hans Redlich. Norman initially wanted to study music. A furious Mr Wilkinson summoned his parents to the grammar school and told them: 'I will not have a boy in this school doing music. It is a subject fit only for girls and sissies.'

Joshua Shia 'Buby' Bornstein was another Letchworth Grammar pupil. During religious studies classes, he and the other Jewish boys used to sit at the back of the class. During one class, when the Jewish boys were not paying attention, the religious studies teacher suddenly said, 'Well, if the class doesn't know, we will ask the Jewish boys. Who were the twelve?' The answer came quickly from one bright Jewish spark: 'Matthew, Mark, Luke, John ......'. Of course, the teacher had meant the twelve tribes.

After the bulk of the Jewish community returned to London after the war, Jewish students at Letchworth Grammar became more of a rarity. Moich Abrahams had attended Hillshott Primary School, where he did not understand what it meant when other children called him 'Jewbag.' Now in the grammar school, he continued to experience some antisemitism. 'Most of my time there, in my older teenage years, I was the only Jewish boy in the school. Rabbi Feuchwanger had arranged for me not to go into the morning assembly. I had to sit outside the headmaster's study, often along with the naughty boys. Even when I revisited Letchworth as an adult, I was called a "Kike."'

'I was a late developer in school, and came bottom in my form in music, but top in art. At about fifteen, I took O level maths and art early, and I won the school art prize. Later, I won the school maths prize. Mr

Yorke, the pure maths teacher, wrote to me personally when I got my A and S level results, saying that I had achieved the best maths results in the history of Letchworth Grammar School. I was awarded the school maths prize.' Mr Yorke was also the private maths teacher to the Sassoon boys.

My brother Marcus Mordechai Fachler attended the grammar school for one year, 1960/61, where one of his classmates was Peter Kenyatta, a son of Kenya's President Jomo Kenyatta.

David Persoff – who had a reputation for conducting scientific experiments at home – in the 1940s, and my brother Chaim in the 1960s, shared an intense hatred of their time at Letchworth Grammar School. Chaim says he suffered from antisemitism. 'I was picked on because I was the only pupil to go home early on Friday afternoon and festival eve in the winter months. I was picked on because I was the only pupil to wear a *kippah* – my "tea cosy" was frequently removed and tossed about. I was picked on because I was different. I was picked on because I was asthmatic. I was picked on because I wasn't into sport. I was made to feel an outsider. I did not yet shine academically, except in maths. I was an easy and convenient target.'

Chaim continues: 'Letchworth Grammar was a very lonely place for me. In hindsight, I now realise that my situation was made worse because I was the only religious Jewish child at the grammar school. If the other Jewish children had been religious, I might not have been so alone and so picked on.'

By contrast, Jean Shindler (Pollock) loved her time at Letchworth Grammar School. She was the only Jewish child in the class, but her experiences were very different from Chaim's: 'Despite my father's strong commitment to his Jewishness, he worked on Shabbat. On Jewish festivals that fell mid-week, my sister Anna and I often attended synagogue in the morning and school in the afternoon.'

Not all of the Jewish children in Letchworth attended grammar school in Letchworth. Some went to Hitchin. Steven Kirsch and Russell Ward were pupils at Hitchin Boys Grammar School. Stella Cukier (Bornstein) was the only orthodox Jewish girl at Hitchin Girls Grammar School. She did not feel comfortable being the only girl to leave early on Friday afternoons or to miss school on Jewish festivals. My brother Meir Fachler has very positive memories of Hitchin Boys Grammar School. 'I somehow felt protected. If anyone made any comment about my being Jewish, or if anyone was tempted to use my *yarmulke* as a football, senior boys took them aside and warned them to back off.' Meir also remembers experiencing culture shock when one of his Hitchin Grammar classmates once asked him to deliberately get a couple of questions wrong in some exam: 'If I don't come top in every subject, I get the strap at home.'

St Christopher School

Letchworth is home to a world-famous co-educational non-denominational boarding school, St Christopher on Barrington Road. Over the years, parents of Jewish children from around the world, including Israel, have felt comfortable sending their children to study at this vegetarian school, among other reasons because their children would not be eating non-kosher food.

David Freudmann insisted that his time at St Christopher was very positive: 'My love for music was instilled by a young music teacher in his early twenties who was only at the school for a year or two. His name was Peter Brough. Great pianist, he used to play at assembly several times a week.' David's younger brother Mickey attended Montessori School at St Christopher: 'I found it a very enlightened and progressive school that encouraged cultural and sporting activities. I learned drawing and painting which I still dabble in, and I learned horse riding. I learned English pretty quickly, and after a while I stopped speaking my native French.'

Mickey remembers only one anti-Semitic incident at the school. 'There was a sports teacher who was a refugee from Czechoslovakia. He once made some disparaging remark about Jews – so my dad went round to the headmaster who called the teacher to order.'

Several other Jewish refugee children attended St Christopher during the war. Peter Harry Gayward (Gayduschek) arrived from Austria with the Kindertransport in 1939, and spent the next four years at the school, before becoming a British Army officer. Another Kindertransport child, Ruth Jackson (born Ellen-Ruth Werner), studied at the school. Her mother survived the war, her father did not. Paul Bertrand Wolfgang Hamburger's father was a paediatrician at the

Charite Hospital in Berlin. When the Nazis came to power, the Hamburger family moved to London. Paul later changed his surname to Hamlyn, a name which he picked out of the telephone directory. Paul Hamlyn went on to become an eminent publisher and philanthropist.

Leo Koppel, whose children Peter and Naomi were boarders at St Christopher, was the owner of the Aero Zip Fastener factory in Wales. Leo fostered Carol Eini (Roth)'s mother Marion. Peter was tutored for his barmitzvah by Dr Heinemann of the Letchworth Hebrew Congregation. Peter also attended *Shabbat* morning services at the Co-operative Hall. Peter has fond memories of meeting Rabbi Sassoon. Peter's daughter Toni remembers the names of several of her father's Jewish contemporaries, including the three Drazin brothers – Michael, David and Philip; Lawrence Hacker; and brothers Gerald and Clive Nathan.

Among the refugee Jewish teachers at St Christopher during the Second World War was former German Olympic discus thrower Eric Schuckardt. In 1944, the school employed a Jewish refugee married couple: Dr Kurt Bromberg was librarian and his wife Katharine was a biology teacher. A Jewish teacher who taught in the school after the war was sculptor Ralph Alexander Beyer. He had been interned in 1940, joined the Pioneer Corps, and taught in St Christopher in the early 1950s.

Jewish pupils at St Christopher in the post-war era include Michael Winner, the filmmaker, writer and media personality; Sir Ralph Mark Halpern, whose parents fled from the Nazis in the 1930s; actor David Horovitch (Jewish father, non-Jewish mother); West End and Broadway theatre producer Sonia Friedman, daughter of the concert pianist and eminent Russian violinist Leonard Friedman, who was leader of the Royal Philharmonic Orchestra; and writer Jenny Diski.

Evelyn Bergman (Isaacs), whose father supplied strip lighting to all the Esso garages, was a St Christopher pupil who became very friendly with the Fachler family. This friendship continued long after Evelyn raised her own family. It was through Evelyn that we met her Highgate neighbour Ann Dawes (Rau.) Ann was a frequent visitor to the Fachlers' Sollershott East home, and she and I have been firm friends for over sixty years. Ann's mother was a née Gestetner, family of the Letchworth Feuchtwangers.

I also remember a St Christopher girl called Borchard whose family were ship-owners, and an Israeli girl called Tirzah whose stunning looks turned many a head among our Shabbat guests.

The biggest impact of St Christopher on the Fachler household was Susie Deutsch (Knight). Her American army father died when she was six months old, and her mother was looked after by her two bachelor brothers, Harold and David Gordon. Susie attended the North West London Jewish Day School. When her mother became unwell, Susie lived with a series of foster parents. David Gordon was into Natural Therapy, and the director of the Kingston Clinic in Edinburgh suggested that Susie should go to the Arundale children's home, attached to St Christopher.

David asked Yitzchak Abrams, Susie's Hebrew teacher at school, if he knew of a Jewish community in Letchworth where Susie could go for Hebrew lessons. Yitzchak referred him to my parents. My mother Chava sent my sister Melanie to Arundale to inquire if there was a little Jewish girl there, and could she come to meet the Fachler family. The housemother promised to send Susie.

Soon after Susie arrived for the first time at my parents' home, they contacted her uncles, and it was arranged that she would leave St Christopher and move in with the Fachlers for the duration of her mother's hospital stay. This temporary arrangement lasted eight years.

Officially, the founding principles and practices of St Christopher include tolerance towards all races and religions. In practice, Susie always claimed that despite the school's egalitarian ethos, Jewish children were regularly picked on. She brought along another young Jewish child, David Barassi, to visit my parents, and I eventually taught him his barmitzvah portion. His grandfather was the sole family member to attend David's barmitzvah celebrations hosted by the Sassoons.

Carol Eini (Roth) tells us: 'David and my father Bernard got on very well, and used to talk for hours. My father's parents divorced when my Dad was quite young and he wasn't allowed to see his father after the divorce, so he had a lot of empathy with David.' Susie witnessed the unspeakable abuse and bullying that David suffered at St Christopher on account of his being Jewish, and she begged the Fachlers to foster David as well.

Susie always described Arundale as an 'awful, awful place.' Anyone who thought that she was exaggerating was put right by the (non-Jewish) *Sunday Times* columnist and former pupil at the school, A A Gill, who described St Christopher as a 'living hell.' In *The Angry Island*, Gill recalled the school as 'a weird and unconventional little place with a high proportion of Quakers, many of whom wore sandals all year round and one of whom wouldn't speak on Wednesdays in memory of those killed in Hiroshima.'

The Letchworth Talmud Torah and Letchworth Yeshiva

"I was privileged to spend Shabbat with the two pyramid houses on Sollershott East."

HARRY LEITNER, CHEDER HEADMASTER

The Talmud tells us that it was the high priest, Joshua ben Gamla, who insisted that every town and village must establish a Talmud Torah, or Cheder, for all children above six or seven. As soon as Jews started arriving in Letchworth in 1939, they organised informal and private Talmud Torahs in private homes and in rented premises. For the duration of the Letchworth Jewish community, the education of the children remained a major priority and preoccupation of communal leaders.

Rabbi Elozor Wahrhaftig was incarcerated in Buchenwald concentration camp after Kristallnacht, but was released a few weeks later. With Rabbi Solomon Schonfeld's help, he arrived in London, where he administered a boys' hostel in Stamford Hill. When the Wahrhaftigs first arrived in Letchworth, they lived with their one-year-old daughter Helen in a tiny room in Cashio Lane. Due to lack of space, the older two children Yankel (seven) and Miriam (five) had to be billeted with a non-Jewish family in Stotfold. Both children caught the measles and were miserable and lonely.

Yitzchak Kaufman, a young refugee working in one of Letchworth's war industries, was on the housing priority list. Because he wanted to stay with an observant family, he managed to arrange for the Wahrhaftig family to be reunited. Yitzchak and all the Wahrhaftigs moved into 77 Hallmead – the next house to number 79 where I would later live.

Rabbi Wahrhaftig plunged into the religious life of the community, and was one of the first teachers in the Letchworth *Cheder*. He was the first person to arrange for kosher (*shoimered*) milk in Letchworth. He would walk with his children to the dairy where he would stamp the milk 'L Wahrhaftig Kosher.' Initially, he did not charge for this service, but Sigi Stern persuaded him to charge a nominal fee to help support his family.

As Sukkot approached, Rabbi Wahrhaftig used all his ingenuity to overcome wartime shortages. Using tenacity and foresight, he successfully obtained a *lulav* and *etrog* from Kew Gardens, becoming the only person in Letchworth with a complete set of *Arba Minim*.

One of Rabbi Wahrhaftig's pupils at 40 Hallmead was Dodi Gurwitz: 'The eleven boys in my cheder class included Rabbi Hammer, Hershel Freeman, Yankel Warhaftig, Moshe Bindiger, David (later Dayan) Kaplin, and Ariel Broch. Rabbi Warhaftig taught me *Chumash*, and Rabbi Nachman Dachs and Rabbi Katz taught me *Gemara*. Later, Abba Bornstein's estate office also served as a classroom.'

Ariel Broch describes Reb Nachman: 'He was the only survivor of his entire extended family in Poland, and had managed to escape via China to England. He was a small thin man, usually wearing a threadbare suit and a worn-down hat. His beard was thin and scraggly. But on *Shabbat*, Reb Nachman would appear in a beautiful black frock-coat and wearing the traditional Hassidic fur *shtreimel*. Nothing was threadbare about him on the Sabbath, even his beard appeared to be fuller.'

Ariel says that he worshipped Reb Nachman, and followed him around. 'Reb Nachman was the Letchworth community's *Shochet*, and I accompanied him on his rounds as he called into anyone with a chicken to prepare for the pot. On Sabbath afternoons, Reb Nachman would take me with him to the *Shalosh Seudos* meal at the table of Rabbi Binyaminsohn, the Zhlobiner Rav. I would sit on the bench at the back.'

One Sunday morning, Ariel and the other boys in the cheder class gathered in the Zhlobiner Rav's home could not believe their eyes. A beautiful young woman came in and kissed the Rabbi's cheek. The boys were in shock. They had never seen the like. The rabbi's niece Beryl Waters assumes that it must have been one of the Rav's other nieces.

Ariel remembers that it was not all plain sailing for the Jewish boys who attended Rav Nachman's Talmud class in the Mullway home of the Zhlobiner Rav. 'After struggling into our coats, we all left together in a group, prepared for any trouble. We were often waylaid on our way out of the class by a gang of youths who would attack us if we were alone or in twos or threes. One Sunday lunchtime, the gang was bigger and braver than usual, and ambushed us as we left the front gate. They showered us with pieces of ice that they had broken off from a static water tank further along the street.

'Charlie Rottenberg, a burly thirteen-year-old and a good all-rounder in sports, took command. "OK. Follow me! Let's charge them!" We formed a sort of scrum and bowled the nearest gang members over as we charged towards the water tank. As soon as we got there, we broke off some ice and counterattacked, throwing huge chunks at our erstwhile tormentors. The gang soon turned tail and scattered under the vicious onslaught. We all got home safely in time for lunch.'

Another pupil of Reb Nachman was Moishe (Maurice) Cohen. 'We all attended a different Cheder under Dr Heinnemann. My first Cheder teacher was Mrs Hildersheimer, who taught a mixed class. Once we were separated by gender, the boys began to learn with the *shochet*, Reb Nachman. When he had a busy Monday at the abattoir, we were given a day off. The language of instruction was Yiddish, a language none of us spoke!

'My parents had lived in Cricklewood before the war, and knew both the Persoffs and Abba Bornstein's family. My maternal grandparents lived in Hallmead, and I *davened Shacharit* with my *Zeida* on weekdays. On Shabbat, I walked with my father to the Howard Hall *minyan* where the *chazan* was Joe Richman, another pre-war friend of my father. Dr Epstein lived opposite us in Mullway, and he and his family also attended the Howard Hall *minyan*. Dr Epstein encouraged my parents to send me away to Aria College in Southsea, which prepared Jewish boys for the ministry. I left Mullway in 1945 for Aria College.'

Some rabbis and teachers taught and tutored students in Letchworth itself during the war. Other rabbis, headmasters and teachers - as well as some students - commuted to London. Coming in the opposite direction was Rabbi Dessler who visited Letchworth to tutor Solomon and Flora Sassoon. Also coming from London to Letchworth was Norman Kass, who was hired by Mr Freudmann as a private tutor for his sons, David and Mickey.

Mickey described Kass as 'a Litvak refugee who spoke a beautiful Yiddish.' He was born in Ponevecz, and had been ordained by the Poneveczer Rav. Rabbi Kass was not comfortable using the Torah as a livelihood, so he enrolled at the London Hospital as a medical student. It was in our Letchworth home that Norman met Frieda Mayer, a refugee from Germany who was employed by my parents to look after my younger brother Edmond (Eddie). I still remember the thrill my brother David and I had when we first saw Norman and Frieda holding hands.'

Vivienne Alper (Gedalla) was one of Rabbi Wahrhaftig's pupils. 'After school every day, I went to cheder in Hallmead. I lived in Mullway, which was not far to walk. However, in the short winter days, walking home in the blackout with my little torch, it was scary and I felt very vulnerable.'

The chairman of the Talmud Torah sub-committee, Elazar Halevy, found an additional teacher and additional teaching space. Dr I Weinstock was placed in charge of second and fourth class, while Rabbi Warhaftig retained first and third class. Dr Weinstock's classes were eventually held in 7 Hallmead, where Elazar Halevy secured suitable desks and benches.

The Education sub-committee cooperated with the Joint Emergency Committee to arrange for religious instruction of the children attending Pixmore school, as well as children evacuated from the Oldfield Road School in Stoke Newington to St Francis College. The Joint Emergency Committee also arranged classes in the Howard Hall taught by Rabbi Barney Klein and Rev I Rosenberg. A post barmitzvah class was taught by Rabbi Klein, Rabbi David Sassoon and Elazar Halevy.

Rabbi David Sassoon's son Rabbi Solomon Sassoon spoke at a special meeting to inaugurate a Letchworth Talmud Torah fund. When Elazar Halevy resigned due to pressures of his job as organising secretary of the national Passover Committee for Evacuees, Rabbi Klein took his place. For a while, Rabbi Isi Broch taught a class at the Vasanta Hall in Gernon Walk.

Chanuka and Purim parties were held for all Jewish children – whether they studied in the Talmud Torah or not, and whether their parents were members of the community or not. At one Purim event, each of the 120 children received a homentachen presented by Mrs Grodzinski (who else?) and a threepenny bit donated by Mrs Kelly.

The prizegiving ceremony for the Letchworth Talmud Torah held after Pesach 1940 was the first of its kind to take place in any designated evacuation reception area. As a token of cooperation, some prizes were given by the Joint Emergency Committee. Rabbi Solomon Sassoon addressed the children, and his mother Selina Sassoon distributed the prizes. The following year, in April 1941, Mrs Sassoon again presented the prizes to pupils of the Letchworth Hebrew Congregation.

In the interim period between the departure of many families back to London and elsewhere in the late 1940s, and the slimmed down community of the late 1950s and the 1960s, the Talmud Torah still thrived. Many rabbis and teachers had joined the exodus from Letchworth, and the amalgamated Jewish community wanted to ensure that no Jewish child in the greater Letchworth area would be denied Jewish tuition.

During the 1950s and early 1960s, the cheder taxi driver was Mr Woods. He would ferry children to and from outlying villages and hamlets, as well as from homes in Letchworth that were too far to walk to cheder. According to all reports, Rabbi Sassoon funded the Woods cheder run all those years.

Carol Eini (Roth) remembers that Mr. Woods lived in Baldock Road in a large house which had an outhouse that served as a small shop. The Roth family used to buy eggs from him. Many Letchworth children remember the Woods taxi, including Lenny Abrahams. It was on Mr. Woods' rounds on Sunday mornings that Carol first met Shulamith Landau (Schischa.)

Shulamith did not attend the Cheder, but had private lessons with her father's aunt Malka Stern in Mullway. On these journeys, Carol and Shulamith discovered that they shared the same birthday, and they became firm friends. Later, the two of them went to Hitchin Girls Grammar, both staying until Senior VI.

The headmaster of the Letchworth cheder was Reb Oosher Feuchtwanger. Like generations of Letchworth and Hitchin children, I too learned my "o, a, e" from Mrs. Rand, the cheder teacher in the late 1940s and early 1950s. Thanks to Mrs Rand, I could read and write Hebrew by the time I was four years old. Like many other of Mrs Rand's pupils, Carol Eini (Roth) still remembers the brown *Reshis Da'as* Hebrew Language primer from which we all studied.

A small *yeshiva* (Talmudical college) was established in 38 and 40 Hallmead in 1951. According to Rabbi Jacob Feuchtwanger, when the Staines Yeshiva folded in early 1951, his uncle Rabbi Sassoon invited them to relocate to Letchworth. Rabbi Sassoon provided the funds, and served as its president. Jacob's father Reb Oosher, the communal rabbi of the Letchworth Hebrew Congregation, served as the yeshiva's principal. The Dean was Rabbi Yitzchok Aussenberg, a Belzer chassid from Cracow whom everyone called Reb Itche. He had been the Rosh Yeshiva in Staines. Reb Simcha Freudiger from Israel and Reb Yankel Benedict were employed as tutors.

Judith Weil's 2011 article in the Jewish Tribune mentions some of the students' names:

Yonoson, Shlomo and Moshe Ezra Hochhauser
Avrohom and Shloime Just
Yossi and Pinny Breuer
Gedallia and Yossi Ebert
Alter Singer
Avrom Hacohen Silber
Moshe Leib Weiser
Asher Steiner
Alexander (Sandy) Halpern
Sinai Halberstam
Shraga Feivish Wohl
Benzion Berkowitz
Feivel Wolgelernter
Levi Lock
Zishe Twersky, the son of the Sassover Rebbe
Ben Harosh
Weider
Krausz
Breslauer.

Rabbi Simcha Freudiger with a class of yeshiva students

Sandy Halpern returned to Letchworth a dozen years later for Yom Kippur because there was a *brit* for a baby boy born locally to an Israeli mother. Very few of us had ever been to a Yom Kippur *brit* before, so it was a real novelty.

Among the documents that Yossel Schischa gave me was a very professionally produced fund-raising brochure, *The Way Letchworth Yeshivah Serves You*. In excellent English, the brochure describes the attraction of Letchworth: 'The quiet and wholesome setting of Letchworth, the First Garden City, with its plentiful fresh air, has in its way contributed towards a concentration and studies not attainable in the turmoil and distracting atmosphere of a big city.'

The brochure emphasises that the curriculum for the junior and senior group conformed with the Education Act, that classes in secular subjects were delivered by highly qualified teachers, and that 'only recently one of HM Inspectors of Schools charged with the examination of the arrangements expressed full satisfaction with the curriculum and class work.'

The brochure informs us that 'students have found it worthwhile coming all the way from Austria, Belgium, Canada, France, Germany and Israel.' Somehow, Britain was missing from the list. Part of the attraction of Letchworth Yeshiva for foreign students is that it afforded them an opportunity to improve their English. At least one of the students had been a 'hidden child' in the Holocaust.

I am not sure how successful this brochure was in raising funds for the Letchworth Yeshiva. Shloime Just recalls that the students themselves were enlisted to go to London to try and collect from Jewish donors. 'We had with us letters attesting that we were legitimately collecting on behalf of the yeshiva, but most people we approached refused to give money, saying "Rabbi Sassoon can support the yeshiva on his own."'

Shloime recalls: 'The yeshiva was run like a five-star hotel. I used to have meals at the Shteinschreiber family. They kept chickens, which meant that we ate fresh eggs each morning.' He remembers how some of the yeshiva boys used to play football on Norton Common on Friday afternoons.

One winter, there was a big snowball fight between the yeshiva students and some local youths. My classmate at Wilbury, Geoff Woollard, who lived opposite the Hallmead yeshiva, gives us his account of the battle:

'One thing that always sticks in my mind is the congregation of "black hats" in the Yeshiva/Synagogue across the road from me. There is one particular incident which I observed from my bedroom window and it is still vivid in my memory. There had been a heavy fall of snow and the Monkland boys, who were pretty fearsome, decided to attack the yeshiva with snowballs. The attack continued for a while. Then suddenly, the doors of the yeshiva flew open and out came all the Hassidic pupils with their robes and *payot* flowing in the wind, carrying dustbin lid shields and armed with snowballs. The Monklands boys couldn't believe what was happening and they beat a hasty retreat to their own territory. As far as I'm aware, they never tried that again!'

Rabbi Sassoon's two sons, David and Haki, then aged twelve and ten, used to cycle every weekday from their Sollershott East home to the yeshiva in 40 Hallmead, where they were taught by various teachers including the son of Rabbi Padwa. Haki remembers an incident when

Group of Letchworth Yeshiva Students

an obviously inebriated gentleman came in off the street and subjected the Rosh Yeshiva, Reb Itche, to a torrent of abuse. Haki was impressed that Reb Itche did not budge.

For a while, the cooks in the yeshiva were Mr and Mrs Beck. Their son Yochanan remembers that yeshiva boys used to walk over to the Sassoons to help make a minyan on Shabbat morning. In 1956, there was a crisis when the Becks suddenly left the yeshiva. At first, some of the yeshiva students ate with local families. I remember that some of the boys ate in our home at 79 Hallmead. Eventually my mother agreed to step in until a new cook could be found, on condition that we Fachler children could eat lunch at the yeshiva every day. This arrangement lasted about 9 months. The yeshiva closed down in late 1957.

During the Letchworth Yeshiva's six-year sojourn in Hallmead, there was a considerable degree of interaction between the yeshiva and the Talmud Torah. Although the Hassans lived in Hitchin, their two daughters Patricia and Margaret attended the Letchworth Cheder every Sunday. Patricia Reifen (Hassan) recalls: 'Both my sister and I were collected by taxi, which Rabbi Sassoon used to send to bring together all the Jewish children in the area. I remember the cheder teacher Mrs. Rand very well, and we all loved her. When she made Aliyah to Israel, we were taught by one of the Yeshiva *Bochers* (students), whose name I do not remember.'

Pamela Tendell retains fond memories of going to Hebrew classes every Tuesday and Thursday afternoon and on Sunday morning. 'I can remember our teacher, Mrs Rand. It must have been difficult with the pupils being of different ages, abilities and convictions. The electric lights sometimes went out, and Mrs Rand had to go up and down the stairs feeding pennies into the meter. I stopped going to Cheder in about 1951, the same year I started studying at Hitchin Grammar School.'

Moich Abrahams recalls that his father employed Mrs Rand to come to the flat above The Arcade to give Hebrew lessons to Moich when he was very young, and probably to Lenny too. 'She first taught me the Aleph Beis. I remember one time she bought me a birthday present - a red lorry with a crane on it. It was very special for me, as basically my main toy was plasticine from Woolworths, and marbles.'

Although most Jewish children who attended the Letchworth Talmud Torah have happy memories, Moich's brother Bernard (Bernie) Abrahams is an exception. As Moich explains, 'Bernie told me that he became disenchanted with learning about the Jewish religion when he was very young. When Bernie couldn't correctly pronounce Hebrew letters, Rabbi Feuchtwanger would wrap him over the knuckles with a ruler. This experience made him lose all interest in studying Hebrew. Even our lodger Mr Gottfried tried to teach Bernie Hebrew, but he had to give up. Bernie really struggled with his barmitzvah, and on the big day, someone stood next to him whispering the words in his ears so that he could say them.'

In the early 1950s, Rabbi Feuchtwanger arranged for all three Abrahams brothers to go to an Agudah summer camp in Bexhill. As Moich reports: 'Bernie hated it, because of the Hebrew lessons. Lenny claims that we seemed to exist on a diet of jam sandwiches. I remember we were taken to Dover to greet the arrival of Rabbi Yoel Teitelbaum, the Satmar Rebbe, who was en route from his historic visit to Israel back to the United States. We queued up, and when I got to him he gave me a blessing.'

Norman Solomon and his wife Doris were a young married couple who arrived in Letchworth in 1955. Norman says: 'Both of my two jobs were financed by the Letchworth Jewish community. One job consisted of running the cheder for the Jewish children of the area. My other job was to teach English to the refugee boys in the Letchworth Yeshiva. After three years in Letchworth, we spent two years in London where I gained semicha - rabbinic ordination - before moving North for my 'first proper job' as rabbi of the recently formed Whitefield community.'

When I was ten or eleven, I used to go with Stella Cukier (Bornstein) every Shabbat afternoon to Norman Solomon's home for Bible study. Getting to his house entailed traipsing through muddy fields. I can't remember much about what we studied, but Stella and I got perverse pleasure in cleaning our muddy shoes on his clean white towels. We thought it was hilarious. I doubt if he was much amused.

Pamela Tendell says that the arrival of Norman Solomon brought new life to the dwindling community. 'In addition to teaching my brother Donald his barmitzvah, Rabbi Solomon started a Jewish Youth Club, amassing all possible Jewish teenagers from the vicinity, including Letchworth, Walsworth, Hitchin and Weston. Thanks to the support and generosity of the Sassoon family, our Youth Club included the Abrahams, Bronsons, Hassans, Yelens and Berisches. We were taken on outings including the Bevis Marks Synagogue and Kew Gardens. Unfortunately, Rabbi Norman Solomon's time in Letchworth was very short.'

Here is a partial list of the children who attended cheder in 1959:

Monica Pressburger
Russell Ward (Barmitzvah preparation)
Cedric Ward
Joel Jaffey (Barmitzvah preparation)
David and Paul Jaffey
Carol and Peter Roth
Mordechai, Chaim and Melanie Fachler
Anne and Jean Pollock
E and G Berisch (two of Ralph Berisch's sisters)
J, K and M Lawlor
A and Beverly Bronson (living in Hitchin)

M Lesnik (living in Hitchin)
M and Richard Lewis (living in Hitchin – their aunt was the singer, Vera Lynn)
Judith Kirsch

Robby Jaffey remembers a Purim play organised by Ruth Keller (Kirsch) and Gail Zivan Neriya (Vanger). 'Rehearsals were held in the Kirsch house. I don't remember the script, but I do remember that I played one half of a cow. I'm not sure if the other part of the cow was Daniel Kirsch or Jonathan Vanger.'

In June 1960, Walter Gottfried, the Hon Secretary of the Letchworth Hebrew Congregation, wrote to all members to inform them of a 'new stage in the development of our community. We are endeavouring to consolidate and further to develop communal, social and educational facilities to benefit all Jewish residents in this district.' The agenda for the general meeting was as follows:

- *Report by Rabbi Sassoon on present communal activities and recommendations for the future.*
- *Treasurer's report.*
- *Proposal to appoint Mr Leonard Daniels as full-time teacher and Assistant Minister for one year.*
- *Adoption of resolution submitted by the Chief Rabbi's Office relating to our eligibility to be represented at the Board of Deputies.*

Rabbi Sassoon was engaged in lengthy – and ultimately unsuccessful – correspondence with Michael Wallach, the secretary of the Office of the Chief Rabbi, over the eligibility of the Letchworth congregation to be represented at the Board of Deputies of British Jews. Wallach had told Rabbi Sassoon that certification would be deferred until such time as 'the Congregation has a separate building permanently set aside for the purpose of public worship and for no other purpose.' A frustrated Rabbi Sassoon, who had already completed a lengthy questionnaire, wrote back to Wallach in August 1960:

'I would like to point out that no. 17 Sollershott East is our permanent synagogue. Prayers are held there regularly every day. The Talmud Torah classes are held there, and my own children are having their instructions and lessons there. Nobody is living at that house and it is being used only for these purposes. These arrangements have been made, since all the Jewish families moved away from the Hallmead area, and thus 40 Hallmead which served as synagogue and for classes for the last 20 years, has become too far for Synagogue goers and for the children.'

Notwithstanding Rabbi Sassoon's arguments, Yossel Schischa reports that the Letchworth community never did join the Board of Deputies. Maybe Wallach regarded Rabbi Sassoon as too much of a maverick who too often followed his own independent courses of action, such as the Shechita booklet that he wrote, published and distributed. My father Eli did become a member of the Board of Deputies - not as the president of the Letchworth Jewish community, but as representative of the Luton Shechita Board.

In 1961, the headmaster of the Letchworth Talmud Torah was Rabbi M Bloom. Jean Shindler (Pollock) still has her report card from the Spring term when she was almost nine years old. Here are some of the written comments from Rabbi Bloom: 'Reading: Her fast and correct reading shows she really practices it in her prayers. General Comments: Jean is very interested and keen in all her work, and here is the fruit of her enthusiasm. Her good attendance only goes to prove this.'

Rabbi Bloom features in a profile on Letchworth in the *Jewish Chronicle* from the early 1960s that describes the town's Jewish population as the 'friendly community whose members were bound by strong ties of cordiality and esteem. This is a £1,000-a-year community. That is the revenue of the synagogue whose minister receives no stipend. A full-time paid teacher, Mr M Bloom, is employed. The annual income from membership fees does not exceed £350. The rest of the budget is defrayed by a dozen conscientious *Baale Batim* [denizens] who have pledged themselves to maintain the £1,000 target. In sum, here is a closely knit community intensely devout yet almost completely Anglicised: essentially European in tradition, yet so very English in outlook and approach to present day problems.'

Harry Leitner, a highly popular headmaster of the Letchworth Cheder in the 1960s, retains very warm memories of his time in Letchworth: 'During the years I spent as rebbe of *Limudei Kodesh* in Letchworth, I was privileged to spend Shabbat with the two pyramid houses on Sollershott East – the home of Rabbi Sassoon and family, and the home of the Fachlers. From both these establishments, I learned the true meaning of nobility, character, joie de vivre, sensitivity to others' needs and how to make guests feel welcome.'

My brother Chaim learned Hebrew grammar from Mrs Rand: 'It is thanks to her that my Hebrew grammar is better than that of my Israeli-born secretaries.' However, Chaim's most rewarding cheder experience was with Harry Leitner. 'I really loved him. He taught me *Limudei Kodesh* to a very high level, so that when I joined Carmel College, I went straight into the top class. To all intents and purposes, I had a private lesson with Mr Leitner – for most of the time, I was the only person in the class. He was a kind and understanding teacher, and even released me early to watch Freddie Truman in a cricket test match on TV.'

Jean Shindler (Pollock) still has the Talmud Torah report card from Spring 1963, signed by Harry Leitner and by the principal, Rabbi Sassoon. 'A model pupil' is how Mr Leitner described Jean. He helped prepare Peter Roth for his barmitzvah, and Peter remembers receiving a set of *Mishna Berura* from his teacher.

As with Ralph Berisch, a major influence on Peter from the age of seven was Aby Van Praagh, who taught him every Sunday morning. Aby was also instrumental in introducing Letchworth to a force of nature by the name of 'Miss Portal' (now Mrs Mimy Santhouse). This colourful and exuberant character taught in the cheder for three years and became a Letchworth institution.

Miss Portal describes how she first encountered 'a most wonderful community – the aristocrats of Letchworth, headed by the saintly Rabbi Suliman Salomon Sassoon and his brother-in-law Rabbi Osher Feuchtwanger.' She was a teacher in the Yesodei Hatorah school in London, and Aby Van Praagh had a garage under her classroom where he stored handbags. One day, Aby suggested that he takes Miss Portal to Letchworth to speak to Rabbi Sassoon with a teaching job in mind.

'We went in his very old van to Letchworth the following Sunday. My meeting with Rabbi Sassoon went so smoothly that I was asked to start teaching twice a week, effective immediately. I was also asked to spend *Shabbos* in Letchworth and take *Shabbos* groups. I asked Rabbi Sassoon if it would be in order to come for *Shabbos* every fortnight, as I had wonderful friends in Golders Green where I spent the alternate *Shabboses*.'

This was only Miss Portal's second job, but she was appointed head teacher of the Letchworth Talmud Torah, which involved teaching all the children, of different ages, and in three different groups. The ages ranged from six years old to sixteen years old.

'I taught them as they returned from school, the younger ones first, then the next group. Rabbi Feuchtwanger introduced me to the shed which was to be my classroom, at the back of the Sassoon's garden. In no time, we had charts of general knowledge and topical pictures of the coming *Yomtov* hanging on the walls. The teaching went extremely well, and I thoroughly enjoyed the children. The teaching did not just stop with the children. I also met their parents in *Shul* after *davening*, for *Kiddush* on *Shabbos* mornings and at Chanuka and Purim parties and other social meetings. A most wonderful experience.

'As I arrived from the train station, both on Mondays and Thursdays, Rabbanit Alice had a full meal waiting for me, often to be eaten in the company of Rabbi Feuchtwanger. The Sassoon's humbleness knew no bounds – their dining room was pure simplicity. Rabbanit Alice, with the sweetest personality, worked very hard, running a most remarkable household and organising the staff in her two kitchens. Mrs Flora Feuchtwanger - a very knowledgeable lady - always had such kind and encouraging words.

'Once, as I was feeling quite tired after a day's teaching, I fell asleep on the train from Kings Cross to Letchworth. I was woken up by the guard at Cambridge station shouting "All change, please. Last stop!" I jumped to my feet! How do I get back to my dear charges? I telephoned the Sassoons. And who do you think came to pick me up from Cambridge and drive me back to Letchworth? It was none other than Rabbi Sassoon himself. What an honour!'

One of Miss Portal's pupils was Carol Eini (Roth): 'Mimy Portal entered our lives like a whirlwind. Since our beloved Mrs. Rand left, we Letchworth cheder children had not experienced a "lady" teacher. We had been taught by serious rabbis, young men and also by members of our own community. Mimy was a breath of fresh air, young, energetic, often late and appeared to be muddled, but she filled us with enthusiasm.

'I was already in my late teens when Mimy started teaching us. I can remember her going through the entire *Shemona Esreh* with us in great detail – word by word. Mimy introduced me to *Hashkafa*, a new and profound way of looking at everything and giving a meaning to our prayers and also thoughts in everyday life.'

More than 50 years since Miss Portal left the Letchworth Talmud Torah, Jean Shindler (Pollock), still has her cheder exercise books. Here is what Miss Portal wrote on one assignment: 'Jean has shown some interest to cheder. Could do better! Did better! Very good! Carry on!'

Gail Zivan Neriya (Vanger): 'My memories of the Letchworth Jewish community always start with the Sassoon's house and the cheder hut at the end of the garden with its round shaped electric heater where we used to warm our hands on chilly days. The furniture, the scent of the greenery outside, the china pots decorating the grass.' Gail's brother Jonathan Vanger also remembers the round shaped heater: 'As kids, Daniel Kirsch and I put a small wooden thermometer on the heater … and yes, it exploded in the cheder lesson.'

Jean Schindler (Pollock): 'We went to cheder three times a week in a shed in the Sassoon garden. It had plain walls and a single bookshelf. Our learning resources were a *siddur* and a *chumash*. We learned in small groups. My class consisted of me, Judy Kirsch and Melanie Fachler. We all loved our cheder lessons. Our teachers were young seminary girls who came from London. My love for classical Hebrew texts and commentaries was definitely built on the wonderful foundations I was given as a child in Letchworth.'

My brother Meir remembers playing Chinese Whispers at the Shabbos Group played by Melanie and Judy. 'It started with Mozelle Gubbay (Feuchtwanger), and the last person said that they had heard "Mashed potatoes in the larder." When Mozelle was asked what she had originally said, it was "Ma Nishtana halayla hazeh" - Why is this night different from all other nights?'

Sue Deutsch (Knight) cherishes her memories of cheder: 'The hut was cold, but the learning kept me warm. In 1971, I earned a Distinction certificate from the Jewish Schools' Torah Council. I was the only Letchworth representative to receive a certificate at the awards ceremony in Munks *Shul* in Golders Green.'

One of the motivations for the Sassoon-Feuchtwanger household to remain in Letchworth for so many years was to supervise the private education of the younger generation: David and Haki Sassoon, and later Mozelle and Jacob Feuchtwanger. As part of a long Sassoon family custom, private tutors from Israel, Chacham Yosef Doury and Chacham Sasson Mizrachi, both of them from the Baghdadi tradition, were (with their wives) part of the Sassoon household. The two chachamim also led services in the Sassoons' private *minyan*.

For their secular education, the Sassoon boys had a series of private tutors, including a retired teacher, Mr West. Haki Sassoon remembers that when it came to the Jewish festivals, Mr West told them: 'Oh, yes, I know all about the festivals. I once taught in a school with Orthodox pupils, including the Adler boy (who later became the famous Golders Green GP). Instead of asking permission to leave school early on the eve of Jewish festivals, they would stay in school until the last lesson. Then they would put down their pencils, leave their schoolbags, and walk – sometimes several miles - to their homes. Mr West was impressed by these orthodox boys who refused to ask for special treatment.'

Jacob Feuchtwanger used to attend private lessons at the Sassoon home, under the same tutors as his cousins. Because he was younger than them, he studied separately. A few months before his barmitzvah, Jacob became the first member of his generation of Sassoon/Feuchtwanger children to attend a regular school when he went to Gateshead Boarding School, before studying at Gateshead Yeshiva like his older Sassoon cousins.

In Gateshead, David and Haki befriended Mumbai-born Yaakov Hillel. They invited him to their home in Letchworth over *Yamim Tovim*. His many visits to Letchworth opened him up to the grandeur of his Baghdadi heritage, and he went on to become a distinguished rabbi in Jerusalem.

An annual visitor to the Letchworth Cheder was Harold Levy, Inspector of Hebrew classes in London and the provinces for the Central Council of Jewish Religious Education. Harold visited over ninety Jewish communities around Britain, and I remember his annual visits to the Letchworth cheder in the 1950s. In the late 1960s and very early 1970s when I was first a teacher in the Luton Cheder under Rabbi Alan Plancey, and then headmaster after his departure, Harold visited every year. By 1970, most of the last remaining Jewish children in Letchworth attended the Luton cheder on Sunday mornings.

Many of Letchworth Talmud Torah alumni went into education, and many rabbis emerged from Letchworth. Prior to 1950, these included Dayan David Kaplin, Rabbi Dodi Gurwicz and his brother Rabbi Avraham Gurwicz, Rabbi Moshe Schwab, Rabbi Dovid Ordman, and Rabbi Boruch Hammer whose parents left Letchworth during the war.

Among the students in the post-war Letchworth Yeshiva who went on to become rabbis are Rabbi Pinchas (Pinny) Breuer; Rabbi Benzion Berkovitz, and Rabbi Sinai Halberstam of the Sanz dynasty. Letchworth children who became rabbis include Rabbi Solomon Sassoon's two sons, Rabbi David Sassoon and Chacham Yitzchak (Haki) Sassoon; Rabbi Feuchtwanger's son Rabbi Jacob Feuchtwanger, and daughter Rebbitzen Mozelle Gubbay; Rabbi Yossel Schischa and Rabbi Refoel Berisch; and the two sons of Stephen Kirsch, Rabbi Danny Kirsch and Rabbi Jonathan Kirsch.

In my own family, two of my brothers received *semicha*, Rabbi Mordechai Fachler and Rabbi Chaim Fachler. My sister Melanie became a *rebbitzen* when she married Ephraim Klyne, and my foster sister Sue Deutsch (Knight) became a *hazzanit*. To this list must be added at least five visiting Cambridge students: Chief Rabbi Jonathan Sacks, Rabbi Benji Cohen, Rabbi Jeremy Rosen, Rabbi Joseph Pearlman and Rabbi Chaim Pearlman.

On a lighter note, this is how Efraim Halevy responded to an email from Carol Eini (Roth) seeking information about Letchworth rabbis and rebbitzens: 'The only rabbi I know is Rabbi Dodi Gurwicz, and I don't know any rebbitzens. However, I am certain that only one head of the Mossad ever emerged from Hallmead!'

Families Kirsch, Pollock, Roth, Ward and Vanger

> *'Mother's reluctance to leave Letchworth, borne solely on having been thrust into widowhood with three children, was a topic which followed her for the rest of her life.'*
>
> NEIL ROLAND

Frederick Kirsch and his wife Liesl came from Chemnitz, a large industrial town near Leipzig, famous for its textiles, gloves, hosiery and knitwear. Educated with a degree in business, Frederick was involved in the management of a large glove manufacturing enterprise in Chemnitz. As a young man, he had worked for two years in England, and spoke English fluently. His language skills came in very handy in 1936 when his contract ran out. His German employer had recently purchased a glove factory in Hitchin, near Letchworth, and he offered Frederick the opportunity to manage it.

Frederick moved to Letchworth immediately, leaving Liesl and the boys, Peter and Stephen (Hans) to stay with relations in Switzerland. The family was reunited in Letchworth in 1938 – and can therefore lay claim to being the pioneers of the Letchworth Jewish community. Subsequently Frederick bought the factory, and when he died in 1952, Peter and Stephen took over and ran the business until they retired in 2001.

When the Kirsches first descended on Letchworth First Garden City, the town had several religious denominations and sects, from Theosophists to Catholics, from Quakers to Church of England. Any Jews who had lived in Letchworth in the First World War had left. The nearest synagogue was in Luton, some ten miles away. The Luton

Stephen and Peter Kirsch with their parents and grandmother

community was orthodox, and although the Kirsches were more used to a Reform service, they soon felt at home in Luton's warm and hospitable community.

It says something about the people of Letchworth that at a time when most golf clubs in Britain were closed to Jews, and would remain closed for many years to come, Frederick was invited to join the Letchworth Golf Club. Liesl was invited to join the bridge club. She recalls that her non-Jewish friends did not understanding the situation of Jews in Germany. One of Liesl's new friends, in her ignorance, thought she had insulted Liesl after making some disparaging remarks about 'Mr. Hitler.'

When the British government ordered the internment of all German citizens in 1940, several prominent gentile citizens of Letchworth vouched for Frederick. There were precious few examples like this of someone avoiding internment.

The Kirsch brothers were very active participants in the famous kiddush at the home of Sali and Bertha Bornstein – and later at the home of Eli and Chava Fachler. When the Letchworth Jewish community ceased to exist in 1971, the Fachlers moved to an apartment in Dunrobin Court on West Hampstead's Finchley Road. Stephen and Janet bought a home in London, but remained in Letchworth while work was being completed on the London home. As Ruth Keller (Kirsch) explains: 'My parents' arrangements for moving house to London coincided with the start of the school year. My sister Judy and I moved in with Chava and Eli Fachler and 4-year old Yossi. When nosy Dunrobin Court neighbours wanted to know who we were, Chava answered, "My nieces." We have all had a good chuckle over this ever since.'

Henry (Hermann) and Florence (Florrie) Pollock joined several other members of London's Adass community when they arrived in Letchworth in late 1939. The Pollocks were accompanied by their adult children, Dennis, Cecil, Derek, Rose (Rosalind) and Joe, and moved into 202 Icknield Way. Henry continued with his dental practice, and generations of Letchworth's Jewish community were treated by him. My personal memory is that the only equipment Henry seemed to possess was a pair of pliers with which he yanked out teeth.

Dennis Pollock started a furrier's shop in Hermitage Road, Hitchin. Cecil followed his father into the world of dentistry. Because of the London bombing, the clinical teaching activities of the Royal Free Hospital / London School of Medicine for Women moved to Arlesey, just a few miles from Letchworth. Here Cecil met and married Estelle, a Jewish student at the school.

Derek, and later Joe, were conscripted into the British Army. Derek served in India and Iraq and then spent several years in army intelligence in Egypt. He returned to Letchworth in 1946, and joined his brother Dennis in his furrier business in Hitchin. In 1949, Derek married Goldie, who had come to England from Malmo, Sweden, and whose family came from Lithuania. Derek and Goldie moved in with Henry and Florrie. Dennis died young, and Derek took over the furrier business. After Henry died in 1952, Florrie joined her children who had returned to London. Derek and Goldie remained in Letchworth.

Their daughter Anna was born in the Benslow Rise Nursing Home in Hitchin in 1950. Younger daughter Jean was born at 72 Leys Avenue, Letchworth, where the family now lived in a flat above a shop. Shortly afterwards, the family moved to 76 Broadwater Avenue. In 1955, Derek

Goldie Pollock and daughters

opened Peter B Jones in Hermitage Road, Hitchin, selling ladies' fashion, linens and curtains. He was joined in the business by his brother-in-law Bert Hassan, who lived in Hitchin with wife Babs, Derek's half-sister. Their two daughters, Pat (Patricia) and Margaret, attended the Letchworth Talmud Torah.

Jean recalls: 'My batmitzvah in 1964 was the first in Letchworth. I gave a *drasha* in our garden, and I still treasure the *Soncino Chumash* given to me by Selina Sassoon. By that time, there were only about a dozen Jewish families left in Letchworth. Every Jewish child had a couple of Jewish friends. In time, there was a Shabbat club – the 'Shabbos Group.' As soon as younger children were able to join in, the older ones became the youth leaders. My parents realised that Anna and I needed a broader peer group, so in 1966 we left Letchworth for the green pastures of leafy Stanmore, a small Jewish community with a handful of people who were more observant.'

Carol Eini (Roth) still remembers an evening in May 1956, when she heard voices in the back garden of her home at 81 Bowershott. 'At about

8 o'clock, when I was supposed to be asleep, I saw my parents – Bernard and Marion – chatting with two people whom I did not know: A tall man, and a lady by his side whose hair was completely covered by a headscarf. I thought this very strange. Little did I know that these two people – Eli and Chava Fachler and their extended family, would be such major influences in my ideology, my beliefs and my way of thinking for the rest of my life.'

The Fachlers welcomed the Roths into their family, and included them in family holidays, Seder nights, day trips, as well as lunch every Shabbat. According to Carol, 'Chava and Eli became our second parents.' The Roths arrived in Letchworth from Perivale in 1954 when Bernard got an engineering job in Works Road. The Roths kept a kosher home, so naturally Marion looked for the nearest kosher butcher. When she found Stern's in the Wynd, she met my father Eli Fachler who worked there. Marion and Eli bonded very quickly over the fact that both these Letchworth residents were from Berlin and had both arrived in England with the Kindertransport. Marion had been sponsored and fostered by the Koppel family in Hampstead Garden Suburb.

Marion was untypical in the Letchworth Jewish community in that she always worked outside the home. Her places of employment included the corset manufacturer, Spirella; Cockerells, the manufacturer

The Roths and The Fachlers

of marbled end papers for bookbinding; Gavin Jones Nurseries; and Marmet, a manufacturer of high quality baby carriages.

Bernard started taking Carol and Peter to Shabbat morning services at 40 Hallmead. Carol recalls: 'This was a very long walk for two small children, so we went in our old Vauxhall, LMX 596, and left it a few streets away and walked to *Shul* which was in a terraced house. I remember that the ladies' gallery was in what would have been the kitchen. There was a gap at the top of the wall so that the service could be heard. Not many women came to *shul* in those days, and I usually stayed with my father. I remember being surrounded by long black coats and a lot of very loud murmuring.'

After the service, Bernard and the children were invited to Sali and Bertha Bornstein's home for kiddush. Carol remembers the children all playing together, and the wonderful spread of food.

When Bernard's employer sent him to Australia for three months, Marion, Carol and Peter spent the High Holidays with the Fachlers at 79 Hallmead. Carol recalls: 'I have a vivid memory of all of us children congregating in one of the small bedrooms that seemed to have elastic walls. Yanky was entertaining us by miming. I remember he plucked a needle out of the air and held it in his right hand and with his left hand took hold of a thread and showed us 'virtually' how to thread the needle. As an impressionable eight-year-old, I was mesmerised by this show.'

During her last two years at school, Carol regularly babysat for Gail and Jonathan Vanger and for the four Kirsch children – Judy, Ruth, Daniel and Jonathan. In the summer of 1966, Carol had a summer job at Kir Gloves, the high-fashion glove factory in Hitchin owned by the Kirsch brothers. Between completing her A levels in June 1967, and starting the Cambridge College of Arts and Technology, Carol worked as a stacker at Richard Vanger's Fox's Stores on the Grange Estate.

In the days before emails and faxes, people from overseas who wanted to get married in Israel had to go through several hoops in order to prove their Jewishness. I remember going to the Tel Aviv Rabbinate a couple of times to testify on behalf of English friends who were marrying Israeli girls. When Carol Eini (Roth) wanted to get married in Israel, she approached the Haifa Rabbinate because her intended, Aharon, lived in Haifa. The Rabbinate demanded proof of Carol's

Jewishness. Their attitude changed completely when Carol produced a certificate of single status issued by Reb Oosher Feuchtwanger. The Haifa rabbis could barely conceal their surprise when Carol nonchalantly informed them that she did not require the services of a duty rabbi because Rabbi Solomon Sassoon would be performing the chuppah.

Letchworth was very well represented at Carol's wedding in 1971, where a Yiddish-speaking Baghdadi rabbi (Rabbi Sassoon) presided over the marriage of another Yiddish-speaking Baghdadi (Aharon Eini) who had been raised in a Yiddish-speaking orphanage in Jerusalem. Several members of the Fachler family were there, and a special guest was Moishe Bornstein. A few days after the wedding, Reb Oosher Feuchtwanger was the guest of honour at the *Sheva Brachot* in the home of Aharon's sister in Petach Tivkva.

Patricia Reifen (Hassan), a graduate of the Letchworth Talmud Torah, also faced difficulties when she wanted to get married in Israel. Rabbi Shlomo Kook of the Rehovot Rabbinate requested a letter from the London Beth Din confirming that she was Jewish. When Patricia asked whether a letter from Rabbi Sassoon would be sufficient, Rabbi Kook was shocked. 'You know Rabbi Sassoon?' The Sassoon and Feuchtwanger families sent Patricia a beautiful Pesach Haggadah which she still has. The commentary is by Rabbi Dr Marcus Lehman of Mainz, Selina Sassoon's grandfather.

Bernard and Marion Roth did not join the 1971 exodus from Letchworth, and Bernard later became a magistrate and served on the Letchworth and Hitchin Bench. The strength of the close Letchworth ties can be seen in the fact that my brother Rabbi Mordechai Fachler was asked to officiate at the funerals of both Bernard and Marion Roth.

When Leslie Ward got a job working on guided missile systems with British Aerospace in Baldock in 1949, he and Ruth and their three-year-old son Russell moved to Letchworth from Manchester. Accompanying them to their home in 33 Broadwater Avenue was Leslie's Latvian-born father, Mike Ward (Michael Herman Wagenheim), who died in Letchworth in 1957. Ruth was very artistic, and an excellent portrait painter. The Wards became very friendly with the Fachlers, and Ruth helped my mother decorate 37 Sollershott East when we moved in there in 1958.

33 Broadwater Avenue, home of the Ward family

Even though Ruth's parents in Higher Broughton, Salford, were orthodox, the Wards were not a practising family. Nevertheless, Leslie and Ruth integrated well within the Jewish community of Letchworth, and both Russell and Cedric attended the Talmud Torah. According to Neil Roland, both of his older brothers retained a strong awareness and respect for their Jewish identity throughout their short lives.

Haki Sassoon remembers meeting Russell when he – Russell – accompanied his parents on their frequent visits to the Sassoons to discuss the arrangements for Russell's barmitzvah. The two boys hit it off, and stayed in contact as young adults. Haki bumped into Russell in London, and visited Russell's ramshackle house. Haki was impressed that Russell was doing the plumbing himself, and he says that he picked up some valuable tips on pipes and plumbing.

Ruth kept a diary. Neil Roland: 'There is a diary entry on 9 February 1962, a Friday, when my Mother and Leslie attended Russell's Hitchin Grammar School to decide Russell's sixth form course. The following day, Saturday, Leslie went to finalise the sale of his yacht, 'Vetiver', which he had decided to sell, returning at 2.30pm. They went together to Letchworth Library, and that evening, Saturday night, Ruth and Leslie went to Letchworth's Broadway cinema to see *Two Loves*, starring Shirley MacLaine and Laurence Harvey. Strange to think that these two actors were, apart from Mother, the last people Leslie ever saw. Mother's diary entry for Sunday 11 February reads simply: "My darling died 7.15am." There is not a single other entry for the year.'

As a painter, and an avid member and exhibitor of Letchworth Art Society, Ruth had painted her most seminal artworks during her Letchworth years. She designed the covers for the Letchworth Adult Education Settlement Social Study group. Ruth worked in her cedarwood studio located a few roads away from their Broadwater Avenue home, to which she escaped from her children to paint. When her son Cedric, on his bicycle, discovered her hiding place, Ruth had the studio rebuilt in the large rear garden of their home at 33 Broadwater Avenue.

Ruth had held her first solo exhibition at the Grabowski Gallery in Chelsea in April 1961, which garnered positive reviews in the national press. I can still remember how proud my mother Chava was of her friend. Neil Roland is convinced that had Leslie Ward not died, and had Ruth remained in Letchworth, her career would have blossomed. When Ruth and the children moved to Sale, Ruth had her Broadwater Avenue studio dismantled and rebuilt in their Cheshire garden.

Cedric's barmitzvah in 1962 was held just six months after Leslie died. Ruth made the barmitzvah on her own and had the party at her home for 115 people, catering it entirely herself. Her son Neil still has his mother's diary/address book containing the details of everyone who was invited: 'With her hallmark exemplary organisational way, she recorded the date they responded, whether able to attend, what had been sent, date of thank you letter – all in easy to see order, yet also peppered with artistic flair – little asides about one person hating pineapple, and another who could not have salmon.'

Ruth's diary entries show that Ellen and Marion Capone, 351 Western Way, Letchworth, attended the barmitzvah, and received a thank you note from Cedric for the £1:1:0d gift. The diary shows that Mr and Mrs Fachler and family at 37 Sollershott East gave Cedric a book on Jewish history, and they also gave books to Russell and Hazel. The Hassans, of The Chilterns, Benslow Rise, Hitchin, gave Cedric a tie pin. Sidney Jackson of 5 Coach Drive, Hitchin, gave Cedric a book, *Discovery and Exploration*. Mrs. Kahn, 16 Cowslip Hill, sent a book about life under the sea. Other attendees at the barmitzvah were the Kirsch family, Dr Harold Maxwell from Luton, the Pressburgers, the Roths, the Sassoons and the Vangers. The Schischas gave Cedric gold cufflinks inscribed with his initials.

According to Neil, Letchworth became synonymous with the pleasures and hopes, the positivity and creativity of a time that Ruth held in the highest esteem. So beloved and profound was Ruth's affection for Letchworth and its community that she imbued Neil – who never lived there – with a real sense of how special the town was. Neil says that he and his father Theo only ever heard good things of Letchworth. 'Mother's reluctance to leave Letchworth, borne solely on having been thrust into widowhood with three children, was a topic which followed her for the rest of her life.'

Ruth's daughter Hazel Schwartz (Ward) lives in Canada, and is a very enthusiastic follower of all things Letchworth. When Theo Roland died in 2020, I was invited by his son Neil – whom I had never met – to conduct a zoom *shiva* session 'because I am so mindful of the Letchworth connection between our two families.'

Long before the Tesco supermarket chain opened its first store in Letchworth in the 1960s, the town had a strong Tesco connection. In 1984, when I was living in Israel, I was introduced socially to English-born Linda. We started playing Jewish geography, and I mentioned that I was from Letchworth. 'I have family in Letchworth,' said Linda, and started rattling off names: 'Cissie Cohen, Sydney Fox, Harry Fox, Celina Wegier and Richard Vanger.' 'So you must be related to the Tesco founder, Jack Cohen,' I said. 'Yes', replied Linda, 'He's my grandfather!' This discovery of a common Letchworth heritage cemented a lifelong friendship.

Jack Cohen was married to Cissie (Sarah), the daughter of Benjamin Fuchs (Fox), a tailor who evaded the Polish military by moving with his wife Chaya Pearl to England early in the 20th century. Benjamin and

Chaya Pearl arrived in Letchworth in 1939. In Maurice Corina's authorised biography of Jack Cohen, *Pile it High, Sell it Cheap*, we read: 'Jack [John Cohen] bought a small property near his mother-in-law – at 46 Baldock Road – for £900. Jack's brother-in-law, Harry Fox, one of the first Tesco pioneers, eventually went into the retail business with his brother Sidney at Letchworth. Sidney Fox eventually opened his own shops in Hitchin, Letchworth, Baldock and Stevenage.' I remember two branches of Fox's Stores in Letchworth – one in the centre of town, and one on the Grange Estate.

Chaya Pearl Fox had a brother, Israel Wegier, in Warsaw. Israel had three children: Celina, Yaakov (Kuba) and Daniel. When Celina was in her early twenties, she wrote to her aunt Chaya Pearl in Letchworth to ask whether she would like some help with the household chores. Chaya Pearl agreed, and in the late 1930s, Celina arrived in Letchworth, a move

Celina Wegier

which almost certainly saved her life. Celina became like a sister to her Fox cousins, Cissie, Hyman, Harry, Phil and Sid.

During the war, Celina's brother Kuba and his wife and son Rishik fled to Belarus, but were placed in a ghetto after the Nazi invasion of the USSR. Kuba secured a permit to work outside the ghetto, and when he learned that the ghetto was about to be liquidated, he smuggled Rishik out of the ghetto, where a work colleague agreed to look after him. After the war, Celina heard that Kuba and his wife had been murdered, but that young Rishik had survived and was now living in an orphanage run by The American Jewish Joint Distribution Committee near Warsaw.

Rishik's aunt Celina in Letchworth decided that she had to bring him to England. She knew of Rabbi Solomon Schonfeld's efforts to bring Jewish orphans to Britain, and she suggested to her cousin Cissie and Jack Cohen that a donation to Rabbi Schonfeld's rescue operation might help save Rishik. In 1946, 14-year-old Rishik arrived at Leith Harbour, close to Southend, on one of the last boats out of Poland before the country turned communist.

Rishik – now called Richard – went to live with Sid and Bessie Fox and their only daughter Cynthia, at 19 Willian Way, Letchworth. Richard rapidly learned English, and attended Pixmore School until he was sixteen. He became the headmaster's regular chess partner. After leaving school, Richard worked at Fox's Stores on Letchworth's Grange Estate. Richard married Lilian Cohen from Hitchin, and they lived in a small flat above Fox's Stores on the estate. Sid and Bessie Fox left Letchworth for London after the war, and their daughter Cynthia married Clive Tanchen. The Tanchens later came to live in Letchworth in Field Lane.

Richard and Lilian had two children, Gail Zivan Neriya (Vanger), born in 1956, and Jonathan, born in 1958. Gail recalls: 'Even though at home our parents may not always have kept an observant lifestyle, it was important for them that we had a strong Jewish identity and that we participated in the Letchworth community's Jewish educational system and that we went to synagogue every Shabbat morning.

'The festivals were extra special occasions, and I remember Purim fancy dress and Chanuka gatherings. In later years, we youngsters used to write and perform our own plays or organize activities, like "All About

Gail and Jonathan Vanger at Purim

Israel" evenings. We wrote to the Jewish Agency, and they sent us pamphlets. On Purim, we watched with anticipation as Rabbi Sassoon set fire to the wonderful picture he drew of Haman.'

Gail remembers the whole family walked home together from services at the Schischas' house, all dressed up in their best outfits. She remembers my father Eli's shofar blowing, and sitting on her great-aunt Celina's knee and measuring how many more pink pages in the prayer book until the end. Gail and her friend Ruth Keller (Kirsch) fasted for the first time when they were nine years old. Yom Kippur services that year were held at the home of the Pollocks.

The Shabbos Group played a formative role in the informal education of many of Letchworth's Jewish youngsters. Gail: 'I remember

Gail Vanger's birthday party

Melanie Fachler and Judy Kirsch leading the way. We used to return to the living room after Kiddush, sit round in a circle and sing, play quiz games and listen to stories. We were all different ages, but we all had a great time. Michael Wieselberg brought information on Bnei Akiva, that for some of us became a stepping-stone to broaden our horizons. We met other Jewish youth at Bnei Akiva camps. Thanks to our Zionist camp experience, Ruth and I started making plans to establish our own kibbutz one day. In the meantime, we learnt Hebrew songs, and even appeared at an old age home with our *Erev Shel Shoshanim* repertoire!'

Gail feels lucky to have been part of a caring community: 'Attending Hebrew classes seemed the most natural thing to do. When the Letchworth Cheder closed, we travelled to the Luton Cheder where Yanky Fachler was the headmaster.'

In 1968, the four Vangers – parents and children – were treated to a holiday in Israel by Sid Fox. It was love at first sight, and the family soon started making plans to move permanently to Israel. In 1970, the same year as the Sassoons made aliya, the Vangers – and Celina - also left Letchworth and moved to Israel. Richard once told me how he went back to Poland long before the fall of Communism to visit the family of

The Fox Family

the woman who had helped him survive the war, Teresa Dolenga-Wrzoseki. He not only helped the family buy their own house, but he also made sure that his wartime saviours were recognised as Righteous Among the Nations by Jerusalem's Yad Vashem Holocaust Memorial Centre.

Letchworth tales: Abductions, Ultimatums and more

"Yossele's abductor was an evil woman."

NORMAN OSTER

'If you go to Letchworth, don't bother coming back.'

Eli Fachler's younger sister, my aunt Miriam Fachler, arrived in London with the Kindertransport in mid-August 1939, and was almost immediately evacuated as part of Operation Pied Piper to Hemel Hempstead in Hertfordshire. She was billeted with a non-Jewish family, who asked Miriam to call them Auntie Alice and Uncle Bert. Miriam recalls: 'In all the five years that I spent living with my non-Jewish foster parents in Hemel Hempstead, I do not remember a single visit from the Jewish Refugee Committee. I certainly felt abandoned. This was a very unhappy time for me.'

Miriam had to wait some thirty months before being reunited with her brother, my father Eli. She had last seen him when he left Berlin in May 1939, and she had not seen him throughout his happy time in his farm school on the estate of Lord Balfour in Scotland. In late 1941, Eli managed to spend a few days in Hemel Hempstead on his way to joining his Buckingham kibbutz. Auntie Alice disapproved of Eli's influence, correctly sensing that he was concerned for his sister's lack of Jewish environment.

Alice had earlier forced Miriam to leave school and work in a factory to help the family finances. She did not want to let Miriam go, and told her that she owed it to her to stay with her. After all, the 'Jews' had not given her shelter and decent living conditions – only Alice had saved Miriam's life.

Every time Miriam visited Eli on his Buckingham kibbutz, Eli's girlfriend Chava Becker was in Letchworth with her parents. Determined to finally meet her prospective sister-in-law, Chava arranged with Miriam to meet in the High Wycombe bus station. Miriam takes up the story: 'We sat in the bus shelter, talking and talking until it got dark. When we kissed good-bye, I started crying. Chava thought she had said something to upset me. 'It's not what you said, it's what you didn't say that made me cry,' I told her. Whenever I had been with religious people, all they had ever done was to berate me for not being more observant. I was so very moved that Chava had never mentioned religious observance. Our friendship started from that moment."

When Miriam first met my grandparents Sam and Melanie Becker and my aunt Marian for the first time at my parents' wedding, they urged her to come and spend Shabbat with them in Letchworth. They fixed a date in February 1945, but Miriam's foster-mother strenuously objected to Miriam going to Letchworth for the weekend. 'Alice basically issued me with a stark ultimatum. She would pack my case and place it by the front door. When I returned from work that Friday lunch time, I had two choices: I could either take the case and enter the house, and nothing more would be said; or I could pick up my case and take the bus to Letchworth, in which case I was never to darken her doorstep again.'

Alice was as good as her word. On the doorstep stood Miriam's suitcase. Alice did not allow her into the house. Miriam caught the first of three buses to Letchworth. 'I was eighteen, I was homeless, and I was penniless. Marian Becker, who was working in Hitchin, happened to be waiting for the Letchworth bus when she saw me sobbing on the upper deck. I poured out my sorry tale. "Now I have no home," I wailed. "Yes you have," said Marian, who was by now also crying. "Our Letchworth home is your home, my parents will never let you go again."'

Marian was right. Miriam became the third daughter in the Becker family home. Letchworth finally allowed Miriam to realize her fervent wish to resume living in a Jewish environment. 'I met so many new people and was welcomed everywhere. I had lost five years of living Jewishly. I worried how I was going to catch up, but catch up I did. I slowly regained my lifestyle and my confidence, and I blossomed in the warm embrace of the Becker family and the Letchworth community.'

The global Letchworth fraternity

One Sunday morning in the early 1950s at about 6am, I was awoken by an unusual sound in our Hallmead home – yelling. It was my father on the phone using a language I did not understand. I was full of questions. Why at 6am? Why Sunday morning? What was the language? Who were you talking to? And why so loud?

My father Eli later explained that he was talking to his uncle Yukel Milchmann in Poland in Yiddish. This was the first time I heard that my father had an uncle living in Poland. Polish Jews, it seems, knew that Sunday morning was the only time that the Yiddish-speaking Polish state censors were not monitoring international phone calls – because they were hung-over after drinking heavily on Saturday night. At a very early age, I discovered Cold War intrigue in Letchworth.

In 1959, the Milchmanns finally received exit visas from the Polish government. Eli travelled from Letchworth to Genoa to meet his uncle and family who were on their way to start a new life in Australia. Eli wanted to give them $100, but he did not have that sort of cash available. Our neighbour Shloime Stern came to the rescue and lent my father the money. Thirty years later, Yukel's son was still carrying the $100 note in his wallet. The family had used it as collateral for raising other funds, but had never spent it.

Almost sixty years after Shloime lent my father the $100, I was staying with Yukel's grandson in Melbourne. I was talking to a member of the Jewish community, who mentioned that his wife had family in London. 'What's their name?' I asked. 'Stern,' he told me. I rattled off all the names of all the Sterns I knew from Letchworth, including of course Shloime Stern. The guy's wife shrieked: 'Shloime Stern is my great-uncle,' and she rushed to show me her late father's autobiography, which included a photo of Shloime, whom I recognised immediately. Yet another example of the global Letchworth fraternity.

Hitchin Ambush – the Dr Sydney Baigel story

In 1955, a young doctor, Dublin-born Sydney Baigel, was about to take up his appointment at the Lister Hospital in Hitchin, the nearest town to Letchworth (and where so many so-called Letchworth-born people were actually born.) Sidney's good friend and mentor Dr Meyer Fisher told him: 'Don't worry. You won't be isolated there. You will soon come across the small Jewish community in Letchworth which is only a few miles away.' Sydney took up his post, but as he said: 'My Jewish life consisted of my weekly copy of the *Jewish Chronicle* and keeping kosher by keeping to a vegetarian diet.'

One Saturday night, in the winter of early 1955, whilst Sydney was on duty in Lister Hospital's Accident & Emergency Department, a tall gentleman came in with a very small boy. The registration card read 'Chaim Fachler, Hallmead, Letchworth.' With no preliminaries, the father told Sydney: 'Coming out of *shul* after prayers, my son fell and grazed his head.' Sydney examined Chaim, and could not detect anything that warranted bringing the child to hospital.

This charade was being witnessed by my mother Chava, who was lurking in the doorway. Sydney turned to my parents and said: 'You know, there's absolutely nothing wrong with his forehead. So why are you really here?' With no hint of an apology, Eli replied with his trademark self-assured smile: 'We knew there was a Jewish doctor here. We left several messages, and finally we had to come in person to find you.'

Chaim himself has only a very hazy recollection of the whole incident. 'I remember falling off my tricycle, but whether I even had a scratch, I don't know.' Sydney became a frequent visitor to the Fachlers' Hallmead home. He was introduced to the Sassoons, the Feuchtwangers, the Bornsteins, the Schischas and many others in the community. In the summer months, he played tennis with Eli in Hitchin on a Sunday afternoon.

When Sydney moved to his next post at the North Manchester General Hospital, he was urged by Chava to contact her sister, my aunt Marian Lopian (Becker). When Sydney failed to call Marian quickly enough, my uncle Yankel went one Saturday night to find Sydney at his hospital. The strong bonds formed in Letchworth now extended to Manchester.

A mystery woman comes to Letchworth

There was something different about the woman who first visited Letchworth in the early 1960s. She was clearly ultra-orthodox. She was very striking, tall, well-dressed, and – dare I say it – not terribly Jewish looking. She spoke excellent English. But she refused to spell out what cause she was raising funds for.

On one of her visits to Letchworth, my brother Meir remembers her declaring that she had dreamt that she would marry a *gadol* – a learned leader of the Jewish community. The only one who fitted that description in our community was Rabbi Sassoon. My mother Chava warned the mystery woman that that Rabbi Sassoon was strictly off-limits!

My father was reluctant to give money for a cause that she refused to divulge. At the weekly kiddush in our home one Shabbat, the mystery guest mentioned that the following day, Sunday, she had to catch a ferry to Calais, in order to attend to important personal matters in Paris. Derek Pollock, a regular at the kiddush, said that he and his wife Goldie happened to be traveling from Letchworth to Paris on the very same ferry, and that they would gladly give her a lift.

At the kiddush the following Shabbat, Derek yelled: 'She's an evil witch, I tell you!!' He explained that they were late for the ferry, and he told her that they would have to wait until the next sailing. She insisted that her Paris meeting was too important to miss, and she demanded that they catch the earlier ferry. Derek told his kiddush audience that a drive that usually takes up to three hours took half an hour – and he repeated: 'She's an evil witch!'

Meanwhile, in Israel, a massive manhunt was underway for a young boy called Yossele Schumacher. His deeply religious grandparents Nachman and Miriam Shtarkes reached Israel in 1958 after years of exile under the Soviet Communist regime. They were soon joined by their daughter Ida and her husband Alter Schumacher. The Shtarkes were unhappy that their daughter and son-in-law were drifting into a secular lifestyle. In late 1959, Yossele's grandparents colluded in his abduction. For two years, no one could find him. His ultra-orthodox abductors decided to smuggle him out of the country.

The person chosen to carry this out was Ruth Ben David, formerly Madeleine Feraille, a 40-year-old French Catholic university graduate who had served in the French Resistance. After divorcing her husband, she and her son converted to Orthodox Judaism, and she began to identify with the anti-Zionist Neturei Karta. Ruth Ben-David disguised Yossele as a girl, and using a forged passport, she managed to get him out of Israel, first to Switzerland, then to France, then to the UK, and finally to a family of Satmar Hasidim in Williamsburg, Brooklyn.

Yossele was finally tracked down by the Mossad in cooperation with the FBI, and reunited with his mother. His uncle was extradited from the UK to Israel, where he was sentenced to jail for kidnapping. The Israel government dropped all proceedings against anyone else involved, including Ruth Ben-David – the mystery woman remembered so vividly by members of the Letchworth Jewish community.

In 1965, Ruth Ben-David hit the headlines again when she controversially married 67-year-old recently widowed Rabbi Amram Blau, the revered founder of the extreme Neturei Karta sect. One Saturday evening, I accompanied my father to an apartment in Jerusalem's Meah Shearim to join the elderly head of the household as he recited *havdala*. The door was opened by the rabbi's striking-looking and much younger wife. It was *Rebbitzen* Blau, previously Ruth Ben-David, who had visited our Letchworth home 10 years earlier. She had fulfilled her premonition that she would marry a *gadol*.

This is not the end of the Letchworth connection to the mystery woman. Norman Oster, who spent several months in Letchworth as a boy in 1941-1942, was the attorney appointed by the Mossad to chase Shalom Shtarkes through the British legal system. Today, Norman is still very friendly with Yossele Schumacher. And when I first asked Norman about Rebbitzen Blau, he used similar language to what Derek Pollock had used in the Letchworth kiddush: 'She was an evil woman!'

An artist inspired by Letchworth's tables

Derek Pollock's daughter Anna Finchas (Pollock) passed away in 2011 at the young age of sixty. Poignantly, the very last time she left her home was when her sister Jean Shindler (Pollock) brought her to visit my brother Mordechai Fachler in his sick bed in London. I was privileged to be present at this sad meeting between two very sick Letchworth-born contemporaries.

Jean says that Anna always credited the Jewish community in Letchworth for making her the artist she became: 'Letchworth instilled in her an early passion for Israel, and she was active in the Soviet Jewry agitation of the early seventies. A chance encounter with the sculptor

Chaim Gross, upon whom Chaim Potok based the teacher of Asher Lev in *My Name is Asher Lev*, led Anna to attend a fine art course at the University of Hertfordshire in Hatfield.'

Anna later won a prize in the Jewish Artist of the Year Award for a work entitled 'Shulchan Aruch' – the Table Laid. As Jean explains: 'It was the laid tables which Anna and I had seen at the Letchworth homes of the Sassoons, Fachlers and others that inspired her art and her own home. Each week, she and I would re-create the Shabbat table that we witnessed at these wonderful families.'

Letchworth – the seventh and final foster home for Sue Deutsch (Knight)

Here in her own words is Sue's story:

Chava Fachler was my seventh and last foster mother. I lived in her home for eight years, the longest of any home in my childhood. In the autumn of 1962, I had just turned 7 years old and was a new boarder at Arundale House, the boarding section for young children at St Christopher School.

Cheder children on Chanukah, with Rabbi Feuchtwanger – (Rabbi Feuchtwanger is standing on the right)

The children of the home who were already residents gathered around me and poked through my meagre belongings in my suitcase. One girl asserted her dominance and demanded that I relinquish all my tuck to her. I was given a drawer for my clothes, and the rest of my things were distributed for common use. It was not a safe environment for a child, particularly if they were Jewish, but we somehow knew not to tell.

On a fateful winter day in 1962, I walked alone in my patent leather shoes already too small for me, with holes in their soles lined with newspaper to soak up the rain, wearing a note pinned to my threadbare coat. The house at 37 Sollershott East had an entrance by a green at the end of a little lane off Baldock Road, with a large iron gate. It was thus I arrived on Auntie Chava's doorstep, after walking down the long tarmac driveway, past a canopy of pine trees.

Afraid to ring the front-door bell, I went around to the side back door and knocked. Auntie Chava opened the door and I briefly looked at her kind and surprised face before lowering my eyes to the ground. If I managed to speak at all, I was barely audible. I mumbled my name, the fact that my daddy died when I was six months old and I that I had been sent by my uncle for cheder lessons. There was a woman standing behind Auntie Chava at the back of the kitchen, who exclaimed something in Spanish. I later learned that this was Felisa, the Spanish au pair, urging Auntie Chava to take me in because I looked so pitiful. Not only was I invited in; I was given food and a pair of Melanie's shoes that she had outgrown.

I still remember the look on Chava's face when she saw me. She told me years later that I looked like a child Holocaust survivor, malnourished, with missing teeth, and my hair falling out. Even though she had five children of her own, she took me in, nurtured me, fought for me and never gave up, despite being told I was a lost cause of subnormal intelligence. She was fierce and kind and refused to accept what teachers, headmasters, and social workers told her was a futile effort. She recognized trauma and worked to heal it.

There is a treasured black and white photograph in my home. In it, Chava is standing in front of the rose garden in Letchworth, with Melanie, Meir and me. I look emaciated, yet I have a shy smile. What the photograph does not show is what came before it was taken – an action that was a defining moment in my life.

The photographer had asked to take a picture of Chava and her children. Melanie and Meir stood with her, and I stepped away, hanging back. Chava turned towards me, extended her arm, and said, 'Come here, Susieleh, you belong in this picture.' At 7 years old, this was the first time I felt that I belonged anywhere. Chava did not just take me into her Letchworth home, she took me into her heart. I would not be who I am today without my time with my Fachler family in the Letchworth Jewish community.

A mystery soldier comes to Letchworth

I first met the mystery visitor to Letchworth in 1969 when I came to my parents for Shabbat. I was introduced to the Israeli boyfriend of my mother Chava's new Israeli au pair, Dahlia – or at least that's the name she gave us. I got chatting to the boyfriend, and he told me he was in the Israel Defence Force (IDF). I asked him where he was serving. I was very surprised by his answer: 'Cherbourg in France.' To the best of my knowledge, Israeli soldiers did not usually do their military service overseas, so I continued questioning the young soldier: 'And what do you do in Cherbourg?'

His answer only served to further puzzle me: 'I sit on top of a hill and I look through my binoculars at the ships in the harbour.' By now, I was scratching my head. An Israeli soldier who spends his week sitting on a hill in Cherbourg and spends his weekends in Letchworth? All very bizarre.

All became clear a few weeks later when the international media broke the story that five missile boats had mysteriously disappeared from their Cherbourg shipyard. They had been ordered and paid for by the Israeli navy, but the French had placed an embargo on them. In a complex subterfuge operation over Christmas, 80 Israeli navy officers and sailors – including the young man I had quizzed in Letchworth – had quietly descended on Cherbourg and spirited the five boats to Israel.

As soon as I heard the news, I realised that Dahlia's sailor boyfriend really had been looking through binoculars down on Cherbourg harbour. And by the time the story broke, he was already almost in Haifa. According to my brother Meir, Dahlia also disappeared at the same time – which leads us to believe that she may well also have been part of the cover story, and that she was not called Dahlia.

British and US soldiers in Letchworth

After the end of the Second World War, the British government soon decided that the post-war peacetime manpower requirements of the British Army were not being effectively met. The National Service Act came into force in January 1949. One of the Jewish boys who joined the RAF in 1957 was John Singer from Birmingham. He was stationed in RAF Henlow in Bedfordshire. Because he came from a kosher home, John was permitted to live off camp. He was billeted with the Angel family in Hallmead. Once we Fachlers managed to overcome his Birmingham accent, John became a permanent fixture in our Letchworth household.

On 2 November 1959, Minister of Transport Ernest Marples opened the M1, the first motorway in Britain linking London and Birmingham. In July 1960, I was a very excited passenger in John's open-top red sports car as we drove from Letchworth to Luton, where we joined the M1 to Birmingham. I stood for much of the journey – no seat belts in those days. I still remember the thrill of the wind rushing through my hair.

Here is John's account of meeting the Fachlers: 'My first memory of Letchworth was arriving at a two-up one-down council house. My stay in this lovely garden city was to last nearly eighteen months, and I found myself in a seriously orthodox community with a *stiebel* just doors away from where I was living. It was here that I met the Fachlers. One *Shabbos*, Eli Fachler took me home from *Shul* and I was welcomed as "the young airman."'

'When the Fachlers moved to the other side of town to a larger property, their home became my second home. I spent many happy hours with the Fachler children, playing table-tennis and more importantly enjoying the wonderful meals served up by Eli's wife Chava.'

There were other connections between Letchworth and military personnel stationed in bases in the area. Johnny Cohen recalls staying with relatives on one of these bases in the Letchworth area - Johnny's father's first cousin Sophie and her husband Philip Camberg. Philip, who worked for US Naval Systems Air Command, was the brother of

Muriel Spark, the Jewish-born novelist (*The Prime of Miss Jean Brodie*) who went to such lengths to hide the fact that she was Jewish.

Chaim Schwartz was a US Army chaplain stationed in a base near Cambridge. Sue Deutsch (Knight) recalls: 'Chaim and his wife Reeva – who I think was Israeli –were regular Shabbat visitors to the Fachler household in Letchworth between 1969 and 1971. He was very easy to talk to.'

Letchworth welcomes the young airman's girlfriend

Sarah Davis (formerly Singer) has very strong recollections of Letchworth: 'My introduction to Letchworth was a visit to the Fachler family when my boyfriend John Singer was doing his National Service and had already become a fixture in the household. So memorable was my visit to the small house in Hallmead that I can still remember what I wore, sixty four years later. I was only seventeen, but as the "young airman's girlfriend", I was made so welcome that I felt I had known Mr and Mrs Fachler and their children for ever.

'By the end of my first visit to Letchworth, my hosts had become Chava and Eli, and a firm bond had been created. The following year, John and I became engaged and we were delighted that Chava and Eli could attend our wedding in 1959 in Birmingham. We made many return visits to Letchworth for Shabbos and other occcasions after the family moved to Sollershot East. When our children came along – Debra in 1960 and Daniel in 1962 – Chava and Eli became surrogate grandparents.

'In my early twenties, Eli and Chava trusted me to "manage" their Sollershott East household with the help of Felicia, the Spanish au pair, on several occasions, so that they could go away. Even though John was my introduction to Chava and Eli, I never lost touch with the family after our divorce. I remarried, to Ron Davis, whose brother Ian in Dublin is a close friend of Yanky. Even though I never actually lived in Letchworth, the town will always hold fond memories.'

When Elijah the Prophet did not visit Letchworth

When I was learning my Bible as a child, I was taught that before the Mashiach – the Jewish Messiah – makes himself known, his appearance will be heralded by the Prophet Elijah. I gained my biblical knowledge mainly from a comic-strip Bible that I read and re-read, sometimes skipping over pages that contained scary images.

This illustrated Bible was the cause of a traumatic case of mistaken identity one Friday evening when I was about eight. I was attending Sabbath prayers as usual in our tiny Hallmead synagogue, when a newcomer entered. As I studied his features, I realised with a shock of recognition that I knew him. He was the Prophet Elijah, straight out of the pages of my illustrated Bible. No doubt about it. And once I convinced myself that it was him, I knew – I simply knew – that he had come to announce the arrival of the Messiah. I could hardly sleep that night. I woke next morning in great anticipation.

Now, I must admit that I did entertain a couple of niggling doubts. Why had Elijah chosen to make his announcement in our small town of Letchworth, of all places? How come I was the only person in our synagogue who recognised him? What was he waiting for? If he was bringing such an important message, shouldn't he be sharing it with our small congregation as soon as possible?

Casting my doubts aside, I reached the logical conclusion that Elijah was waiting for the three stars to appear in the night sky marking the end of Shabbat. That's when he would reveal himself to the astonished congregation.

Elijah did not proclaim the coming of the Messianic Age that Saturday evening in Letchworth. Nothing happened. There was no big announcement. No rejoicing. Just a damp squib. My comic-strip Bible had misled me. The mysterious stranger was not Elijah. He was, as Monty Python might have said, 'just a naughty boy.'

A road trip to Letchworth

After Ruth Roland (Ward) died in 2011, her second husband Theo and their son Neil made a road trip from Manchester to Letchworth. This was Neil's first-ever time in the town about which his mother Ruth had waxed lyrical for 50 years. Here is Neil's description of the visit:

'When we reached Letchworth, we drove to Broadwater Avenue, to look again at number 33, which is still an elegant, attractive early Garden City home. The current owners who have lived there for a number of years, appeared in the garden. We introduced ourselves, and they showed us around their home. I noticed that the front door was modern and not at all in keeping with the rest of the house. They told me that when they added their porch, the Letchworth Garden City Society had told them that the front door which had been on the house was not the original, and they therefore did not allow the family to put it back.

'This was clearly nonsensical. The old front door was still in the back garden, awaiting an uncertain future. As soon as I saw it, I recognised it from the family photos taken outside the house. With its hand-blown bubble glass and wonderful arts and crafts brass door knocker, there was no mistaking that this was the original door.

'When the current owners offered the door to me, I jumped at the opportunity, and this bit of Letchworth is now proudly part of my Manchester home. On the other side of the door are the memories of those thirteen happy years that my mother Ruth spent amongst the very unique Letchworth community.'

Tangiers meets Bournemouth in Letchworth

In 1962, Louise Benoliel arrived in England from Tangiers in Morocco. She came from an orthodox family, and had received a scholarship from the American Jewish Joint Distribution Committee to study nursing at the London Jewish Hospital. Louise had no family in England, and the atmosphere in the hospital was not great. The only friend that Louise made was another Jewish student nurse, Marion Capone from Letchworth.

In early 1963, Marion invited Louise to visit Letchworth, telling her: 'Although we don't keep a kosher home, friends of ours, the Fachlers, will be happy to put you up for Shabbat.' And so it was. Louise began visiting my parents' home regularly, and she made a big impact on all my family. During her weekend visits to Letchworth, Louise befriended Chaim Lader from Bournemouth. Chaim was working in Letchworth for a Jewish boss, Mr Curran, and he boarded with a non-Jewish family. My mother Chava made Chaim an offer he could not refuse: 'I will provide you with supper every evening if you give Hebrew lessons to my children Melanie and Meir, and to a few other children in the community.' A deal was struck, and Chaim would often spend Shabbat with my parents.

Love blossomed, and Louise and Chaim married in December 1966 in Tangiers. Their wedding was attended by Trevor Fenner and his wife Inge – Trevor had been a regular visitor in Letchworth from Cambridge. Another Cambridge student who arrived in Tangiers one day after the wedding (but in time for the Sheva Berachot) was Michael Wieselberg, a regular feature in Letchworth. Louise and Chaim had really wanted Chava and Eli to attend their wedding. However, the Fachlers were precluded from flying to Tangiers because they had flown to Israel for another wedding that same week – mine!

Wartime Letchworth barmitzvah

Ariel Broch retains detailed memories of the 'very difficult and important year' leading up to his barmitzvah in wartime Letchworth. 'My barmitzvah preparations were in addition to my normal school activities, my evening Talmud classes, and my usual homework. I was not the first boy in my class to turn thirteen, so I knew what proficiency was expected of me. For nine months leading up to my barmitzvah, all my social activities were curtailed. No going out with friends, no cinema, no cricket –nothing except the studies to prepare myself for the day.

'I had a team of helpers at my disposal. Reb Nachman Dachs was there to teach me two speeches, one to recite in the synagogue, and the other at the celebration dinner. Reb Nachman would come once a week, and sip a glass of lemon tea, as he declaimed by heart the part we had just learnt. Every now and again, he would softly inject a word or rephrase a sentence, or emphasize a particular word.

'Then there was the very musical Mr. Dresner, a young man from Manchester who had volunteered to form a choir from the boys in the Hebrew classes. He helped me to prepare my Torah portion.

'On the Shabbat morning of my barmitzvah, I woke up early, got dressed slowly, savouring my new suit and new size-14 shirt with the detachable collar. In the synagogue hall, I sat in the front row between my father Rabbi Broch, and the Zhloviner Rav, who served as the ministering rabbi. I completed all the readings, followed by the final blessings, shouts of "Mazal Tov" from all quarters, and sweets raining down on me.

'I remained standing as the Zhloviner Rav took to the lectern and turned it around to face the congregation. He spoke in Yiddish for about twenty minutes, regaling the gathering on matters of law and tradition. Finally, he called me to stand in front of him and blessed me: "May the Lord keep you as Ephraim and Manasseh...."

'After the service, we all moved to a smaller hall where a kiddush was laid out. I went to a small dais, cleared my throat, and recited the first of my speeches. It went well, and I joined the family in walking home. We had borrowed long tables and benches and set them up in the long living room, to seat about sixty people. All the food had already been prepared, the herring, the pickles and salads were all in big bowls in the pantry, kept cool by a large block of ice.

'I sat at the head of the table between Father and the Zhloviner Rav, who both spoke. The president of the shul presented me with a book on behalf of the community. I stood up, cleared my throat. It was time for my second speech, which I delivered in Yiddish.'

The Bexfields of Letchworth

One morning in 1960, a toddler started climbing the stairs at 37 Sollershott East. While it is true that youngsters were not exactly a novelty in the Fachler home – Meir Fachler was just two at the time – this particular toddler was a stranger. No one knew who he belonged to. With great presence of mind, my mother Chava picked him up, and went out into the street to see if anyone was looking for him. Someone was – his frantic mother, Katherine (Kate) Bexfield, who lived over the road at 22 Sollershott East with her husband Arthur, Simon the runaway stair climber, and Daniel. Young Simon had crawled out of his home, crossed the road, and made his way through the open back door of the Fachler home and up the stairs.

This was the beginning of a lovely friendship between the two families. Meir and Simon were inseparable, and they eventually went to Hitchin Grammar School together. Apart from being very friendly neighbours, the Bexfields also happily assumed the role of Shabbos Goy – turning boilers on or off on Shabbat.

As my parents were chatting to Kate one day, she mentioned in passing that her maternal grandmother's name was Rosenblum. My parents did not want to press the point too far, but it is quite conceivable that Kate was halachically Jewish, since Jewishness passes down through the female line.

When the Fachler family left Letchworth for London in 1971, it was our neighbours the Bexfields who bought our Sollershott home. Over the years, many Fachler children and grandchildren have made the sentimental pilgrimage to 37 Sollershott East.

Letchworth, city of sanctuary

Letchworth had the reputation as a city of sanctuary for people who were often in quite dire and dramatic circumstances. But occasionally, Letchworth became a temporary city of sanctuary in a less dramatic context. One hot summer day in August 1962, sisters Judith and Sharon arrived home in London a day early from their month-long, international Bnei Akiva summer camp in Holland. They found the solid-oak front door to their Tudor-style Victorian house firmly locked. Judith takes up the story:

'I acutely recall feeling very alone in the world. Looking everywhere we could think of for half an hour, it slowly dawned on us both that our dear parents had forgotten all about us. Our family's timekeeping had always been notoriously lax. I wracked my brains for what to do.

'I will never know how or why I suddenly came up with the inspired idea of contacting the Fachler family. Yanky and I had been teenage pen-pals when he was at Carmel College. The Fachlers suddenly loomed large on my mental horizon. Where did they live? Letchworth? Where on earth was Letchworth? Somewhere miles away! Did I have their telephone number? No! How was I going to reach them? No idea!

'My mind was racing. Sharon and I were both so tired and hungry from the long journey home from Holland, and we wondered where we'd sleep that night. Ever-practical, I headed to our next-door neighbours, none other than Roger Moore of James Bond fame. I had occasionally baby-sat for his stunningly beautiful Italian second wife Luisa. Thankfully, Luisa immediately agreed to my using their telephone. In those days, telephones 'out in the sticks' were not yet direct-dialling.

'I had to sweet-talk the operator into looking up the Fachler's Letchworth phone number for me: 1454. Eventually, I somehow managed to make a collect call to the Fachlers. I heard the welcoming boom of Eli's voice: "Yes, of course I will accept the charges. Judy, how wonderful to hear from you. Yanky's still at home with us for the holidays and would love to see you. How would you like to meet up?" I almost cried with relief, and told him what had happened. I'll never forget his immediate reaction. He guffawed with laughter, and yelled out to his wife, "Chava, our old friends have forgotten all about their children returning from holiday, and the girls are sitting on their doorstep with nowhere to go!"

'Chava came to the phone, and I can still hear her loving, firm voice ringing in my ears today, "You and Sharon must come and stay with us in Letchworth for as long as you want. Just take a taxi and we'll pay for it." Pure, heartfelt generosity when it mattered most. I'll never forget it. I can't recall that taxi journey, apart from the fact that it was long. By late afternoon, we reached Letchworth. We were both welcomed with open arms and a bowl of hot chicken soup in the sprawling Letchworth home which was teeming with boisterous and happy children.

'On the next day, I can vividly remember sitting in the Fachler's fragrant, flower-filled garden, happily chatting to Yanky about our adventure, and why I'd even thought of calling the Fachlers in Letchworth. Fifty years later, when I visited Eli and Chava for lunch in their Jerusalem apartment, they kindly gifted me with the original photos of me and Sharon chatting with Yanky in their Letchworth garden. I will never forget the laughter, kindness and warmth we encountered that summer of 1962 in Letchworth.

Letchworth Pen Portraits

'If you saw a car driving towards you, and it looked as if no one was at the wheel, you knew it was Dr Jaffey.'

RUTH ROLAND (WARD)

The Hildesheimers

Scholem and Martha Hildesheimer lived in Mullway, opposite the Heinemanns. Martha was a granddaughter of Rabbi Marcus Lehmann of Mainz and was therefore a cousin of Selina Sassoon. The Hildesheimers' nephew Osher Lehmann spent eighteen months in Letchworth with his uncle and aunt, and mentioned Letchworth in his memoir, *Faith at the Brink*.

Actually, there was another Hildesheimer in Letchworth. When the Nazis came to power in 1933, Unilever Germany arranged for its Jewish employees to seek safety in Britain. One of these employees was Arnold Hildesheimer, grandson of a former Chief Rabbi of Germany, Rabbi Azriel Hildesheimer. Arnold's son Wolfgang attended St Christopher school.

The Abrahams family

Margaret Abrahams was born in Hungary, and after two years in Antwerp, she arrived in London in 1931. She spoke no English – but she did speak Yiddish, as well as German, Hungarian and Czechoslovakian. She worked as a cook for the Stamford Hill family of Harry Goodman, and in 1933 she married Harry Abrahams. Although he came from a very orthodox family, he personally was not at all orthodox. In late 1939, the Abrahams family arrived in Letchworth.

Moich Abrahams explains: "I always understood my mother to be of Chassidish stock. She maintained a kosher home, and bought her meat from Stern the butcher, who had a shop next to my father's upholstery in The Wynd. Later, the arrival of the Luton Kosher Foods van was always a notable event in our household.

"My mum lit Friday night candles and organised the correct meals and rituals for Passover and other festivals. Both my parents insisted that all three of their children – Bernard, myself and Lenny – went to Cheder. My mum occasionally attended services at the Sassoon, and I remember that Flora Sassoon used to write to her."

Walter Gottfried

I only learned from Moich Abrahams that Mr Gottfried had a first name. Throughout my childhood, he was only ever known as Mr Gottfried. I still remember one chag when we were short of a minyan, and Mr Gottfried must have overslept. A bunch of us accompanied Mr Schwab as he stood in the street outside Mr Gottfried's upstairs window in Hallmead. I don't remember whether Mr Schwab's extremely loud 'Ahems' did the trick.

Mr Gottfried had been an industrial chemist in Vienna, and arrived in England just before the war, only to be interned as an enemy alien. I remember him as a very quiet and unassuming man. My sister Melanie Klyne (Fachler) remembers: 'Mr Gottfried was a maths genius and a chess genius. When I did two maths A levels in one year, he used to come to the house and tutor me.' My foster sister Sue Deutsch (Knight) was taught chess by Mr Gottfried: 'He always let me win.'

Moich Abrahams recalls: 'Mr Gottfried came into our lives when I was twelve in 1953, and he lived with us for the next nineteen years until he could no longer manage the flights of stairs up to our second floor flat. He would join us for a meal on Friday nights or Shabbat. Thanks to him, I was able to become more academic. He was quite a chess master, the Hertfordshire champion, and he taught me to play.

'I asked him to help me with my homework, and he did, looking everything up in our newly acquired Encyclopaedia Britannica that I had nagged my dad into buying when I got into the grammar school. I did not mind how long it took to do my homework. Mr Gottfried taught me how to study. I repeatedly asked him for help, and gradually I got brave enough to ask a question in class when I didn't understand. Mr Gottfried helped my confidence grow.

The Schwabs and the Lichtigs

Leopold (Yehuda) and Henny (Hanna) Schwab had moved from Frankfurt to England in the 1930s. They arrived in Letchworth in 1940, and lived in Hallmead. Among their children was Herman – an insurance broker – and his Swiss-born wife Betty. Herman was a pillar of the community, and the Schwabs were among the families who delayed their return to London after the war until the early 1950s.

In the Jewish community at that time, it was rare to see a woman driving. Betty was an exception. I still remember my mother telling me that Betty was once delivering a cake to a friend and was so worried that the cake might fall that she took her eye off the road and ended up in someone's front garden.

Mr Lichtig was Joe Richman's brother-in-law. Mrs Lichtig and Betty Schwab gave birth on the same day in 1942 at the Hitchin Nursing Home: Mrs Lichtig to Joyce Hanna Kahn (Lichtig) and Betty Schwab to Esther. Joyce Hanna says: 'Esther and I are therefore "twins" and we have remained in touch until today.'

Because the Schwabs had a nasty landlord, the Lichtigs took the Schwabs into their home in Redhoods Way. The two families lived together until the Lichtigs returned to London, and then sold their house to the Schwabs.

The Jaffeys

The Jewish doctor in Letchworth was Saul Jaffey from Scotland. For a while, he had a Jewish colleague, Dr Ross. Saul and Frieda Jaffey were married in the Giffnock synagogue by Rabbi Kopul Rosen, and they had four boys: Joel, David, Paul and Robert. Robert (Robby) recalls: 'On Fridays my mother always lit the Shabbat candles, and continued to do so right up to the age of ninety five. We always made kiddush and had a Friday night supper. I always looked forward to one or more of my brothers coming home for the weekend.'

Dr Jaffey ran a baby clinic with very modern equipment and methods. My mother Chava recalls: 'No appointments were necessary, and mothers would just turn up with whichever baby needed looking at. His clinic was especially important for young mothers in Letchworth who – like me – did not have mothers of their own to help them with new babies.' According to my brother Chaim, every time Dr Jaffey made a house call, he always said reassuringly: 'I remember having that.' This seemed to calm everyone in the Fachler household.

Dr Jaffey was very short. Neil Roland says that he heard from his mother Ruth that if you saw a car in Letchworth driving towards you, and it looked as if no one was at the wheel, you knew it was Dr Jaffey.

Nobby Clark

Nobby Clark was a local Letchworth plumber who was employed by my father Eli to get 37 Sollershott East fit for habitation before our family moved in the summer of 1958. When Carol and Aharon Eini were visiting England in 2006, they made a trip to the USA. Carol continues with story: 'Our usual taxi driver couldn't take us from Letchworth to Gatwick Airport, and sent a colleague, a Mr Clark. During the journey to Gatwick, we got chatting, and the driver told us that he was known as Nobby Clark. "Oh," I said, "I knew a Nobby Clark about fifty years ago in the 1960s – he was a plumber who used to do work for my parents."

'That plumber is me. I now do part-time taxiing,' Nobby Clark said to Carol, 'I knew from the address it was you, but I was reluctant to say anything.' Nobby then asked Carol about the Fachlers, the Sassoons, and other Jewish families for whom he had worked.

The Reed family

Moich Abrahams remembers with sadness the scandal surrounding the Reed family, which owned a furniture store at the bottom of Leys Avenue. Apparently, the Reeds – father, mother, and three sons: Raymond, Norman and Peter – had been well integrated into the Letchworth Jewish community. There is a photograph of Raymond together with Moich's older brother Bernard, Stella Bornstein, Judy Stern, Mrs Rand and Rabbi Feuchtwanger and others.

When it became time for one of the boys to have his barmitzvah – he had already been tutored for the big day – Rabbis Sassoon and Feuchtwanger suddenly discovered that Mrs Reed was not halachically Jewish. There was no longer any question of a barmitzvah, and the family disappeared from the communal scene. Moich thinks that they may have held the barmitzvah at the more liberal community in Welwyn Garden City. The furniture business thrived in Letchworth for several years. Suzanne Freedman (Pressburger) remembers bumping into one of the Reed boys in London several years later.

Reuven and Sophie Angel

Reuven and Sophie Angel came to live in Letchworth during the 1950s when Reuven went to work at the Stern & Greenbaum meat factory and abattoir. Reuven had fought with the British Army under General Allenby in Palestine in the First World War.

Sophie Angel was a cook in the Letchworth Yeshiva for a while. Their rabbi son Chaim grew up in the East End of London, but never lived in Letchworth, although he visited frequently.

Tobi, Reuven and Sophie's granddaughter, was a frequent visitor to Letchworth: 'I loved to come and visit my grandparents while they lived in Letchworth. I used to come very often, either by train on Sundays or I was given a lift by people going up to Letchworth for *Shabbos*, usually Mr. Aby Van Praagh, often accompanied by his mother. I used to like to visit the Fachlers very much, but I was very shy. I also often visited the Sassoon family, and sometimes was invited to 'Tea' with Rabbi Sassoon's mother Selina. I was friendly with Shulamith Schischa, but after my grandfather passed away in early 1967 and my grandmother left Letchworth, I lost all contact with the community until Yanky's talk in Jerusalem.'

Laura Kahn

Rudolf Khan from Vienna arrived in Letchworth in the 1940s to work at the Anglia Match Company on Works Road. Huge poplar tree trunks were used for making matches and matchboxes. The company used to put reject matches out in the yard at the back, and children used to climb over the fence and take the matches home. The company was founded in 1935 by brothers Jacob and Julius Gourary and Mr Gershonnen from Salzburg. When the manager of the factory, Mr Cohen, died in 1950, Rudolf Kahn was promoted from district manager to manager, but he died soon after, and the factory closed in 1953.

Rudolf's widow Laura Kahn lived in Cowslip Hill, and was a frequent visitor to the Sassoons, Schischas and Fachlers. She was a regular shulgoer, and my sister Melanie remembers that she attended Ladies Guild meetings held in 37 Sollershott East. As my brother Chaim Fachler puts it: 'Mrs Kahn looked after us when mum and dad went AWOL to Israel and elsewhere. Strangely, we only ever called her Mrs Kahn. Everyone else in the entire Letchworth community was auntie this or uncle that. Marion Roth was Auntie Marion, Bertha Bornstein was Auntie Bertha. Moishe Bornstein was Uncle Moishe, and Ossy Pressburger was Uncle Ossy. Mrs Kahn always remained Mrs Kahn.'

My sister Melanie reports: 'I was eleven or twelve when our parents travelled to Detroit for the barmitzvah of my cousin David Litke. For three weeks, Susie, Meir and I were left alone. Mrs Kahn moved in to look after us, which included cooking our meals. I was shocked and outraged that Mummy, who never left us and spent all day long looking after us, would abandon us like this. I remember tearful and whispered conversations with Susie about how awful this was.'

Fely and Chris Robson

On one occasion, the Fachlers' Shabbat morning kiddush also doubled as a wedding reception. My mother Chava's Spanish au pair Fely (Felicia) met a local Catholic boy, Chris Robson, in Letchworth's International Club. Chris takes up the story:

'We were married on Saturday, 27 October 1962 at St. Hugh's Catholic Church in Letchworth, incidentally Mr. Fachler's birthday. The Fachlers very generously offered their home for the wedding reception. The reception coincided with the weekly kiddush that the Fachlers hosted every Saturday after morning prayers at the Sassoon synagogue. I will never forget the solemnity and the warmth with which Rabbi Sassoon greeted and shook hands with every one of the wedding guests.

This must have been the only Catholic wedding with one Catholic priest and three rabbis!'

Ellen and Marion Capone

On 5 December 1958, Queen Elizabeth II inaugurated the era of STD – subscriber trunk dialling – by directly dialling Edinburgh from Bristol. Until then, phones in the UK did not have dials. If you wanted to make a call, you picked up the phone and waited for the switchboard operator to ask: 'Number please'.

In the 1950s, Ellen Capone worked as a switchboard operator in the Letchworth telephone exchange. Here is a typical phone call:

Operator (Ellen): 'Number please.'

Marion Roth: 'Letchworth 1454 please.'

Operator (Ellen): 'Sorry Marion, Chava (Fachler) is talking to Gisa (Pressburger). I will call you back when the line is free.'

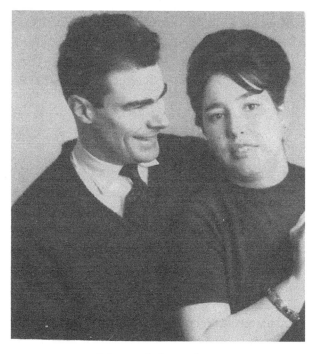

Felicia and Chris Robson

Neil Roland remembers his mother Ruth telling him of an occasion when she needed to speak to Frieda Jaffey, only to be informed by the operator – Ellen – that Mrs Jaffey was out having a dress fitting and would be back at 5pm! Says Neil: 'Mother said you had to be careful what you said on the phone – there was zero privacy.'

Ellen's daughter Marion was a regular fixture in our home from her teens. She went on to study nursing, and it was Marion who introduced Louise Benoliel to Letchworth.

Agnes and John Kaposi

Another frequent visitor to our home in Sollershott East was Dr Agnes Kaposi, who was very friendly with my mother Chava. Her recent book, *Yellow Star – Red Star*, tells her story of having survived the horrors of the Holocaust and Stalinist Hungary. Carol Eini (Roth) comments: 'In the sixties, my parents made friends with John and Agnes Kaposi, who had moved to Stevenage. In 1967, when Agnes was teaching at the Cambridge College of Arts and Technology, she took me personally for an interview with the Head of the Secretarial Department just before my A levels. I was accepted for the advanced Secretarial Course at the College. I am still in touch with Agnes, who now gives regular talks to raise awareness about the Holocaust. Agnes retains fond memories of Letchworth.'

Herman and Yetta Kaffel

Haki Sassoon recalls: 'Herman and Yetta Kaffel lived in Field Lane, and they were the first people I knew who owned a television. Herman was a retired tailor from Minsk who had arrived in Letchworth via the East End. On their diamond anniversary in 1952, the couple received a telegram from the new queen, even before her coronation. Herman was the oldest person to attend the Sassoon synagogue and used to converse with my father in Yiddish. My brother David and I both picked up Yiddish from the Yiddish-speaking visitors to the Sassoon home. Mr Kaffel's son had an antique shop in London, and Mr Kaffel was related to Celina Wegier.'

Doug Gifford

Many Jewish residents of Lethworth learned how to drive with Doug Gifford. He managed my father Eli's Hadassa Wine Company in Hitchin, and later borrowed enough money to buy a Morris Minor with which he started the Gifford School of Motoring. My mother Chava passed her driving test under Gifford's tutelage. So did Marion Roth, Peter Roth, my brother Mordechai (who passed his driving test first time) and myself (who didn't).

When my aunt Miriam and uncle Yoel Litke made their first visit back to England in 1959, my father hired Gifford to drive us to London Airport to greet the family. Gifford got lost, and we got there late, by which time the Litkes had already made their own way to Yoel's family in London.

'Sollerposh East' – the new centre of gravity

"I understood something else that afternoon on the first of many visits to Letchworth: the Fachlers were very sure about how they lived their Jewishness."

ISAAC BENOLIEL

The third and final chapter in the story of the Letchworth Jewish community began effectively when the Fachlers joined the Sassoons in Sollershott East in 1958, thus creating a new centre of gravity for the community. My father Eli explains the rationale for this move:

'Moishe and Ann Bornstein with Stella were moving to Edgware, and Sali and Bertha Bornstein with Buby were moving to Golders Green. We were walking from Hallmead to the Sassoons every Friday night and Shabbat for prayers. Hallmead and Mullway were now almost 'Judenrein' (bereft of Jews). We felt it was time to move to the other side of Letchworth, closer to the Sassoon household.'

Eli found a house at 37 Sollershott East with six bedrooms, two lounges, a kitchen/morning room, a large dining room with beams in the ceiling and a bay window, and a garage. The house itself was fairly run down, with leaking roof and a very dilapidated interior. During the summer of 1958, while the rest of the family was in Cliftonville, Eli supervised the repairs. Chava handled the interior decorating, with the able professional help of her good friend Ruth Ward. The two of them used to take trips to London to choose materials.

The move to 37 Sollershott East represented a sea change for the Fachler family. My brother Chaim remembers: 'I used to cycle from Hallmead to Sollershott with my older brother Mordechai to look at the new house before we moved in. We had to pinch ourselves. Not just the house but the whole neighbourhood could not have been more different to where we had been raised. Uncle Moishe Bornstein had another name for Sollershott East: "Sollerposh East." Mordechai and I definitely agreed with this description.'

The erstwhile Bornstein Shabbat morning kiddush in Hallmead relocated to 37 Sollershott East, and became an important magnet for the community. Marion Roth, the secretary of the Letchworth Jewish Community's Ladies' Guild, used to skip the prayers at the Sassoons. However, she always turned up for the kiddush where she would indulge in her weeky 'tipple,' courtesy of Eli Fachler. One week, Eli gave Marion a new liquer to try out. Carol Eini (Roth) explains: 'As per usual, the noise level in the room was very high. As my mother held her liquer glass poised in her hand, she suddenly drowned out all the voices by blurting out: "Would you all bloody well shut up – I can't taste my drink!"'

La spécialité de la maison at the Fachler kiddush was a combination of cherry brandy and Advocaat egg liquer (or 'yellow wine,' as we used to call it.) My father may have borrowed this tipple from the Bornsteins.

37 Sollershott East

Margalit Fachler (Cohen) recalls: 'Who can forget the Letchworth yellow wine ritual. The children were only allowed one small glass. If they wanted more, my father-in-law Eli always had the same retort, which I had never heard before: "You only want it because you see it."'

When Susie Deutsch (Knight) started frequenting pubs after she returned to London in the 1970s, she once asked the barman for a cherry brandy and Advocaat. The look she received from the barman was a signal that this particular Letchworth mixer had not yet broken into the wider world.

Most Jews in Letchworth were not involved in local or national politics. Bernard and Marion Roth were an exception. As staunch members of the Labour Party, they met Harold Wilson and other leading party members, and campaigned vigorously and successfully to get Shirley Williams elected to Parliament in our constituency in 1964. They even persuaded her to come along one Shabbat to the Fachler kiddush. I remember the occasion well, because at the kiddush I challenged her loudly about the British Government's massive arms sales to Saudi Arabia.

Sunday was a day when streams of visitors descended on 37 Sollershott East. The visitors included my parents' friends from school and from their kibbutz days. Uncles, aunts and cousins. Friends of me and my siblings. Frequent visitors from London included the art dealer Siegfried Oppenheimer, whose wife Nettie was my father's aunt; my mother's first cousin Margot and her husband Manfred, their son David, and Manfred's cousins Sonia, Zelma and Gala; and my mother's uncle Alec Levius and wife. My mother's cousin Peter Gordon Foster would often come for *Lel Haseder* – in fact, he was the first visitor whom my parents 'allowed' to return home by car after the seder.

From overseas, my mother's first cousins Leo Wolpert and Ezra Pratt visited from Israel, and my father's cousins from Belgium, Joseph and Erich Fachler, came over for my barmitzvah.

Naturally, we saw my mother's sister Marian Lopian (Becker) and her husband Yankel, but more often than not, this happened when the two families were on holidays together in the summer. It was their children – my cousins Dovzi, Malka and Shimmy, who would often spend time with us in Letchworth during school holidays – first in Hallmead and later in Sollershott East.

One Sunday afternoon in the early 1960s, a van-full of Gruners – Feyge Gruner was my aunt Miriam Litke (Fachler)'s sister-in-law – arrived in Letchworth from Stamford Hill. After they tumbled out of the van, the children scattered around the house and the garden. That afternoon, a variety show was being broadcast on TV, featuring a chorus line of leggy ladies. As a bunch of us were sitting chatting in the garden, one of the Gruner kids rushed out of the house yelling in Yiddish: 'Nakete Nekevos' – literally, 'Naked Females.' Nakete Nekevos became a catchphrase in the Fachler family. In her final days, in Jerusalem in 2018, my mother was still able to chuckle at the memory.

Television was a novelty in the Fachler household. My parents had not wanted a TV in our small Hallmead home, but in Sollershott, they went to the other extreme. My father loved buying bargains, and we ended up with a TV in almost every room. My brother Chaim learned an early lesson in the power of advertising. 'I was sitting watching TV one day with Mordechai, when a commercial for the Mars bar came on the screen. Mordechai left the room, cycled to the nearest corner store, and came back with a Mars bar.'

My sister, Melanie Klyne (Fachler) remembers: 'As a child growing up in Letchworth, I enjoyed a lovely big warm house, set in huge gardens. There was always plenty of delicious food on tap. There were also paid lodgers, who inevitably became like family. One was William Adam, for whom the Fachlers would later host a *sheva brochas* when he married. Our home was filled with many and varied visitors: *Shabbos* guests, house guests, Sunday day trippers of all ages and from many walks of life. A special attraction of our home was the spacious garden.'

The departure of Bertha Bornstein from Letchworth to London in 1958 meant that my supply of comics was now cut off. My understanding parents took up the slack. In the early 1960s, I became an avid reader of the more upmarket *Eagle*. Mordechai and Chaim read its sister publication, *Swift*. And Melanie read *Robin*. We all eagerly awaited the arrival of our comics through the letterbox.

A frequent visitor to 37 Sollershott East was Josh (Shia, Buby) Bornstein, who had lived in Letchworth with his parents Shloime (Sali) and Bertha Bornstein until 1958. Buby often joined us on our summer vacations. At about 6 foot 6 inches, Buby definitely stood out. Suzanne Freedman (Pressburger): 'Buby tutored me in maths before the eleven plus exam and he gave me Hebrew lessons. He was very short sighted but very long in stature.' Hazel Schwartz (Ward) remembers Buby as 'tall, thin, and so short sighted that he had his nose up against the TV to see it, effectively blocking others from viewing.'

One Friday evening, Buby was strolling through the streets of Letchworth with his distant cousin, Cambridge student Jeremy Rosen, son of Rabbi Kopul Rosen, principal of Carmel College. A couple of yobos made the mistake of muttering some anti-Semitic slur as they passed. Within seconds, short-sighted or not, Buby had them both on the ground, writhing in pain.

Although I left Wilbury School in 1957, and I left Hallmead in 1958, I stayed friends with Geoffrey Woollard, and he was a frequent visitor in our Sollershott home. Geoff says: 'I recall the *succah* that your dad built in the garden of 79 Hallmead. For some reason, I remember having to drive your dad's new car off the drive at 37 Sollershott on the Sabbath. And of course, it was in the Fachler home that I developed my love of *Matzos* each Passover. My wife Ann and I now eat *Matzos* all year with our cheese!'

Margalit Fachler (Cohen): 'I remember that we arrived one Friday in Letchworth to discover that our usual room at my in-laws' home at 37 Sollershott East was unavailable. The "Swedish Camp" had taken over, and we had to sleep with friendly neighbours.'

My brother Meir explains the background of the Swedish Camp. 'When I was 8 or 9, my mother informed us that the following week, a group of London *madrichim* – counsellors – from the Ezra youth group would be running a camp to teach a bunch of Swedish Jewish kids about *Yiddishkeit*. I don't think anyone anticipated the upheaval. The Swedish Camp was the initiative of the maverick community macher from Stamford Hill, Abba Dunner, a friend of the family. He had asked my parents to handle the logistics, including meals and accommodation. I think my mother was in her element, and probably felt that she was back on kibbutz. She did all the cooking, and made certain that every space was filled with mattresses.

'The Swedish Camp lasted a few days, and totally took over our home. The Swedish kids looked and spoke quite strange. I think they were Russian kids who spoke no English. But as big as the upheaval was, it was really only a bigger version of what happened in our Letchworth home every week.' Meir claims that he only realised how untypical and unique was his Letchworth Shabbat when the family moved to London.

Louise Lader (Benoliel) also has very distinct memories of the Swedish Camp: 'There were people sleeping in every nook and cranny in the house. I was reluctant to come to Letchworth that Shabbat because of the chaos, but the Fachlers insisted. I think that the Swedish Camp experience left an indelible impression on everyone present that weekend.'

Louise served as a sort of advanced party for several other members of the Benoliel family. My parents travelled to Paris to attend the wedding of Louise's sister Estrella. Louise's brother Asher became a regular visitor to Letchworth. He was extremely tall, and my mother Chava did not like seeing him wear shirts where the sleeves did not reach his wrists. Her solution was to order made-to-measure shirts from Susie Deutsch (Knight)'s shirtmaker uncle, David Gordon, who supplied all the men in our family with his 'David Gordon' shirts.

When Louise's brother Isaac sent us his memories of Letchworth, he thanked us for the opportunity to relive his happy experiences from almost sixty years ago. 'I first entered the Fachler Kingdom on *Tish'a BeAv* on a late July afternoon in 1963. I was on my university vacations and my sister Louise wanted to introduce me to a "wonderful" family, something different from what I knew before. Mrs Fachler was sitting in the garden with a few children playing around her. We talked about my vacation and my trip to London. After a while, another guest came and sat with us. This guest was not Jewish, and Mrs Fachler offered her some tea and biscuits.

'This scene could not have happened in Morocco at my parent's home. I was astonished. Such experiences taught me to appreciate the qualities of the Fachlers and the Letchworth *"minhagei hamakom"* – local customs. In Morocco, our contacts with the people around us were very limited, or almost non-existent. Particularly on Tish'a BeAv, we would not have anybody eating in our house. As Jews, our lives centred around our family and our synagogue.

'Tish'a BeAv was a day of sadness, and it was inconceivable to sit, talk and enjoy life as it comes. I had grown up in an atmosphere of antagonism between Jews and Arabs. The Fachler's Letchworth way of life forced me to recalibrate my thinking. I saw a day when we remember sad things, without meaning that the whole of life stops. I saw that life carries on in the context of the place where you find yourself. For the Fachlers in Letchworth, this included not only mourning and fasting, but also talking, laughing and playing. It was a place full of life, human feelings and communication at all times and in all circumstances.

'I understood something else that afternoon on the first of many visits to Letchworth – that the Fachlers were very sure about how they lived their Jewishness. You can be Jewish and live your life without limitations. You can fulfill all you believe in, while living in the world around you. At the Fachlers, there was room for differences, for opinions and for life choices. There was a freedom to express the power that lies in each of us.'

A very colourful addition to Letchworth in 1962 was Claudine Fachler from Belgium, the daughter of my father's cousin Joseph. Claudine wanted to perfect her English at a language school. My mother Chava recalls:

'We loved her, especially Yanky, who met her on all his holidays from Carmel College. We welcomed her with open arms. She was a beautiful, tall and leggy young lady in her teens and although she had never lived in a religious atmosphere before, she fitted in and adapted very well. It was while she was with us that her father Joseph died in Antwerp. Eli and I went with Claudine to the *levaya*, and to our great surprise after a couple of weeks she was back in Letchworth to finish her studies.'

Another colourful character who lived for a few months in Letchworth in the very early 1960s was Chen Barsky from Tel Aviv. My mother Chava learned through the grapevine that a young Israeli family was looking for an apartment, and she used her detective powers to track them down. Chen's wife Ziva had given birth to a daughter Ze'ela before they arrived in Letchworth, and my brother Meir and Ze'ela became inseparable. The Barskys came to Letchworth because Chen had a job in nearby Stevenage.

The Barskys became like family. For us children, Chen will always be immortalised for his bubble car, in which he travelled from Letchworth to the Edinburgh Festival. It was the first bubble car we ever saw – and maybe the first that Letchworth ever saw. The idea of driving this car to Scotland seemed as brave and foolhardy as driving it to the moon.

The rose bed in our Sollershott garden looms large in the collective memory of everyone who lived or visited the Fachler abode. My brother Chaim remembers: 'I was quite a lonely child in my early teens, and I had not yet become the confident person I later evolved into. I would spend a lot of time walking round the rose bed, trying to solve the problems of the world, and having important discussions with myself as I tried to work out my place in the world.

'In the weeks before the Six Day War, I obsessively collected press cuttings, and I was very worried that Israel could be wiped off the face of the earth, as the Arab states were threatening. And it was during my perambulations round the rose garden that I suddenly knew for certain that God would not have allowed us to establish the State of Israel, only to allow it to be destroyed 19 years later.'

In the run-up to the Six Day War, my father Eli experienced the same tightness around his chest that he remembered from Kristallnacht. He sat the family down and told them that he wanted to volunteer for the Israeli Army for the duration of the emergency. At the age of forty four, he felt at the peak of his physical prowess. In the end, Eli's experience was not required.

The garden in 37 Sollershott made a big impression on Margalit Fachler (Cohen): 'Coming from the very centre of Tel Aviv, near Dizengoff, I remember Letchworth as very green, very quiet, with not too much traffic. The Fachler garden on a Sunday was full of friends and family lounging around on deckchairs, with the children in the inflatable paddling pool. I raised my son Ashi at the same time as my mother-in-law Chava was raising her youngest son Yossi. Every Shabbat, the two kids cycled around the garden on their little tricycles, sitting at the Shabbat table in their respective highchairs, and having fun confusing visitors as to who was who.'

Robin Leigh describes the time that he was sent on a training course in Letchworth. He needed a temporary home for eating and sleeping, and the Fachlers offered him their hospitality. 'My life experiences during the eight months I spent at 37 Sollershott East had a significant effect on me and on my later life. To this day, on my bedside cabinet, I keep three books: the Chumash, the *Tanya*, and a copy of *The Vow*, Yanky Fachler's book about his parents.'

My cousin Dovzi Lopian's memories are of an open, friendly home with lots of visitors. 'There were friends from London, students from Cambridge, pupils from the local vegetarian boarding school, locals coming in for a chat - you name it, they all came to the welcoming Fachlers. Auntie Eva cooked delicious meals but, above all, the friendly warm welcoming atmosphere that pervaded the home was the magnet. The highlight of the week was the Shabbat Kiddush.'

Dovzi's sister, my cousin Malka Pine (Lopian), recalls: 'As my mum Marian Lopian (Becker) and her sister Chava were very close, my brothers and I were often dispatched down to Letchworth to spend time with our cousins, in their fabulous, big, rambling country-style house, set in a large garden with fruit trees and vegetable patches. For city kids like us Lopians, who lived in the cool, wet, industrial north of England, Letchworth was heaven. We enjoyed the peaceful and picturesque Letchworth countryside, but we also enjoyed meeting different types of people - newly religious families, not-yet religious families, young people without supportive families, exotic-looking Jews from India, and more.'

David Alexander is the son of Yisrael and Chaya, close Kindertransport friends of Chava and Eli from their wartime kibbutz days. In 1959, the Alexanders came to spend three years at Carmel College, where Yisrael taught Hebrew and German. David and I became firm friends. Here is what David says about the Sollershott East days:

'For the three years that we lived in England, we spent almost every *chag* and school vacation in the huge Fachler family home in Letchworth Garden City. It was there, even more than at school, that our finest mutual memories played out. It was there that I learned to appreciate our hosts, whose way of life expressed an all-embracing hospitality. At the Fachlers, the term "open house" was no cliché. "Let all who are hungry come and eat" was no empty phrase.'

David's father Yisrael was not the only Carmel College teacher who was a regular visitor to our home in Letchworth. Dr Alexander Tobias, known universally as Toby, was the headmaster of the Carmel prep school. He had a photographic memory and a mastery of many different disciplines. I think that Toby found in Letchworth an intellectual stimulation and accepting warm welcome that may have been lacking for him at Carmel. His visits to Letchworth came to an end when he left

Carmel in 1964, when he took up a position in the library of the Jewish Theological Seminary in New York.

Carol Eini (Roth) says of my mother: 'Auntie Chava was an integral part of my Jewish education. Practically everything I know about the Jewish kitchen I learned from her. I also learned first-hand the true meaning of *Hachnassat Orchim*, welcoming visitors. I even remember one Shabbat when she was devastated because there were only seven people around her Shabbat lunch table.

'She came up with the wonderful idea of bringing all the young Jewish girls in Letchworth to form a Knitting Club, every Tuesday afternoon in her home. Mozelle Gubbay (Feuchtwanger), Shulamith Landau (Schischa) and myself were among the club's graduates.

Ruth Keller (Kirsch) says about the Fachlers: 'Down the road from the Sassoons lived the indomitable Fachler clan. Theirs was a truly open house. The level of kindness and hospitality to everyone was extraordinary and made a tremendous impression on me. Here the adults of the community, people of all levels of observance, would meet after prayers every Shabbat for a wonderful home-made Kiddush and join in the lively discussions which followed.'

The move of the Fachlers from Hallmead to Sollershott East marked a new era of friendship and cooperation with the Sassoons and Feuchtwangers. An intricate web of warm connections between these two Letchworth households was woven between 1958 and 1970 when our neighbours left for Israel.

When I was studying at Brunel University in the late 1960s, I met Vivienne Schonfeld, who introduced me to her first cousin Jonathan Schonfeld. Jonathan is the son of Rabbi Solomon Schonfeld, and grandson of Chief Rabbi Hertz. When Jonathan started coming regularly to my parents' home in Letchworth, it was the closing of a circle. My mother Chava had joined Rabbi Schonfeld's community in London when she had arrived from Germany in 1938, and my father Eli had encountered Rabbi Schonfeld when he worked for Stern in Letchworth and when he was setting up Luton Kosher Foods.

Jonathan seemed to serve as a catalyst for a stream of young men and women who regularly came from London when Letchworth was the place to be. My brother Meir remembers: 'One Sunday morning, we woke up to find Jonathan sleeping in the lounge. He had arrived the previous evening, quite late, to find the front door locked – an unusual occurrence in our Sollershott home – so he had prised open a window and gone to sleep in the lounge. Jonathan was also part of the group of young London and Cambridge people who helped with the Shabbos Group.'

The Letchworth branch of Cambridge University

'One day on the Cambridge Buffet Express, Michael was minding his own business. Mum opened the door, his yarmulke she saw, To her six kids she added one more.'

FROM YANKY'S SONG FOR THE SHEVA BERACHOT OF
MICHAEL AND HUGUETTE WIESELBERG

During the final phase of the Letchworth Jewish community in the 1960s, an encounter took place on the Cambridge Buffet Express – the train from Kings Cross to Cambridge via Letchworth – that in retrospect probably helped to extend the community's sell-by date by several years.

Individual Jewish students at Cambridge had already discovered Letchworth in the past, including Jeremy Rosen, son of Rabbi Kopul Rosen. The ditty at the opening of this chapter is part of a song that I composed for the *Sheva Berachot* that my parents hosted in Letchworth in honour of Cambridge student Michael Wieselberg and Huguette Azoulay after they got married. The refrain of the song was:

'We're gathered at 37,
to the scene of the crime we have come.
They might make shidduchim in Heaven,
but they're helped along by Dad and Mum.'

The back story is that my mother Chava was on the Cambridge Buffet Express from London to Letchworth in the early 1960s. I will let Michael describe what happened next:

'My Letchworth experience began serendipitously on a train ride from my London home as a fresh Cambridge undergraduate. Sitting quietly alone, I was startled to be approached by a *besheitelled* woman asking where I was headed. The link was obviously my *kippa seruga* – knitted yarmulke – so I told her. She asked quite unashamedly about my background, and on learning I had just returned from six months in Israel as a 'mature' Bnei Akivanik, she explained that some stops ahead there was a small post-war remnant Jewish community in need of someone to run a weekly social group for children to reinforce their *Yiddishkeit* and Zionist interest.

'She had introduced herself as Chava Fachler, and was so pleasantly enthusiastic that I cautiously agreed to try it out, coming by train on Sundays in term-time. Thus began a significant set of relationships which changed my life, and perhaps influenced the lives of one or two others. I was invited to spend the first of many Shabbatot in Letchworth and discovered a warm open multi-cultural welcoming group of people centred on the Ashkenazi Fachler household and the old-world patrician Sephardi Sassoons.

'There was the brilliant original thinker Rabbi Solomon Sassoon at one pole, and a peripatetic paternalistic kosher butcher to southern England's outlying communities, Eli Fachler, at the other. The Fachler household was always focused on children and young people. On top of their own six children, Chava and Eli fostered Susie from a troubled background for several years, reshaping her future. One way or another, all their children have made substantial communal contributions as adults.

'*Minyanim* in Letchworth were formally Orthodox, but included very disparate traditions held together by warmth, tolerance and generosity. As a simple example, I once mislaid my *Tallit* bag at the Sassoons. Returning a week later, still no sign of it. A month afterwards, Rabbi Sassoon's son Haki modestly presented me with a vibrantly coloured replacement he had personally embroidered. I still treasure it.

'This pattern of inclusive leadership and hospitality, embedded in Torah and *Derech Eretz* in an assimilating world, was rather unusual. Many if not most of the ten to fifteen Letchworth children (Fachlers, Kirsches, Pollocks, Roths, Vangers and others whose names I sadly no longer recall) in quite a wide age range who came to my groups, ended up living Orthodox lifestyles, many in Jewish leadership positions in later life, many coming to live in Israel.

'One of the features of this small community was its ongoing ability to bring others, mainly older teens and young adults to come for weekend visits to the key households. Shabbat mealtimes at both Fachlers and Sassoons could continue for hours, with youngsters chatting, arguing, singing, exchanging *Divrei Torah*. This hospitality was hugely enjoyable. Both houses seemed to have plenty of guest rooms and generous gardens.

'Being the 1960s, women and men still mixed easily, but as far as I was aware, always chastely. Alongside the social explorations were the intensely intellectual discussions with Rabbi Sassoon. He loved having bright young people around. Letchworth was an extraordinary haven for young singles from so many backgrounds, brought together to experience a stimulating family plus group Shabbat in a suburban cocoon. It was a unique concoction designed by Eli and Chava together with the brilliant other-worldly and eccentric Rabbi Sassoon, to keep the flame of *Yiddishkeit* and Jewish identity alive for their children in an alien environment. A sort of original private *kiruv* movement emerged.'

From Michael's initial visit, a pattern emerged. Up to half a dozen Cambridge Jewish students – male and female – would descend on Letchworth every weekend. My mother and Alice Sassoon would liaise in advance which students would eat in which home for Shabbat meals. Michael formed the Letchworth Jewish Youth Club, and his engagement with the community lasted for the duration of his stay at Cambridge.

It was during this period that Rabbi Sassoon and Rabbi Feuchtwanger acted as invigilators for students who required close supervision over Shabbat while their Cambridge contemporaries were sitting exams. The Jewish students were then allowed to sit the exams the next day.

Cambridge student Charles Heller was a regular weekend visitor to Letchworth: 'It was customary that guests staying at the Fachlers would have Shabbat tea at the Sassoons, and vice versa. The odd thing was that the Sassoons had a *milkhik* lunch and *fleyshik* tea, so your entire Shabbat was either *fleyshik* or *milkhik*.'

Meir Fachler remembers one seuda shlishit at the Sassoons when Rabbi Sassoon expounded on how the brain works. 'The Cambridge students – including several science students who were studying physiology – were agog at Rabbi Sassoon's incredible knowledge. On

Sundays, Rabbi Sassoon often gave guided tours of his library to visiting groups, such as the Cambridge Jewish Society, and Ezra and Bnei Akiva groups from London.'

One of the Cambridge students who came under Rabbi Sassoon's spell was Jonathan Sacks. When he arrived in Cambridge in the mid-1960s to study philosophy, he had no thoughts of becoming a rabbi. As many of his biographies and obituaries tell us, while he was a student at Cambridge, he travelled to New York in order to discuss a variety of issues relating to religion, faith and philosophy with two of the most prominent rabbis in the world: Rabbi Yosef Ber Soloveitchik, the Orthodox rabbi, Talmudist, and modern Jewish philosopher, who challenged Jonathan to think; and the Lubavicher Rebbe, Rabbi Menachem Mendel Schneerson, the Sorbonne-trained leader of the Chabad-Lubavitch movement, who challenged Jonathan to lead.

Charles Heller, Jonathan's contemporary at Cambridge, recalls: 'Jonathan was a year below me when I was an undergraduate at Trinity Hall. I remember being in and out of his rooms at Caius on friendly visits. He was set on a career in philosophy, but his life was turned round after a visit to the Lubavitcher Rebbe in New York, who with his penetrating gaze persuaded him to devote himself to *Yiddishkeit*.

'On his return, Jonathan put up a large portrait of the Rebbe on his wall and his path was set. Rabbi Shmuel Lew valiantly drove up from Stamford Hill to Cambridge every Sunday to give a *shiur* to the students. He persuaded Jonathan to visit the Rebbe, and the rest is history. When Jonathan was appointed Chief Rabbi, I sent him a letter of congratulations, to which he replied: "Heaven knows what I've let myself in for. I keep saying it's a bit like Cambridge Jewish Society, only bigger."

What the biographies and obituaries fail to mention is the decisive role of Rabbi Sassoon and Letchworth in influencing Jonathan's decision to become a rabbi. On his regular weekend visits from Cambridge to Letchworth, Jonathan would spend so much time closeted with Rabbi Sassoon that Alice, Rabbi Sassoon's wife, used to beg my mother Chava to wean him away from the Sassoon home.

My sister Melanie recalls: 'I used to see Jonathan and Rabbi Sassoon walking round and round the Sassoon garden engaged in intense conversation.' It is clear that Jonathan's exposure to the genius of Rabbi Sassoon exerted a powerful influence on his ultimate decision to change his career trajectory and become a rabbi.

One Shabbat, Jonathan sheepishly asked my mother – of whom he was very fond – whether he could bring his girlfriend Elaine to Letchworth on the following Shabbat. Elaine Taylor was studying radiography in Cambridge. Although she did not usually mix in university circles, she attended the Jewish Society, where Jonathan was president. Elaine always claimed that it was love at first sight.

My brother Meir recalls that when our mother saw Jonathan and Elaine together in Letchworth in the early stages of their courtship, both of them were very shy. Chava could be very plain speaking, and she apparently pushed Jonathan to get a move on.

When Torah scholar and author Avivah Zornberg (Gottlieb) first started visiting Letchworth with her sister Freema as Cambridge students in the 1960s, Avivah already had a special aura. Her father was the head of Scotland's Rabbinical Court, and her uncle was the chief rabbi of Romania. Avivah had taken the unusual step of studying for a year at the Gateshead Girls Seminary before starting her studies at Girton College.

Here is Avivah's eloquent recalling of Letchworth: 'Through the blur of the years, those many *Shabbatot* spent in Letchworth crystallise into a few memories. The three magical families – the Sassoons, the Feuchtwangers, the Fachlers. The first two are in a brocaded, carpeted and shadowy world, of learning and prayer and melodies from an unknown tradition. Most prominent is the image of Rabbi Sassoon, eager and eloquent, balancing on the balls of his feet, as he propounds his theories and readings of traditional sources. We were young and startled but open to revelation.

'The contrasting image is of afternoons with the Fachlers, sunlit vitality. The larger-than-life personalities of Eli and Chava, their stories, their well-earned wisdom – a world centring on young people, the Fachler children, just out of the nest. The older generation and the younger, which included us, visitors from Cambridge, full of our own experiences, questions, desires, turning our faces to this intense Shabbat world of immigrants from other lands, from Baghdad and from Germany. Like my own parents, they addressed us in foreign accents, but different foreign accents. They were strange but intimate – they live on within me, like a dream.'

Another frequent visitor from Cambridge to Letchworth was Dr Henry Knopf, whom we all knew as Chanoch. Dr Knopf was not a student – he was a librarian for the Taylor-Schechter collection at Cambridge University Library. This collection was part of the Cairo Geniza, hundreds of thousands of Jewish manuscript fragments found in the storeroom of the Ben Ezra Synagogue in Old Cairo.

It was Dr Knopf who informed Cambridge student Raymond Ludwin about Letchworth and 'the very special Jewish families making up the Jewish community there.' Raymond decided to check this out: 'When I visited Letchworth for the first time with a group of fellow Jewish students from Cambridge, I was especially struck by the hospitality. That summer, the university exams fell on Shavuot. For observant Jews, this posed a serious problem, since writing is not allowed on Jewish festivals.

'The solution was for Dr Knopf to supervise us in Letchworth, with Rabbi Sassoon giving his personal guarantee that none of the students would receive any communication from the outside. That Shavuot for me was lifechanging. I saw a modern and open approach to traditional Judaism, with families hosting Jewish students not for personal benefit but because it was the right thing to do.'

Raymond continued visiting Letchworth for weekends after he graduated from Cambridge, and even brought his parents to visit. One Friday, in 1969, when Raymond arrived at the Fachlers for Shabbat, my mother Chava said to him: 'This is Hanna Ktorza, our new au pair from Israel.'

Hanna was in England to learn English. As Hanna explains: 'Mrs. and Mr. Fachler were like second parents to me. They were so caring, giving, warm and lovable people. Every morning, Mr. Fachler used to come to wake me up like a father if I wasn't up on time. I was soon calling Mrs Fachler Auntie Chava, and I felt part of the family. I used to love babysitting for Yossi the youngest son, and for Ashi, Yanky and Margalit's son. Both boys were two years old. It was quite an experience for me to see an uncle and a nephew the same age. I was very impressed by how the Fachlers treated Susie as their own daughter.'

Raymond takes up the story: 'There were several Cambridge students in Letchworth that Shabbat, and after the Friday evening meal, we all went out for a walk. Mrs. Fachler took me aside and told me that Hanna did not speak much English, and would I please talk to her. For the entire walk, Hanna and I hung back, talking non-stop. We started dating. Sixteen months later, Hanna and I were married in Israel.'

In 1993, I saw the movie *Shadowlands*, starring Anthony Hopkins as the famous author C S Lewis, the chair of Mediaeval and Renaissance Literature at Magdalene College, Cambridge. Debra Winger played the Jewish poet Joy Gresham nee Davidman, who had converted to Christianity. In this moving story, we are introduced to Joy's son Douglas, who is adopted by Lewis. The film is not always accurate, because in fact Joy had two sons from her first marriage. The other son David was airbrushed out of *Shadowlands*.

When I mentioned to my mother how much I had enjoyed the movie, I was not at all certain that she had ever heard of C S Lewis. Much to my surprise, she said nonchalantly, 'Oh yes, Joy's son Douglas often visited Letchworth fom Cambridge to explore his Jewish background.' Douglas' spiritual quest eventually led him away from his mother's Jewish roots to become a Christian evangelical. Douglas' brother David, on the other hand, became an Orthodox Jew, with the encouragement of Lewis. One of Lewis' Oxford colleagues, the Jewish History scholar Cecil Roth, helped source kosher food and religious services for David. As far as we know, David never visited Letchworth, but Carol Eini (Roth) remembers him from when she studied in Cambridge.

There were several dozen other Cambridge Jewish students who visited Letchworth in the 1960s. My sister Melanie remembers the following: George Friedman, Trevor Fenner, Francis Landy, Lesley Berkley, David Greenberg, Stuart Jackson, Karen Zamet, Neil Ross, Roger Kingsley, Malcom Lewis, and Joanne and Jonathan Greer.

In the 1960s, a non-Jewish Cambridge student, Brian Jennings, decided to become Jewish. He frequently joined his Jewish friends when they visited Letchworth for Shabbat. Brian made tentative enquiries about converting, but like many people, he found too many obstacles being placed in his path by the London Beth Din. It was Letchworth's communal rabbi, Reb Oosher Feuchtwanger, who wisely advised Brian to go to Israel, and complete his conversion there under the auspices of the Israeli Rabbinate. Brian followed this advice, underwent orthodox conversion in Israel, married Ettie, and lived in Petach Tikva where I often met up with him in the 1970s. Brian was tragically killed in an industrial accident, leaving two young children.

In 2016, my brother Meir in Jerusalem called the Bezeq telephone company to solve some cabling issues. When the Bezeq technician turned up, Meir discovered from his name tag that he was Amos Jennings – Brian's son. The long arm of the Cambridge-Letchworth-Israel connection was there for all to see. We arranged for a very emotional reunion between Amos and my mother in her Jerusalem care facility.

Another example of the long arm of the Cambridge-Letchworth-Israel connection concerns a very popular student who was a frequent visitor to Letchworth, Benji Cohen. His Cambridge contemporary Elliott Berry contributed this memory of Benji:

'There was no-one quite like Benji. He was always smiling and interested in you and all matters Jewish at Cambridge. He was ever-present. He gave me private lessons in Jewish Halachic History which were accompanied by personal tales. His knowledge was deep, broad and formidable. He was friendly with everyone.'

Here is Michael Wieselberg's description of Benji. 'Sometimes on Shabbat I was joined in Letchworth by a dear friend, Benji Cohen. Not too excited by the Cambridge economics he was meant to be studying, his head was more often buried in a *Gemara*. His *shiurim* were always sprinkled with warmth and witticisms, and he bore his earlier Gateshead experience lightly when with less knowledgeable friends. It was a particular pleasure for him to go head-to-head with Rabbi Sassoon. Benji was a precious, gentle soul.'

After my parents moved from Letchworth to London in 1971, we heard that Benji had made aliya, married an Israeli girl, and was living in Israel. I bumped into him in Zichron Yaakov in the late 1970s. My sister Melanie Klyne (Fachler) takes up the story:

'In the early eighties, our young family was living in Glasgow where my husband Ephraim attended the *kolel*. I heard that Benji had been appointed student chaplain in Scotland, and soon after he arrived in Glasgow, we enjoyed a great reunion, reminiscing about the good old Letchworth days. Our two families became very friendly, and our children and Benji's children went to *cheder* together.

'In October 1987, on *Chol Hamoed* Sukkot, Benji and his 7-year-old daughter called in to us. Benji told me that they were driving to visit a

Jewish student who lived somewhere in the Scottish Highlands. Benji was taking along a *lulav* and *etrog* to enable the student to say the blessing. I gave Benji some cake and biscuits for himself, his daughter and the student.

'That evening, we received a phone call from a hospital informing us that Benji had been tragically killed in a car crash, and that his daughter was unconscious. The doctors had very little expectation that she would recover. Ephraim drove immediately to the hospital, and despite the protestations of staff, he insisted on performing the Jewish religious ritual of watching over the body.'

Ephraim spent the night praying for the welfare of the little girl. His prayers must have helped, because in the morning she miraculously regained consciousness. Ephraim helped organise Benji's funeral, which was attended by practically the entire Glasgow Jewish community. A few days later, Benji's widow gave birth to a baby boy, and my parents Chava and Eli travelled from London to Glasgow for the highly emotional *brit*.

Fast forward to 2008. Melanie's oldest son Gedallia was living with his young family in Jerusalem. One very stormy evening, there was a knock on the door. Two strangers, a young man and an older man, asked whether they could seek shelter from the rain. They had arranged to meet someone in the apartment across the corridor, but he was not yet home.

Melanie takes up the story again. 'After Gedallia welcomed them in, the older man told him that the young man was getting married, and showed Gedallia the wedding invitation. Gedallia did a double take. The bridegroom's name in Hebrew was Binyamin Yedidya ben Binyamin Cohen – Benjamin Yedidya the son of Benjamin Cohen.'

The penny dropped. Gedallia realised that the young man who had randomly sought shelter from the rain in a stranger's home was none other than the baby boy born in Scotland just days after his father, Benji Cohen, died so tragically in the car crash. Gedallia himself had attended young Binyamin Yedidya's *brit*. Here, quite randomly, stood the same Binyamin Yedidya. A Cambridge-Letchworth connection with a powerful wallop.

'No Minyan in Letchworth'

'One of Britain's most unusual provincial communities is dying.'

JEWISH CHRONICLE

The headline to the Jewish Chronicle article on 24 September 1971 describes the demise of the Letchworth Jewish community: 'One of Britain's most unusual provincial communities is dying. The community is Letchworth, and it is unusual because since the early days of the Second World War, it has been a stronghold of Orthodoxy. The congregation in recent years revolved around the Sassoon family. It was at their home that services were held twice daily with the family servants joining in the prayers. But the Sassoons have emigrated to Israel and other members of the congregation have left the garden city too. Now one of its leading members has moved to London – because he says he can no longer get a minyan in Letchworth on Shabbat.'

The 'leading member' in the article is my father, Eli Fachler. As Letchworth's Jewish population continued to shrink in the late 1960s, there were usually enough guests to help make up the Shabbat minyan at the Sassoons. On the death of Selina Sassoon in 1967, both the Sassoons and the Feuchtwangers set about fulfilling their long-held wish to move to Israel. Once both families left Letchworth for Jerusalem in 1970, the weekly minyan became increasingly unsustainable. The community was living on borrowed time.

As my father Eli writes: 'For nine long and difficult months, we tried to keep a Shabbat minyan going. We had to rely on visitors from London and Cambridge to make up a minyan. Though we continued to hold services mainly at the Schischa's, the end was near. Yossi was reaching the age where he would have to enter primary school. This prompted our decision to move to London, and we informed our fellow congregants in Letchworth of our intentions. Most of them signalled that they would only stay in Letchworth while we remained there, and that once we left, they too would eventually leave.'

The departure from Letchworth of most of the remaining families effectively marked the end of the glorious 32-year history of the Letchworth Jewish community. On 20 December 1970, my father Eli, in his capacity as honorary treasurer of the community, formally wrote to Rabbi Yossel Schischa as follows:

'I hereby wish to confirm your appointment as rabbi of our community. Now that Rabbi Feuchtwanger has given up his duties and is going on aliya, we are pleased that you have accepted the position. Having seen you grow up within our community, we feel a certain pride as well as honour to have you as our rav, and we wish you a successful, trouble-free and satisfying term of office.'

Here is how Yossel describes the formal ending of the Letchworth Jewish community. 'Mr Fachler spoke to me concerning his suggestion that I become the Rav of the community. He had probably discussed it with my late father and the few others who were still there. In reality, it was only a sinecure, as there was not much to do. I *leined* most *Shabosos*. I arranged the sale of *chometz* for Pesach 1972, and that same year I gave a *Shabbos Hagadol* drosho – the final one in the history of the community. One *Shabbos* there was a kiddush for Bernard and Marion Roth's silver wedding, and I recall saying a few words.

'Even after we left, I would visit Mr Gottfried who remained in Letchworth in sheltered accommodation on the Grange Estate. I was also involved in his funeral, and later also the funeral of Mrs Abrahams, who also did not move away.

'There was no official end to the Letchworth Jewish community. It finished when there was no Shabbos Minyan anymore. When my parents left, just before Pesach 1972, there was no one else still there to give them a farewell kiddush!'

In terms of longevity, the only unbroken Jewish presence in Letchworth from the mid-1940s to the present day is Leonard (Lenny) Abrahams: Over the years, he has unsuccessfully tried to persuade

Jewish families to rebuild the Jewish community in Letchworth. Here is his description of the afterlife of the Letchworth Jewish community.

'It was hard when most of the Jews left Letchworth for London and Israel in the 1960s and 1970s. When it was just Peter Kirsch and myself left, we used to go to the shul in Welwyn Garden City. After Peter died, I decided it would be better to go to London. Since then, I have spent every *Shabbos* and *Yom Tov* in Stamford Hill. Twice a year, before Covid, I organised a minibus of men from Stamford Hill to come to Letchworth so there could be a *minyan* for me to say *kaddish* for my parents."

The last Fachler family simcha in Sollershott East before my parents left Letchworth was in February 1971, when my brother Meir celebrated his barmitzvah. My brother Chaim was summoned from his Israeli yeshiva to teach Meir his *parsha*. When he was not teaching Meir, Chaim studied at London's Etz Chaim Yeshiva.

The Friday night service on the barmitzvah weekend was held in the Fachler home. The Shabbat morning service – including Meir reading from the Torah scroll – was in the Schischa home. My sister Melanie Klyne (Fachler) remembers the barmitzvah: 'The main physical work for this fell on Mummy, but I do remember a delightful Mrs Mergut helping with some of the cooking. We had huge, lavish meals in the big room. We had to set out tables and chairs in one of the upstairs rooms to accommodate the overflow.'

In May 1971, Rabbi Sassoon wrote to Bernard and Marion Roth from Jerusalem: 'We are beginning to settle down, but miss all our friends in Letchworth and London very much indeed... I hear that the Fachlers have found a flat in London and that the Schischas are looking hard for a house. It seems a pity that communal life in Letchworth is coming to an end, but that was bound to happen, as we did not succeed in attracting sufficient Jewish families to Letchworth to take the place of those who were leaving.'

If Theo Cowan was one of the first Jewish children to be born in Letchworth in 1917, the last Jewish birth in the Letchworth Jewish community was 55 years later in 1972 when Carol Eini (Roth) gave birth at the Hitchin Maternity Hospital. 'A couple of days after I had my daughter Tzippy, Uncle Eli turned up to visit me with a huge bunch of grapes. He had been informed by the hospital that a Jewish mother had given birth, in case I wanted kosher meals. The Pressburgers had not yet left Letchworth, and were still living in Cross Street. Gisa and Ossy were Tzippy's first babysitters when she was a few weeks old and Aharon and I took ourselves off to Hitchin for some shopping."

An outstanding legacy

*'Above all, I recall the wonderful people.
Their tolerance and understanding were, without doubt,
Letchworth's most outstanding legacy.
There will never be another Letchworth.'*

DEREK POLLOCK

By April 1941 when Chief Rabbi Dr Joseph Herman Hertz visited Letchworth, it is estimated that up to 1,500 Jews resided in the garden city. It is probably fair to say that the impact of the Jewish community was predominantly inwards. Despite constituting close to ten percent of Letchworth's total population during the war, the community did not leave a lasting legacy in the town itself. To this day, many people in Letchworth are not aware that a Jewish community thrived there during the war years, and continued to exist for a further quarter of a century.

Letchworth touched the hearts and souls of so many members of the Jewish community. This is how Jean Shindler (Pollock) sums up the Letchworth experience: 'Above all, the handful of religious families – the Sassoons, the Feuchtwangers, the Fachlers and the Schischas – were exceptional role models to those of us whose upbringing was different. The adults exuded Jewish values and were totally non-judgmental. Each religious home had an open-door hospitality.

'Every little girl growing up in the Letchworth Jewish community wanted to be like Chava Fachler or Flora Feuchtwanger. By the age of twelve, I aspired to keep Shabbat. Looking back on my years of growing up in Letchworth, I realise how much of my adult life has been influenced by those experiences. Being part of such a small yet strong Jewish community surrounded by a much bigger non-Jewish population, with such an emphasis on Jewish learning and values, clearly defined my Jewish identity. It is no coincidence that, like so many other Letchworth children, I went into Jewish education.'

David Alexander from Israel was an occasional visitor to Letchworth between 1959 and 1962: 'I was not born in Letchworth. Nor was I raised or educated in the Garden City. I haven't been there for more than sixty years, and I admit to remembering precious little about the town itself. Even though Letchworth is undoubtedly very different from anything I was familiar with as I was growing up in Israel – it's not a city, not a town, not a village, not a kibbutz and not a moshav – I freely acknowledge that the planning that makes Letchworth so unique totally bypassed my consciousness. I don't remember the streets, the landmarks, the tree-lined boulevards, the roundabouts or the green spaces.

'But what my 13-16-year-old self remembers about Letchworth is two houses. The Fachler house – warm, spacious, friendly, and always extending a welcome to any and every visitor. And the Sassoon house – maybe I should describe it as the tribal grounds of the Sassoon clan. I still remember the in-house synagogue, the library, and the aromas that imbued the rooms.

'My visits to the Sassoon household left an indelible impression on my developing imagination. This was the first time in my life that I found myself in the presence of the truly rich, in the presence of a wealthy lifestyle that I had only read about in books. The tribal atmosphere – I'm not sure whether to describe it as Eastern, Sephardi or Baghdadi – enveloped everyone in an aura that was so very different from any of the Ashkenazi families that I had ever met throughout my childhood and early teens.'

Gail Zivan Neriya (Vanger) also recalls the diversity of the Letchworth community: Ashkenazi, Sephardi, Indian and Iraqi. 'There were those who kept Shabbat more and those who kept Shabbat less. We lived in a natural harmony. We were all part of a Jewish people. I did not feel any friction between my own Shabbat experience and my family's different Shabbat experience.

'The only downside of this coexistence is that when our family moved to Israel, I could not understand why the country's educational system was not based on the Letchworth model, with both orthodox and less orthodox children studying together. Letchworth taught me a natural tolerance and acceptance of my new neighbours wherever I found myself in Israel. Above all, Letchworth taught me the meaning of responsibility towards our community.

'I had several role models for this. Melanie Fachler, our *madricha* in *Shabbos* Group. Her parents Eli and Chava Fachler who invited the adults to their home after Shabbat morning prayers for a kiddush. Our rabbis who made sure that everything required for our Cheder lessons was provided. Growing up in Letchworth made us feel special – and so proud of our little Jewish community.'

Judy Oppenheimer (Kirsch) paid tribute to the strong women of the Letchworth Jewish community: 'They were wonderful wives and mothers and homemakers. They were also such remarkable personalities in their own right, able and willing to teach the younger generations so much, both formally and informally.

Judy's sister Ruth Keller (Kirsch) remarks: 'It says a lot about this cross-section of Jews, from English-born to Continental to Eastern, and

Gathering of friends at the Fachlers

from highly orthodox to highly unorthodox, that they were able to create such a tightly knit and cohesive community.'

Ruth's comments are echoed by so many others. Here is Esther Broch: 'We were all war refugees. There was tremendous unity among the close-knit Jewish community.' And here is Esther's sister Deborah Emanuel (Broch): 'I have such happy memories of living in Letchworth and have been back there from time to time to re-visit the past.' Gita Miller (Bindiger): 'The *achdus* – unity – of all the different Jewish people who lived in Letchworth at that time is memorable. People from all backgrounds – German, Chassidic, Litvish – not to forget Bahgdadi - got on well.'

David Freudmann: 'I always have had a very soft warm spot in my heart for Letchworth.' Ray Kornbluth (Bornstein): 'My years in Letchworth were some of the happiest years of my life.' Sue Deutsch (Knight): 'The eight years I lived in Letchworth gave me a home and the family I so desperately needed.' Frances Israel (Richman): 'I remember the warmth of the community. We were always in and out of one another's homes.'

Shloime Just: 'For me, Letchworth had a special charm.' Vivienne Alper (Gedella): 'After living in such a close-knit community, it was a shock to go back to London at the end of the war.' Zippy Rosenblatt (Persoff): 'I truly believe that the phenomenon of a substantial, cohesive Jewish community being transported en masse to Letchworth was Divine Providence.'

Clive Toberman: 'I will always remember the many happy times I spent in Letchworth all those years ago. I was always made welcome. Such happy days.' Ann Dawes (Rau): 'I remember those days vividly. The Fachlers were very hospitable and their doors were always open to visitors, many of whom stayed with the family for Shabbat. The Fachler Letchworth experience was a mixture of an honour, a pleasure and something that I treasure.'

The headmistress of the Letchworth Talmud Torah, Mimy Santhouse (Portal) pays tribute to the Fachlers' 'most significant role in that *Kehilla* – their *Hachnosas Orchim* was extraordinary. They always invited students and others to their *Shabbos table*. My personal gratitude goes to Uncle Eli for all the lifts he gave me from the station to Cheder and back again.' The headmaster of the Talmud Torah, Rabbi Norman

Solomon: 'I experienced first-hand the warm welcome from the Letchworth community. I recall exemplary intercommunal harmony.'

Murray Cohen: 'Looking back on my 7-8 years in Letchworth, I have very happy memories.' John Singer: 'My stay in Letchworth was probably one of the best memories of my early life.'

Sarah Davis (Singer): 'Letchworth will always hold fond memories for many people for many reasons.' Robbee Jaffey: 'My experiences and the daily routines in the small Letchworth Jewish community positively affected me in the eventual path that I took.' 'Hazel Schwartz (Ward): 'I was only eight when I left Letchworth, but I have happy memories. Letchworth houses were all different and original and lovely. I'd happily live back in Letchworth if it was full of Jewish people again.'

Shulamith Landau (Schischa): 'I treasure the friendships I have with girls I grew up with in the 1950s and 1960s. The Letchworth kehilla was an oasis of Torah and *Ahavat Yisroel* in an especially lovely English country town. I remember the warmth and mutual respect, the unity within the community, and the fact that we all knew each other's extended family so well. I feel truly privileged to have experienced such an example of pure goodness, kindness and unbelievable hospitality that emanated from the Sassoon / Feuchtwanger and Fachler homes.'

Referring to Pharaoh's biblical dream, Hanoch Knopf says: 'I enjoyed seven "fat" years of Jewish contentment, with the Sassoon and Fachler families providing a homely environment in Letchworth.' Judith Lebrecht: 'I have fond memories of the very relaxed atmosphere in Letchworth. The community felt like one big family.'

Avivah Zornberg (Gottlieb) speaks of 'the three magical families – the Sassoons, the Feuchtwangers, the Fachlers.' Isaac Benoliel described Letchworth as 'a corner of paradise where you could find yourself and others. Letchworth is now in my heart.'

Meir Fachler: 'Looking back, I am always struck anew at just how special, how unusual and how unique my Letchworth childhood really was.'

Derek Pollock: 'The Jewish families I encountered in Letchworth when I returned from the war included every type of Jew, from the most liberal to the most orthodox. The fact that so varied a group could form themselves into a tightly knit and coherent community says much about our life. Even now after fifty years of living in London, I share many pleasant memories of the friendship and almost family feeling of those years in Letchworth. Above all, I recall the wonderful people. Their tolerance and understanding were, without doubt, Letchworth's most outstanding legacy. There will never be another Letchworth.'

Michael Wieselberg speaks for many when he says: 'It is a fitting tribute to this Letchworth community, that decades later, those of us touched by it, now in our sixties and seventies or older, still retain especially fond memories, some remain in touch, and enjoy sharing our appreciation.'

At the beginning of WW2, when the fate of Britain was still uncertain, Rabbi Dr Isidore Epstein wrote the following: 'Letchworth is an exemplar of organised Jewish life. None of us can tell whether our stay in Letchworth will be long or short, but it is to be hoped that when we return "each man to his camp and each man to his standard," we will be able to recall with pleasure and satisfaction our contribution to this embattled island fortress.'

The Jews of Letchworth did indeed eventually return each to his or her camp and each to his or her standard. Some remained in Letchworth for longer, some for shorter, and some just passed through. Half a century after this microcosm of the Jewish world ceased to exist, the special aura of the Letchworth Jewish community remains.

Mickey Freudmann finds it incredible that at a time when Jewish communities in Europe were being destroyed, Jewish life in Letchworth flourished. 'For my family, Letchworth was an island of calm and almost complete tranquility in a war-torn world. It was a haven for us.'

In 2000, Chief Rabbi Jonathan Sacks wrote to my parents: 'Your letter brought back marvellous memories of the old days in Letchworth, which were an important part of my own spiritual development.' My brother Meir suggests that something that Sacks wrote in his book *Radical Then, Radical Now* is key to understanding the Letchworth phenomenon.

In his book, Sacks describes the scary period before the 1967 Six-Day-War, and the extraordinary ways in which Jews throughout Cambridge University suddenly became visible. Students and dons who had never before publicly identified as Jews could be found there praying. Everyone wanted to express their solidarity and their identification with Israel's fate.

Sacks says that what he witnessed had nothing to do with politics or war or even prayer: 'It had to do with Jewish identity. Being Jewish meant being part of an extended family. By being born into the Jewish people, I was enmeshed in a network of relationships that connected me to other people, other places, other times. I belonged to a people. And being part of a people, I belonged.'

I believe that this intense feeling of belonging helps explain why, 50 years after the Letchworth's Jewish community's sell-by date, so many people are still basking in its afterglow.

- -

I am happy to report that the quirky spirit of Letchworth Garden City is still alive and well. Ebenezer Howard encouraged people to grow their own food. Proof that his influence still hovers over the town is evident in the makeshift handwritten sign that appeared in one of Letchworth's quiet and leafy streets during the 2020/2021 covid pandemic lockdown. Above a cardboard box filled with freshly cut pink rhubarb stalks was this sign:

"Hello, dog walkers, bike riders, exercisers, strollers and all fellow-isolators! Please help yourself to the rhubarb and enjoy cooking it at home!
Be safe and well!"

Yanky Fachler
Selected Bibliography

- The Vow: Rebuilding the Fachler tribe after the Holocaust, DavMor, 2018
- Yanky's Doodles – the authorised memoir, DavMor, 2018
- 6 Officers, 2 Lions and 750 Mules – with a preface by Benjamin Netanyahu, DavMor, 2015
- A Tale of 4 Cities: Frankfurt, London, Letchworth, Jerusalem, self-published, 1992
- Balfour, Boycotts, Blood Libels and Black Books, DavMor, 2017
- Gentile Heroines and Heroes, DavMor, 2014
- God's Little Errand Boys, DavMor, 2012
- Ignite your Chutzpah, DavMor, 2016
- Kaleidoscope: the colourful characters who helped shape the Irish Jewish community, Jewish Historical Society of Ireland, 2013
- Zooming through Covid: A selection of Yanky Fachler's zoom talks, Jewish Representative Council of Ireland, 2021
- Co-editor: Redemption and Revelation: Essays on Pesach and Shavuot, by Rabbi Mordechai Fachler, Renana Publishers, 2013
- Co-editor: Shalom Bayit: Torah insights into family relationships, by Rabbi Mordechai Fachler, Renana Publishers, 2014
- Chapter on Innovation and Enterprise: Ireland and Israel, in What Did We Do Right? Global perspectives on Ireland's 'Miracle,' ed. by Rory Miller and Michael O'Sullivan, Blackhall, 2010
- Chapter on Kristallnacht in my Family, in The Irish Context of Kristallnacht: Refugees and Helpers, ed. by Gisela Holfter, University of Limerick, 2014
- Chapter in The Rabbi in the Green Jacket: Memories of Jewish

Buckinghamshire, 1939 - 1945 UK ed. by Vivien and Deborah Samson, Matador, 2015
- Chapter in A Chapter in the Book – Generations sharing narratives of courage, sadness and positivity, ed. by Ralph M Kley, 2019
- Chapter on Marcus Witztum, the Irish Schindler, in Out of Zion: An Anthology of Papers first delivered at the Israel Branch of the Jewish Historical Society of England, ed. by Gabriel Sivan and Kenneth Collins, 2022

Saluting 4 generations of proud Letchworthians:

Sam and Melanie Becker

Eli and Chava Fachler

Yanky Fachler, David Fachler, Mordechai Fachler, Chaim Fachler, Melanie Klyne, Meir Fachler and Yossi Fachler

Ashi Fachler

With sincere thanks to Yanky Fachler for writing and compiling the Letchworth Book, thus providing a platform to remember all those who built, invested in and left their mark on one of the most unique Jewish communities of the twentieth century; and in Loving Memory of our Dear Parents

Bernard and Marion Roth

יחיאל דב בן חיים הירש ופייגא (פני)
ומריון בת אלזה וקארל (שלמה)
יהיו זכרם ברוך

Pillars of both the Letchworth Jewish Community and the wider Community of North Hertfordshire

Carol Eini (neé Roth)
Peter Roth

In honor of our dear and esteemed parents,
Rabbi Solomon and Mrs. Alice Sassoon
and our grandmother,
Selina Sassoon.

These extraordinary, dedicated individuals initiated Jewish community interests, advanced Jewish education, and served as role models for the entire Letchworth Jewish community.

David and Elsie Sassoon
Letchworth - Jerusalem

In appreciation of the role Letchworth played in our formative years.

Haki Sassoon

In recognition of cousin Yanky's literary and
broadcasting skills, along with our fond memories of
the many times we stayed at the Fachler home in
Sollershott East, Letchworth;

and in memory of our beloved parents
to whom we owe so much:

ר' יואל יעקב בן מוה"ר אליהו ז"ל
וזוגתו הא' מרים בת שמואל שלמה ע"ה

Yankel and Marian (née Becker) Lopian,
who met while both families were resident in Letchworth

ר' מנשה בן חיים יהושע ז"ל
וזוגתו הא' פיגא בת אברהם חיים ע"ה

Menashe and Itza (née Motzen) Eder

Dedicated by their children
Dovzi and Anne Lopian

Dedicated to the memory of my sister,
Anna Finchas,

my parents, **Derek and Goldie Pollock**,

my grandparents **Henry and Florrie Pollock**,

and all the members of the Pollock family who lived and thrived in Letchworth.

The Letchworth Jewish community provided an idyllic childhood for me and Anna. The yardstick of its leadership was to give and not to take, to accept and not to judge, to put others before themselves. These were the values - the Jewish values - with which I grew up and have guided me throughout my life.

Letchworth was an education outside school and shul. Its participants have now dispersed far and wide, to the four corners of the earth, but for all of us, Jewish Letchworth continues to live on in our hearts and deeds.

Jean Shindler (née Pollock)

As a token of our appreciation to

Mr Eli and Mrs Chava Fachler

for their ongoing and so generous hospitality.

Benoliel Family:

Estrella Ohayon,
Isaac Benoliel
Louise Lader
Messod Benoliel
Evelyn Bensimhon

Dedicated in loving memory
to our parents

**Shlomo ben Yitzchak Hacohen
and Devorah bat Eliezer**

Janet and Stephan Kirsch

Letchworth 1938-1972 was a place of transition in which exceptional families and individuals, in a unique community, changed the lives of so many in a permanent positive way.

For my children and grandchildren – some memories of myself as a young girl.

Vivienne Alper

Wishing Yanky great success,

Jerry Klinger

President and founder, Jewish American Society for Historic Preservation
www.JASHP.org

ANONYMOUS

In memory of my grandparents,
Hugo and Celine Lunzer,
who lived in Letchworth during the war years.

The stories of life at 56 Chillingswood
as retold to me by my father
Jack Lunzer
reverberate to this day.

Margaret Rothem

"Give me the child until he is 7 and I will show you the man."
Aristotle

Thank you, Uncle David Gordon, for imbuing me with
a love of God, music, learning, and for teaching me
how to listen. Thank you for sending me to St. Christopher's
in Letchworth at the age of 7, where I would meet my
Fachler family. Huge love and gratitude to Eli and Chava
Fachler who saw the good in my 7-year-old self and
nurtured more of that good, embracing me into their
family and holy community, modelling for me in the
tiny town of Letchworth how to show up
and be God's hands and heart in the world.

Sue Knight Deutsch
www.CantorSue.com

Dedicated to the memory of my parents,
Rabbi Asher and Rebbitzen Flora Feuchtwanger,
my husband,
Rabbi Avraham Gubbay,
and my brother
Rabbi Jacob Feuchtwanger.

I am privileged to have grown up in such a warm-hearted community, surrounded by such amazing people who genuinely cared for one another.

Mozelle Gubbay

In loving memory of our parents
Harry and Margaret Abrahams
whose family lived above the Arcade in Letchworth for half a century 1939-1989, and who ran an upholstery business in The Wynd; and in memory of
Walter Gottfried,
our friend and houseguest for many of those years.

Lenny (Shlomo) Abrahams
one of the last few Jewish people
still living in Letchworth;
Martin (Moich) Abrahams,
artist, www.moichabrahams.co.uk;
Bernard (Baruch) Abrahams
Wishing this book great success,
and offering best wishes to all who read it.

Wishing the Jewish Letchworth book much success:

Miriam Fachler Litke

Efraim Halevy

David Walker

Shimmy and Pearl Lopian

Shimmy and Malka Pine

Huguette and Michael Wieselberg

List of Illustrations

1 Hand drawn map of Hallmead by Sammy Hollander
2 Road Sign for Broadway
3 Stella Bornstein's 3rd birthday party, 1948
4 Golda Bornstein and the Bornstein clan
5 Bertha and Sali Bornstein in Switzerland
6 Sheila Kritzler in 2022 holding the birthday date book she received from Joe Pollock in 1941
7 Pollock House, Icknield Way
8 The Freudmann Family
9 Group of Children in Norton Common
10 Frances Richman in her pram in Hallmead
11 Spirella Factory near Letchworth Rail Station
12 Howard Hall
13 The Synagogue and Yeshiva at 38 and 40 Hallmead
14 Rabbi Horowitz giving a shiur
15 Parents and Children 1949
16 Mr Abraham's Upholstery shop in the Wynd
17 2 Cross Street
18 The Abrahams Family
19 Flyer for Purim Party, 1960
20 Sassoon House
21 Cheder pupils
22 Rabbi Sassoon in the garden of 15 Sollershott East
23 Rabbi Feuchtwanger
24 The Coppice, home of the Schischas
25 The 5 Fachler children
26 Coronation street party, Hallmead, 1953
27 Rabbi Simcha Freudiger with a class of yeshiva students
28 Group of Letchworth Yeshiva boys
29 Stephen and Peter Kirsch with their parents and grandmother
30 Goldie Pollock, Anne and Jean
31 The Roths and The Fachlers

32 33 Broadwater Avenue, home of the Ward family
33 Celina Wegier
34 Gail and Jonathan Vanger at Purim
35 Gail Vanger's birthday party
36 The Fox Family
37 Jean Pollock
38 Felisa and Chris Robson
39 Fachler House, 37 Sollershott East
40 Gathering of friends at the Fachlers

GLOSSARY OF HEBREW/YIDDISH TERMS

ABUI – Father
ACHDUS – unity
ADON OLAM – Prayer at end of Shabbat morning service
AGUDA – Orthodox political movement
AGUDAT/AGUDAS YISRAEL – see AGUDA
AHAVAT YISRAEL – love of fellow Jews
ALEF BET – first two letters of Hebrew alphabet
ALIYA – Moving to Israel
ALIYA – Being called to make a Torah blessing
ALIYA BET – Clandestine immigration to Palestine
AMOUD – Literally, "Arise"
ARBA MINIM – 4 species used on Sukkot
BA'AL TEFILLA – Layman who leads the service
BA'ALEI BATIM – denizens of the community
BABYLONIAN TALMUD – see TALMUD
BACHAD – Modern Orthodox Zionist youth movement
BALAGAN – Chaos, fiasco
BARMITZVAH – When a boy reaches age 13
BAT BAYIT – Frequent guest in someone's home (female)
BAT MITZVAH – When a girl reaches age 12
BELZER CHASSID – Member of the Belz Hassidic Court
BEN BAYIT – Frequent guest in someone's home (male)
BES (BET) HAMEDRASH - study hall, synagogue
BESHEITELLED – Woman wearing a wig
BETH DIN – Jewish Court of Law
BNEI AKIVA – Modern Orthodox Zionist youth group
BODEK – Inspector of slaughtered meat
BRIT – Circumcision ceremony
CHACHAM – Sephardic equivalent of Rabbi
CHAG (pl. CHAGIM) – Jewish holiday
CHALLOT (sing. CHALLAH) – Loaves of bread on Shabbat
CHAMETZ - Foods with leavening agents
CHANUKAH – 8-day Festival of Lights
CHAREDIM – see HAREDIM
CHATAN BERESHIT - Person honoured to be called up to the first portion of the Torah

reading on Simchat Torah
CHATAN TORAH – Person honoured to be called up to the last portion of the Torah reading on Simchat Torah
CHAZAN – Synagogue cantor
CHEDER – see TALMUD TORAH
CHOL HAMO'ED – Intermediate days of Pesach/Sukkot
CHOSSEN - Bridegroom
CHUMASH – Book containing the 5 Books of Moses, the Pentateuch
CHUPPAH – Wedding canopy
DAVEN – To pray
DAYAN – Judge in Jewish religious court
DAYANUT – Examination to become Dayan
DERECH ERETZ – Good manners
DRASHA – Sermon
DROSHO – see DRASHA
DVAR TORAH – Talk related to weekly Torah reading
EIDA HACHAREIDITH – Ultra-orthodox community
ERUV TECHUMIN – distance limit on Shabbat
ETROG – citron used on Sukkot
FLEYSHIK – Meaty (after eating meat dish)
FRUM – Religiously observant
GADOL – A great and saintly rabbi
GEFILTE FISH – Chopped fish dish
GEMARA - Component of the Talmud comprising rabbinical commentary on the Mishna
GEMUTLICHKEIT - Geniality
GENIZA – storage area in synagogue for worn-out religious books and documents
GLATT KOSHER – Unblemished kosher meat
HACHNASSAT ORCHIM - Hospitality
HACHSHARA – Preparation for living on a kibbutz
HAFTARA – Additional reading at Shabbat service
HAGGADAH - Text with the order of the Passover Seder
HALACHA – Jewish law
HALACHIC – Pertaining to Orthodox Jewish practice
HALACHICALLY JEWISH – Jewish according to Halacha
HAPOEL HAMIZRACHI – see MIZRACHI
HAREDI – Ultra-Orthodox person
HAREDIM- Ultra-Orthodox community
HASHKAFA – Worldview
HAVDALA – Ceremony to mark end of Shabbat
HEIMISH – Traditional
HOMENTACHEN – Three-sided cookie for Purim
HORA – Communal dance

IMI – Mother
IVRIT – Modern Hebrew language
KADDISH – Mourning prayer
KASHERED – Meat that has been made kosher
KASHRUT – Kosher dietary laws
KEHILLA – Jewish community
KIBBUD AV – Honouring one's father
KIBBUD EM – Honouring one's mother
KIDDUSH – Repast after Shabbat morning service
KINDERTRANSPORT – Rescue operation that brought 10,000 children from Nazi-occupied Europe to Britain in 1939
KIPPA (pl. KIPPOT) – Skull cap, yarmulke
KIRUV – Bringing secularised Jews back to Orthodox Judaism
KISLEV – Jewish month, usually coincides with December
KITZUR SHULCHAN ARUKH – Book containing laws of daily life
KOL NIDRE – Eve of Yom Kippur prayer service
KOLEL – Talmudical college for married students
KRISTALLNACHT – State-sponsored pogrom of 9 November 1938
L'CHAIM – To Life!
LEINING – The act of reading from Torah scroll
LEL HASEDER (see SEDER)
LEVAYA - Funeral
LIMUDEI KODESH – Jewish studies
LITVAK – Jew from Lithuania
LITVISH – of Lithuanian-Jewish origin
LULAV – Palm branch used on Sukkot
MACHER – Mover and shaker
MADRICH(IM) – Youth group counsellor(s)
MATZOS – Matza flatbread consumed on Pesach
MAZAL TOV – Congratulations
MECHITZA - Partition that separates men and women in synagogue
MIKVEH – Ritual bath
MILKHIK – Milky (after eating dairy dish)
MINCHA – Afternoon service
MINYAN – Quorum of 10 men for prayers
MISHLOACH MANOT – food gifts distributed on the festival of Purim
MISHNA – First section of Talmud
MITZVAH – Commandment, good deed
MIZRACHI – Modern Orthodox Zionist Movement
MOHEL (pl. MOHELIM) – Circumciser
MOSHAV – Communal agricultural village in Israel
MUSSAF – Additional service on Shabbat and festivals
MUSSAR MOVEMENT - Ethical movement

NE'ILA – Service at close of Yom Kippur
NUSACH – Style of prayer
OSTJUDE – Jews from Eastern Europe
PARSHA – Weekly Torah portion
PAYOT – Side curls
PESACH - Passover
PIDYAN HABEN – Redemption of first-born male child
PIKUACH NEFESH – Preservation of human life
PILPUL – Talmudic dialectic
PIRKEI AVOT – Ethics of the Fathers
POLACK – Jew from Poland
PURIM – Festival celebrating thwarting of Haman's genocidal plot to kill the Jews
RABBANIT (see REBBITZEN)
RASHI – Medieval Bible and Talmud commentator
RAV – Rabbi
REB – Honorific alternative to Rabbi or Mr
REBBE – Teacher
REBBITZEN – Rabbi's wife
ROSH HASHANA – Jewish New Year
ROSH YESHIVA – Head of a Yeshiva
SANDEK – Godfather at circumcision
SCHLEP – Tedious or difficult journey
SCHNORRER – Beggar, sponger
SE'UDA – Celebratory meal
SE'UDA SHLISHIT – Third meal on Shabbat
SEDER (NIGHT) – Celebratory meal on eve of Passover
SEFER TORAH – Torah scroll
SEMICHA – Rabbinical ordination
SH'ATNEZ – Cloth containing mixture of wool and linen, which is prohibited under Jewish law
SHABBAT – The Sabbath, Saturday
SHABBAT SHALOM – Greeting on Shabbat
SHABBOS (see SHABBAT)
SHABBOS GOY – Gentile who switches on lights or heating on Shabbat
SHADCHAN – Matchmaker
SHADCHANIT – Female matchmaker
SHALOSH SEUDOT/SEUDOS – see SEUDA SHLISHIT
SHECHITA – Method of Jewish ritual slaughter
SHEMONA ESREH – Prayer recited 3 times a day
SHEVA BROCHES/BRACHOT – Celebratory meal on the 6 days following a wedding
SHIDDUCH – Match between a bride and a groom
SHIUR (pl. SHIURIM) – Lesson
SHIVA – Seven-day mourning period after a person is buried

SHOAH – The Holocaust
SHOCHET – Ritual slaughterer
SHOFAR – Ram's horn blown on Rosh Hashana
SHOIMERED MILK – milk that has been supervised at the milking parlour
SHTREIMEL – fur hat worn on festive occasions by Hassidic Jews
SHUL – Synagogue
SIDDUR – Prayer book
SIMCHAT TORAH – Festival of Rejoicing of the Law
STETL – Small village in Eastern Europe
SUCCAH/SUKKAH – Temporary booth used for meals during the Jewish festival of Succot Sukkot
SUCCOT/SUKKOT – Jewish festival
TAHARA – Ritual preparation of the dead for burial
TALLIT (pl. TALLITOT) – Prayer shawl
TALMID CHACHAM – Learned scholar
TANYA – Early work of Hasidic philosophy by Rabbi Shneur Zalman of Liadi
TEFILLIN – Phylacteries
TEKIA GEDOLA – Long blast of the shofar
TISH'A BE'AV – The fast of 9th Av
TORAH VE'AVODA – Modern Orthodox youth group
TREIF – Unclean, not kosher
TU B'SHVAT – New Year for Trees, 15th Shvat
YAHRZEIT – Anniversary of the death of family member
YEKKISH – Pertaining to Jews of German extraction
YESHIVA – Talmudical college
YIDDISHKEIT – The Jewish way of life
YISHUV – Pre-state Mandatory Palestine
YOM KIPPUR – Day of Atonement
YOM TOV (pl. YAMIM TOVIM) – Jewish festival(s)